SKIING IN THE MAD RIVER VALLEY

FRONT COVER: Extreme skier John Egan lofts himself into an area known as The Church at Sugarbush. Reached from the Long Trail between Paradise and Castlerock at Lincoln Peak, The Church seeks worshippers of daredevil adventure. (Photograph by Sandy Macys, courtesy of John Egan.)

COVER BACKGROUND: Lincoln Peak looms larger than life over Warren and Waitsfield. No matter where one may travel within the 20-mile confines of the Mad River Valley, either Lincoln Peak, Mount Ellen, or Mad River Glen are visible, and in some places, such as Bragg Hill, all three resorts may be seen, a constant reminder, along with cows, barns, and pastures, of what this beautiful valley is about. (Photograph by Ellie Hilferty.)

BACK COVER: Ski schools were necessarily large in the days when people were first learning the sport. European instructors were popular in the beginning, with many coming from Austria, Norway, and France. Many in this group at Glen Ellen would have served under directors Neil Robinson, Pierre Stamos, or Jonathon Jenkins. (Photograph by Sewall Williams.)

SKIING IN THE MAD RIVER VALLEY

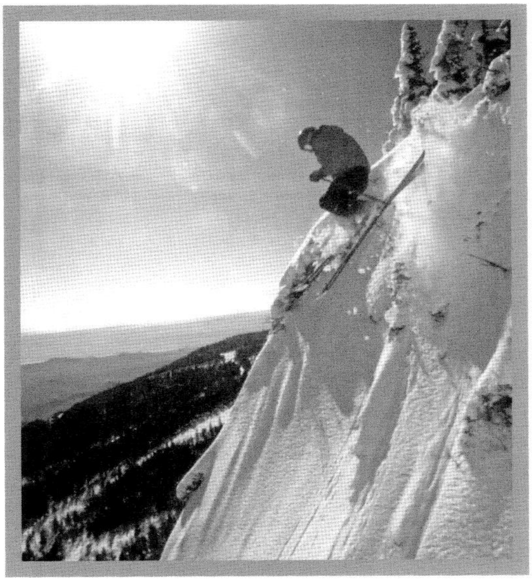

John and Ellie Hilferty

ARCADIA PUBLISHING

Copyright © 2010 by John and Ellie Hilferty
ISBN 978-0-7385-7365-6

Published by Arcadia Publishing
Charleston, South Carolina

Printed in the United States of America

Library of Congress Control Number: 2010924555

For all general information, please contact Arcadia Publishing:
Telephone 843-853-2070
Fax 843-853-0044
E-mail sales@arcadiapublishing.com
For customer service and orders:
Toll-Free 1-888-313-2665

Visit us on the Internet at www.arcadiapublishing.com

CONTENTS

ACKNOWLEDGMENTS

The authors wish to acknowledge these resorts and organizations that greatly helped in the creation of the book: Blueberry Lake Cross Country Center, Green Mountain Valley School, Mad River Glen, National Ski Areas Association, New England Ski Museum, North American Telemark Organization, Ole's Cross Country Ski Center, Ski Vermont, Sugarbush, U.S. Ski Team, and Vermont Ski Museum.

And these individuals: Henri Borel, Bill Bozack, Willy Bozack, Charlie Brown, Holly Buck, Jen Butson, Pat Clark, June Cook, Dennis Curran, Ann Day, Lee Hall Delfausse, John Egan, Tony Egan, Newcomb Eldredge, Dave Ellison, Henry Erickson, Erin Fernandez, Gene Foley, Rosie Fortna, Barb Frascella, Eric Friedman, Rick Hale, Dickie Hall, Al and Jane Hobart, Rich Jones, Mary Kerr, John Kerrigan, Doug Lewis, Lisa Loomis, Sandy Macys, Ron Majorell, Peter Miller, Edith Thys Morgan, Diana Mosher, Cindy Mumford, Ken Quackenbush, Judy Reiss, Malcolm Reiss, Mike Riddell, Lenord Robinson, Ginny Roth, John Roth, Meredith Scott, Peggy Shinn, J. J. Toland, Sally Knight Utter, Felix Von Moschzisker, Mike Ware, Chan Weller, Liz Weller, Candace White, Peter Wicklund, Ann Williams, Arthur Williams, John Williams, Mark Wooley, Kevin Wry, Jean Wry, and Kelly Murphy Wood.

A special thank you goes to the Williams family, who contributed the voluminous collection of photographs taken by Sewall Williams.

Books and publications of note: *A Mountain Love Affair: The Story of Mad River Glen* by Mary K. Kerr, 2008; *Boston Globe*, *Holiday Magazine*, *Life Magazine*, *Newsweek Magazine*, *New York Pops*, *The New York Times*, *Ski Magazine*, *Skiing Magazine*, *Sports Illustrated*, *Times Argus*, and *Valley Reporter*.

INTRODUCTION

Prior to the arrival of alpine skiing in Vermont in the 1930s and 1940s, prejudices about the little Green Mountain State bounced about the large urban areas elsewhere in the Northeast.

One publication intoned that "In small towns and on failing hill farms, life was particularly bleak. Two things have made living in Vermont bearable for much of the population: central heat, and television. Before central heat, winter was one long battle to stay warm. And before television, winter was long, dark, and very isolating."

Those critics appear to have never sat by a glowing wood stove on a cold winter night nor stopped by woods on a snowy evening. They had somehow forgotten, or were never aware of, Vermont's physiognomy: scenery and clean air that exalted one's daytime spirits to giddy heights. The critics failed to see that beneath the flintiness and glum veneer of Yankee farmers was a kinship with a place unmatched in scenic grandeur anywhere else on earth.

When the skiers came, there began a dependency and relationship that came to benefit both the visitors and the home folks. For the skiers, the mountains offered thrills, joy, and relief from stressful lifestyles in the cities. For the locals, it was an uplifting caused by something they had not seen much of before—money.

Thus was born a tourist economy that superseded dairy farming, logging, and sugaring. The Vermont Tourism Board in Montpelier noticed the changes and, by the 1950s, produced a series of films and advertisements to boost the influx. In the Mad River Valley, though the focus now concentrated on skiing, it was through the lens of the valley's rural charm: its inns, its country stores, and its generations-deep residents—who were not that unhappy after all. The latter opened their farmhouse doors, put in bunk beds, and cooked mighty breakfasts for the strangers.

It was not all pretty snowflakes at first. In fact, Mad River Glen started in 1948 as a resort full of mud, with so very little snow to ski upon, any innovator other than Roland Palmedo might have quit and gone back to Wall Street.

But Palmedo persisted, and soon Mad River's oddball Single Chair lift began clicking to the top of Stark Mountain amid bounteous snowfalls, with blankets, and even raccoon coats, draped over the knees to fend off the sharp winds.

Ten years later, Damon Gadd, who visited Mad River frequently, foresaw a different angle, and at his new place, Sugarbush, skiers stayed warm in an enclosed three-passenger gondola imported from Italy. But the contrivance was a magic carpet that swept up famous Broadway and Hollywood stars to the newly nicknamed "Mascara Mountain" to ride this novel wonder.

The difference between Mad River Glen and Sugarbush was, from the beginning, glaring. Mad River stood delightfully still while Sugarbush expanded. In 1978, the new owner, Roy Cohen, bought Glen Ellen, which had opened in 1964 as the third alpine resort.

But history has overlooked four tiny rope tow operations that lasted no more than one or a few years each. The first was the Warren Outing Club's operation on the Austin farm in Warren prior to World War II. Another was the rope tow at Tucker Hill, which augmented a cross-country operation that involved several inns. The third was a peewee rope tow in 1963 at the Alpen Inn on Route 100. The next year, the developers, George and Ann Day, installed a new, 1,500-foot-long rope tow on the site of the present-day Shaw's supermarket in Irasville. Powered by an old Buick engine, it sped uphill towards the Knoll Farm, but it lasted only a year.

An example of how well old Vermont had come to mingle with the rich and famous outsiders was when the movie star Kim Novak spent weekends with George and Ann Day at their Knoll Farm on Bragg Hill Road. By 1960, the flow of glittering show business people was on.

Then came college graduates, and many liked the trade-off in lifestyles so much that they decided to stay. No ski bum suffered a diminished social status in the Mad River Valley. High-paying jobs were exchanged for a quality of life with a nearly perfect place to raise families, trumping high-salaried careers in an office.

The folksiness of Mad River Glen, in particular, appealed to both the new arrivals and local, longtime residents alike. Mad River became a mountain very personal to the people who skied there—except for the snowboarders, who are not allowed. Visit any snowboarding Web site and search for mention of Mad River Glen. Make sure the children are in bed. The epithets are toxic.

The first two chapters of this book are snapshots of the growth of both resorts, offering glimpses of the mountains and the personnel who worked there, as well as the more loyal visitors who, in some cases, made the resorts a second home. Today great-grandparents show little ones where the best snow stashes are.

The third chapter is fat with the sporting life of ski racing champions who were both native to the valley and from abroad. The Green Mountain Valley School was started, an academic school aimed at producing racers whose fame would rise far beyond the valley in World Cup and Olympic venues.

The fourth chapter traces—in old photographs, maps, and menus—the growth of the hospitality side of the ski industry. By the 1960s, about 40 inns and restaurants were doing business. Many did not last but changed hands as the booms and busts of the nation's economy dictated.

The final chapter could easily have been the first, because it covers cross-country and telemark skiing, whose roots are in Norway many centuries ago. Cross-country trails run freely throughout the Mad River Valley; there are actually more trails than there are roads. Chief among them are those at Ole's Cross Country Ski Center and Blueberry Lake, both commercial operations begun by men who are now in their 80s, Ole Molseson and Lenord Robinson. Ole spends most of his time in his native Norway, where his family's fishing guide business goes back decades. Lenord is a deeply rooted dairy farmer who has watched his grandchildren progress on skinny skis and into championships as racers.

Not at all least in this package are those skiers who call themselves "pinheads," after the type of binding that goes with their telemark skis. They have the best of both worlds—cross-country and alpine—and boast that they can ski anywhere there is snow. The North American Telemark Organization (the other NATO) is firmly headquartered in Waitsfield, and every year, scores of devotees gather at Mad River Glen to ski and to party.

In fact, as you look through the pages of this book at some wonderful old photographs, you might question which stands out the most—the skiing or the partying. The correct answer is both.

1

Dearly Beloved Mad River Glen

The best skiers come from Vermont and from the East, because they have all the challenges here—the terrain and the conditions.

—Stein Eriksen

Over the long haul, several wizards held the same magic wand that fixed the tradition of Mad River Glen, chief among them Roland Palmedo, the founder; Ken Quackenbush; and Betsy Pratt. Stubbornly rejecting profit and benignly nurturing the mountain's rugged nature year after year, they let the precipitous land remain as it was created by the Ice Age 20,000 years ago, with its nooks, crannies, rivulets, and fall lines.

The crazy mix of fast and steep trails amid boulders and trees was a skiing experience that was honest to both the terrain and the people who skied there.

The skiers knew what they were getting, and the fact that it was not corduroy-easy made the challenge better for its excitement, and, more importantly, its intimacy. What Palmedo created became very personal to the skiers who visited and returned, time after time, virtually raising their families there for as many as three and four generations. The result is an iconic mountain resort unequaled in time or place, with a reputation of uniqueness that has bounded around the world.

By the time Betsy Pratt handed over ownership to the cooperative of skiers who were part of that family, the tradition was fixed. But now there were hundreds of owners, a democratic, cooperative concept that could have become a chaotic free-for-all tempted by "improvements." It has not happened. That all of those owners resisted change was memorialized with the cloning and restoration of the old, beloved Single Chair that continues to click and clack its way smoothly to the summit, one passenger at a time.

The most beautiful aspect of Mad River is that, when all of those who have lived and loved the place to this date are gone and new generations take over, things will remain the same. The place is haunted by loving ghosts who will not allow man-made advancements to mar its traditions and natural beauty.

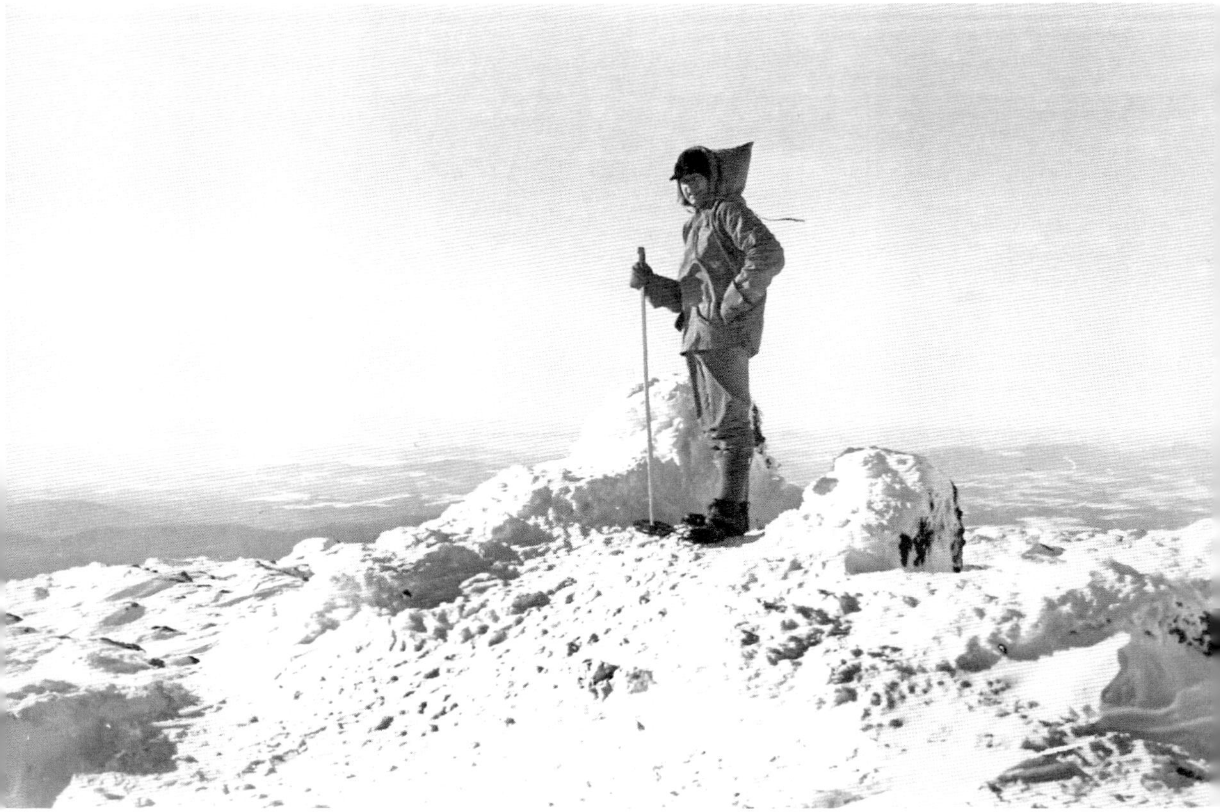

People who climb mountains earn the sobriquet "visionary," both literally and figuratively. What did Roland Palmedo see on this trip to the summit of Mount Washington in 1916? A sport where participants would go downhill an awful lot faster than it took him to go up the East's tallest mountain? Certainly, World Wars I and II again took him to the clouds. As a wartime pilot, that vision must have sharpened, and a job on Wall Street gave him capital to fulfill some dreams. Palmedo helped found the ski resort at Stowe and took to the air again in the 1940s to scout a mountain 25 miles to the south. The result, Mad River Glen, opened on December 11, 1948, but the festivities were largely ceremonial because of disappointing amounts of snow cover. (Courtesy of Mad River Glen.)

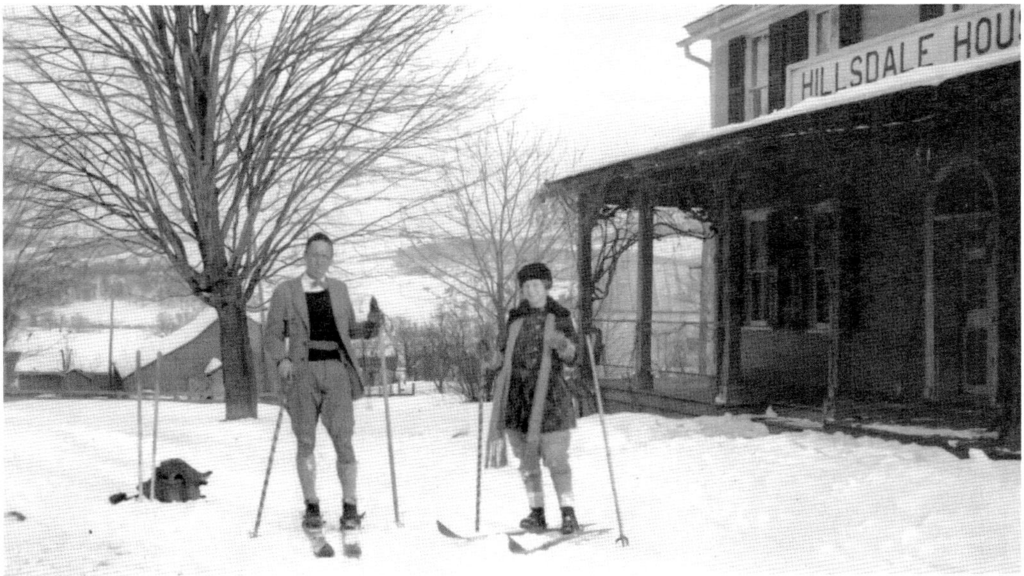

Palmedo's first experiences with the sport he loved began in the Alps more than 30 years before he founded Mad River Glen. After World War I, in which he was a U.S. Navy pilot, he succeeded on Wall Street as an investment banker, and, for relaxation, enjoyed winter sports at Hillsdale in the Adirondacks, dragging along several Wall Street friends, whom he then enticed into skiing at Stowe in the 1930s. (Courtesy of Mad River Glen.)

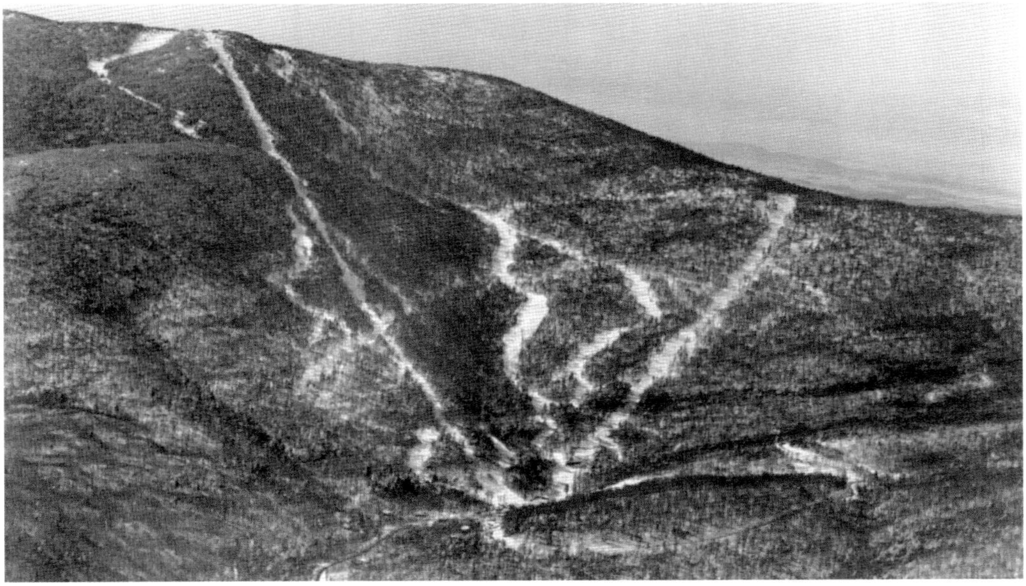

The 1,730 acres of mountainous property pictured here that became Mad River Glen was actually chosen by Roland Palmedo and his partners after they had considered a location in Warren near the Lincoln Gap Road. The Warren site was turned down for several reasons, including the lack of lodging in the neighborhood and a very much impaired Route 100. (Courtesy of Mad River Glen.)

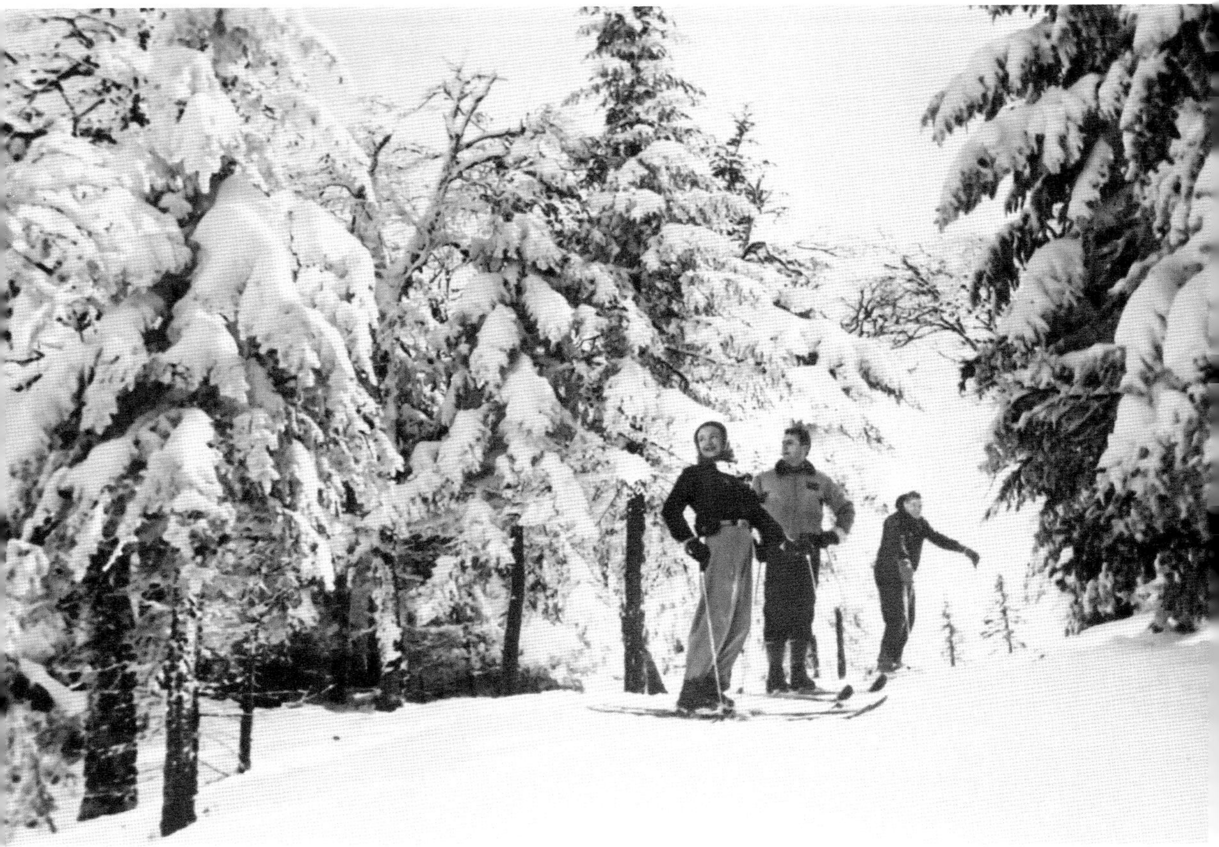

Finally, after a decrepit first season of little snow and mild weather, the heavens blessed Mad River Glen. "All kept their chins up," wrote Palmedo, "and richly deserve the extra-good, real old-fashioned Vermont winter in the snow corner of New England." The first trails that were cut were Catamount, Lift Line, Fall Line, Canyon, and Porcupine. But the fickleness of Vermont winters seemed in full swing. Ironically, when Palmedo wanted to open the place in 1947, a fierce snowstorm in November buried the mountain, but it did not continue, and the opening had to be postponed until the following year. The first really good snow was in February of 1949, and then Mad River Glen took off. The mountain's challenge led to a unique race called "No Stop, No Fall," and it became a tradition carried out annually. (Courtesy of Mad River Glen.)

Construction of the Single Chair at Mad River Glen was done in the late 1940s. As lift lines increased, 68 new chairs were added, nearly doubling the capacity in 1955. Nine years later, another 25 chairs made for a total of 158. (Courtesy of Mad River Glen).

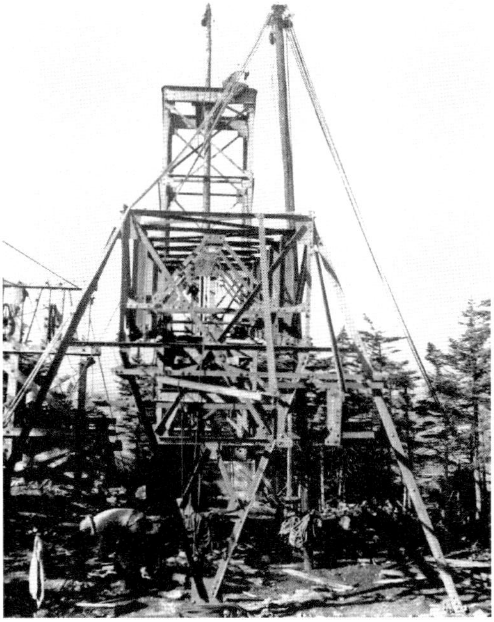

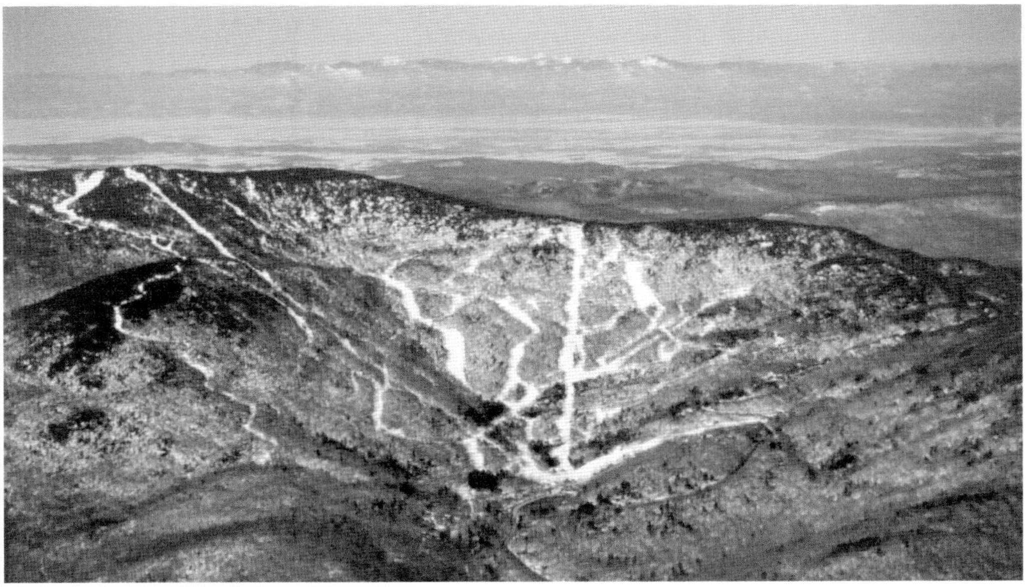

The configuration of Stark Mountain fit nearly perfectly with the ambitions of Mad River Glen's founders. Trail designer Charlie Lord, in a letter to Roland Palmedo in 1946, wrote that the mountain in Fayston was one of the best locations "for good snow conditions for it has protection from the wind as well as the sun, and snow will last two to three weeks longer than an East to South location." (Courtesy of Mad River Glen.)

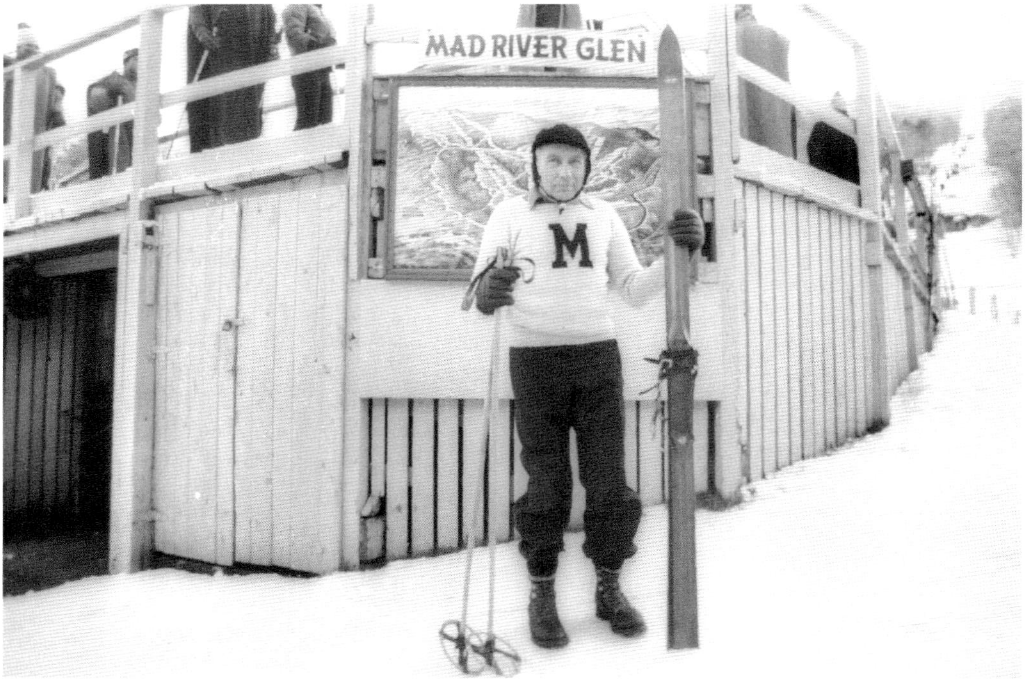

Ken Quackenbush, shown here in vintage garb at the 40th reunion of Mad River Glen in 1988, carried on Roland Palmedo's goals as president/general manager for 45 years. Those goals were to keep development simple and let the mountain set the style. (Courtesy of Mad River Glen.)

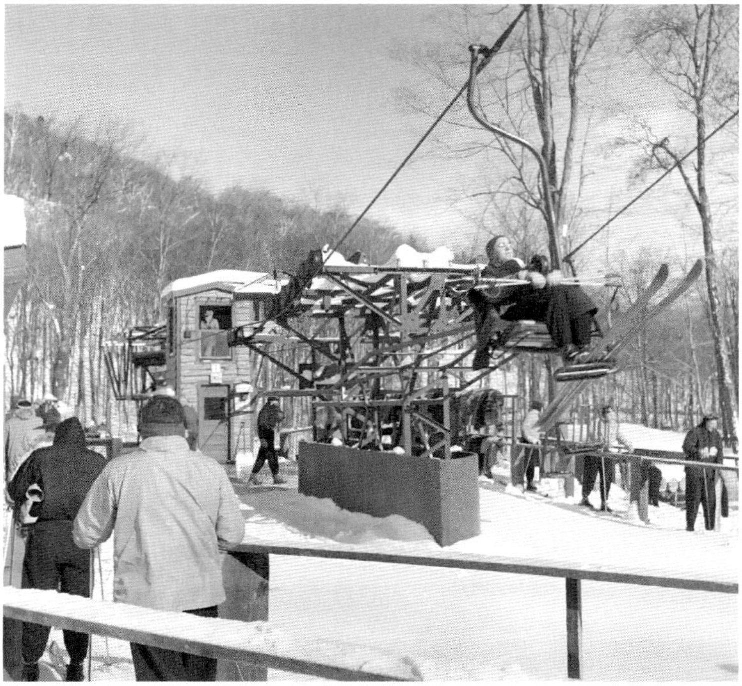

Anywhere in the Mad River Valley, an offhand remark about the Single Chair brought smiles of recognition. So beloved was this creaky old darling—the last one operating in the United States—that the $1.7 million needed to restore it was quickly raised by cooperative owners of the resort, including the sale of more than 140 of the old chairs at up to $1,500 each. (Courtesy of Mad River Glen.)

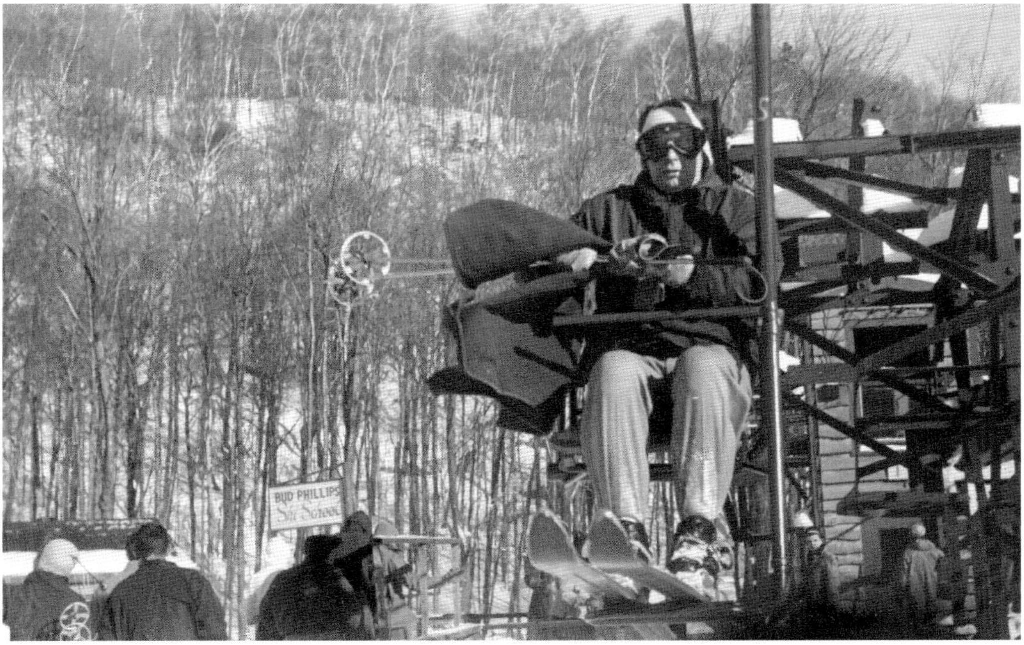

The long chilly ride to the top can thwart enthusiasm. For warmth and comfort, Sugarbush had its gondola, Mad River its blanket. Both the gondola and the blanket are gone, but the world-famous Single Chair at Mad River Glen is the last in the country still in use, having been rebuilt in 2007. (Courtesy of the Charlie Lord collection.)

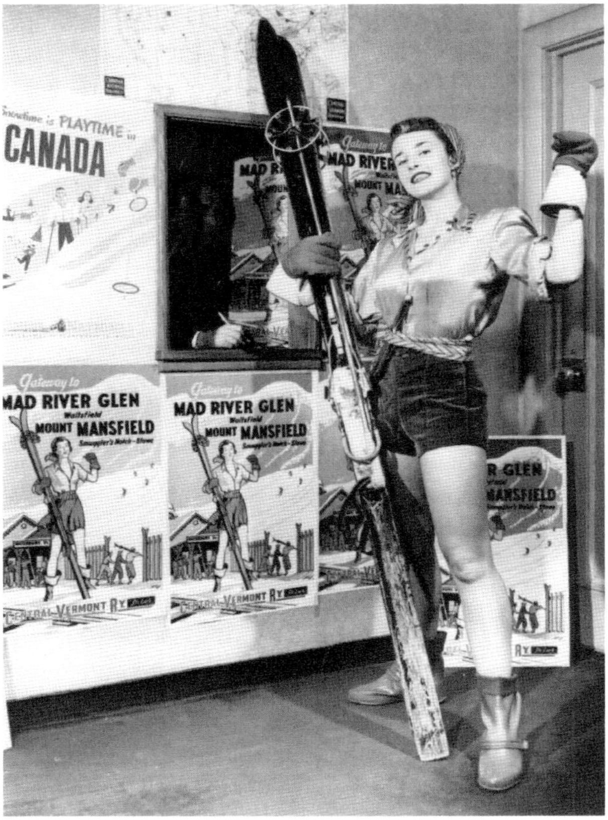

Mad River Glen and the valley were established as a big-time destination resort area, thanks in part to the *Ski Lark*, the weekend passenger train that hauled enthusiastic skiers from New York City to Waterbury, beginning in the late 1940s. Joan Smith was the Mad River Glen poster girl in this promo photograph, which was published in newspapers as far away as New Mexico and Alabama. (Courtesy of Ski Vermont.)

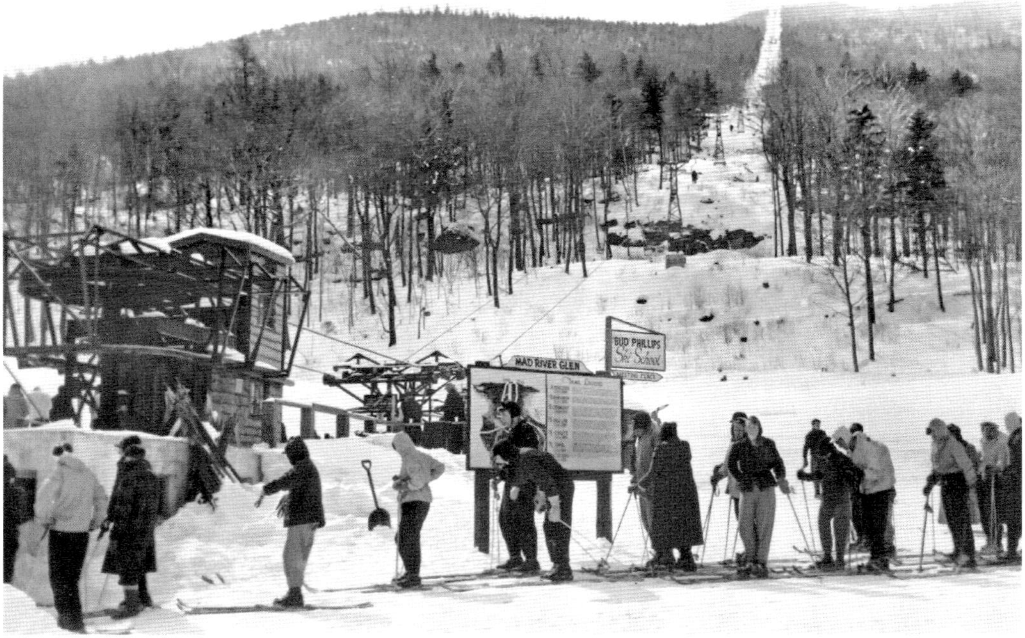

The lift line extends beyond the gathering place for novices and experienced skiers to meet for the Bud Phillips Ski School at Mad River Glen. Phillips directed the classes from its inception in 1948 on up to 1966. Phillips was one of the World War II members of the legendary 10th Mountain Infantry Division that was the vanguard of the skiing industry as it is known today. (Courtesy of Ski Vermont.)

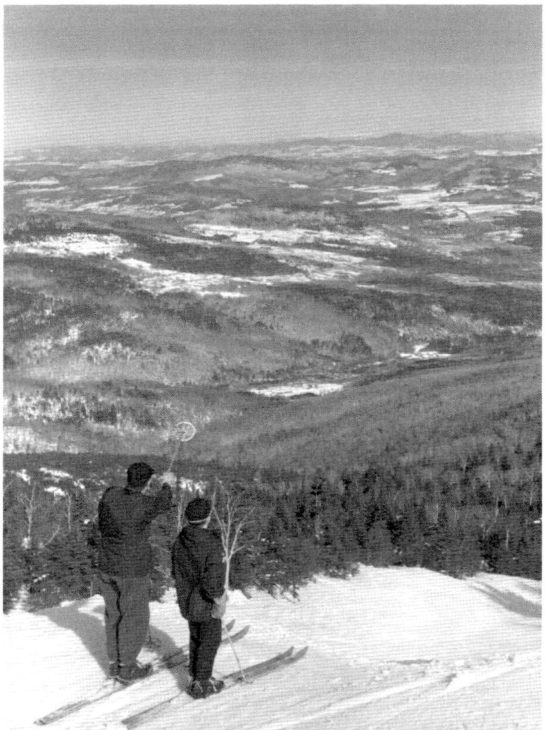

Lean years turned to good years, depending on the weather. During the Christmas holidays of 1955, more than 10,000 passengers made it to the top of General Stark Mountain, marking the beginning of a remarkable year. The lift shut down April 17 after 124 days of operation, with 119 of them being consecutive. (Courtesy of Mad River Glen.)

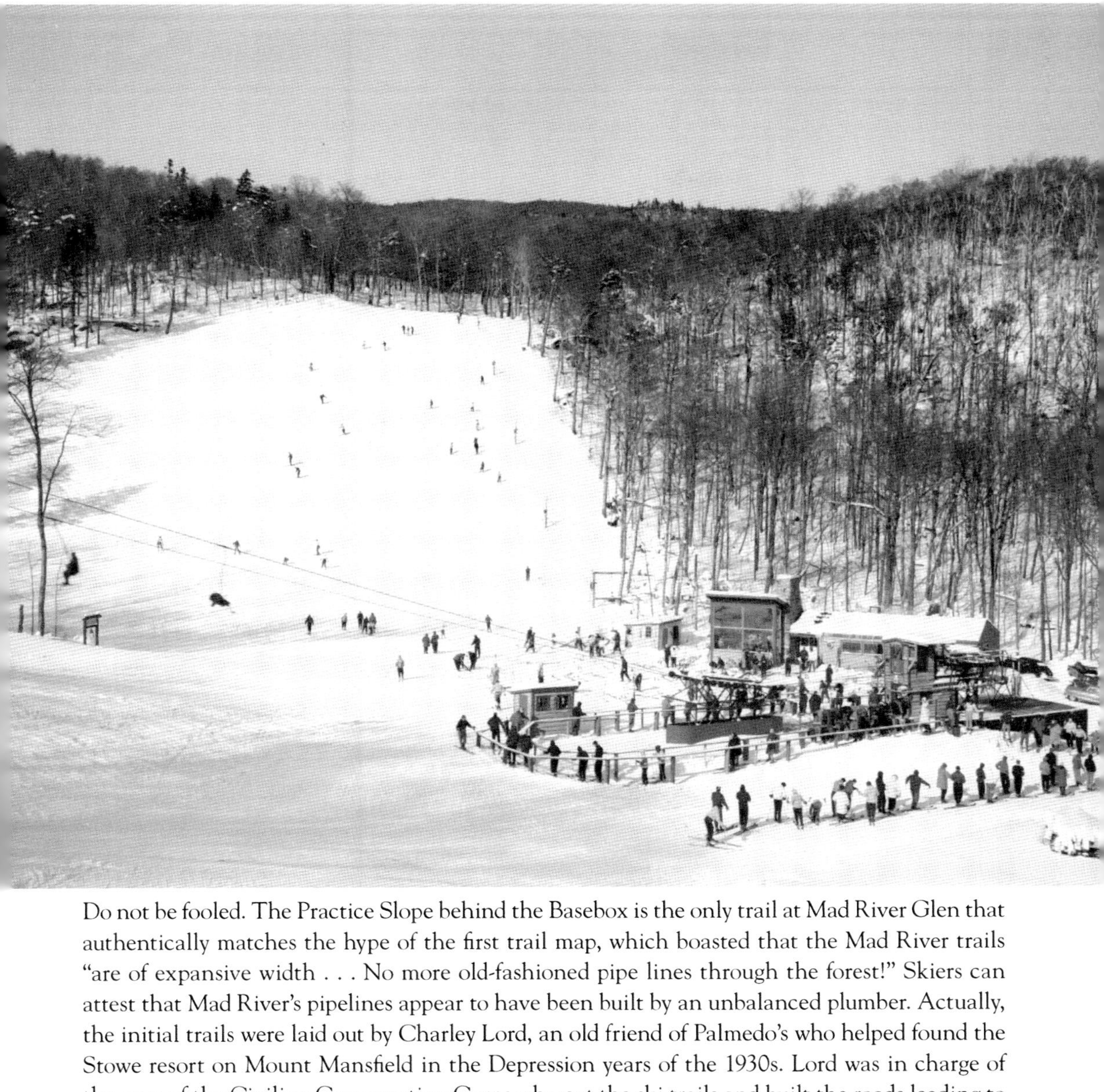

Do not be fooled. The Practice Slope behind the Basebox is the only trail at Mad River Glen that authentically matches the hype of the first trail map, which boasted that the Mad River trails "are of expansive width . . . No more old-fashioned pipe lines through the forest!" Skiers can attest that Mad River's pipelines appear to have been built by an unbalanced plumber. Actually, the initial trails were laid out by Charley Lord, an old friend of Palmedo's who helped found the Stowe resort on Mount Mansfield in the Depression years of the 1930s. Lord was in charge of the men of the Civilian Conservation Corps who cut the ski trails and built the roads leading to Mount Mansfield. Stowe was a natural place for a ski resort because tourists had been coming to the mountain since the 1850s. (Courtesy of Mad River Glen.)

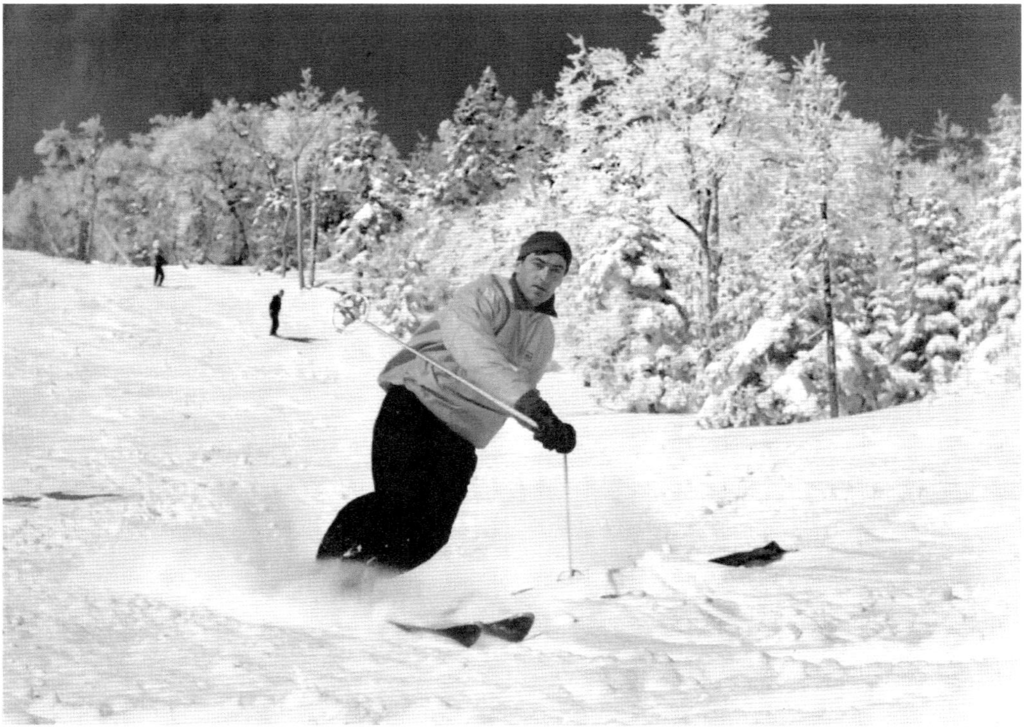

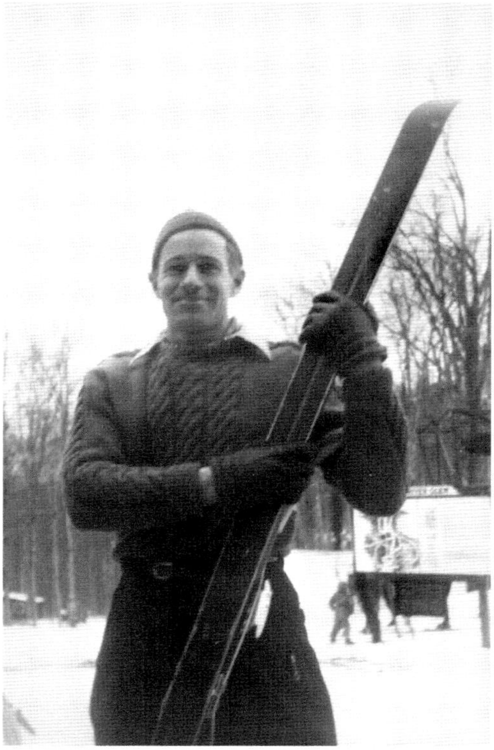

If the instructor cannot make a turn look easy, who is to trust him? But Bud Phillips, who ran the first ski school at Mad River Glen, never had that problem. Keeping up with him, however, was a challenge. He taught fall line skiing, in tune with the precipitous terrain of the mountain—tight, fast, and narrow. (Courtesy of Kelly Murphy Wood.)

Cliff Taylor was an instructor in the Bud Phillips Ski School, which operated from the beginning of Mad River Glen until the 1965–1966 season, when it was taken over by Rudi Maier. At about the same time, the resort opened the trails in Birdland. (Photograph by Sewall Williams.)

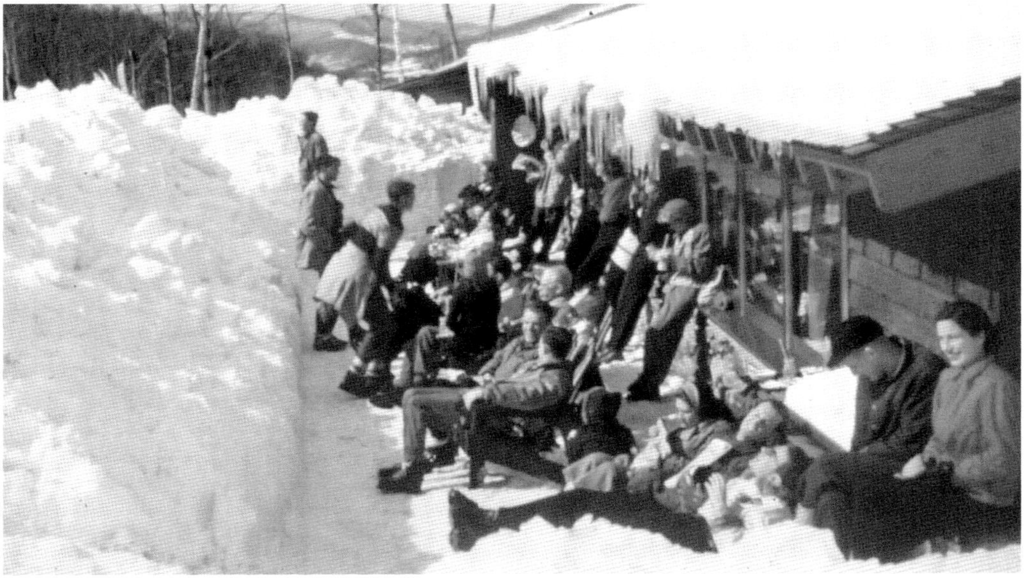

This is an "answered prayers" photograph showing scads of snow piled up against the lodge at Mad River Glen. The resort was cursed in the beginning by two miserable snowfall seasons (1949 and 1950). In January of 1949, there was practically no snow, and for the season, the lift operated only 55 days, which was about half the normal expectancy. (Photograph by Sewall Williams.)

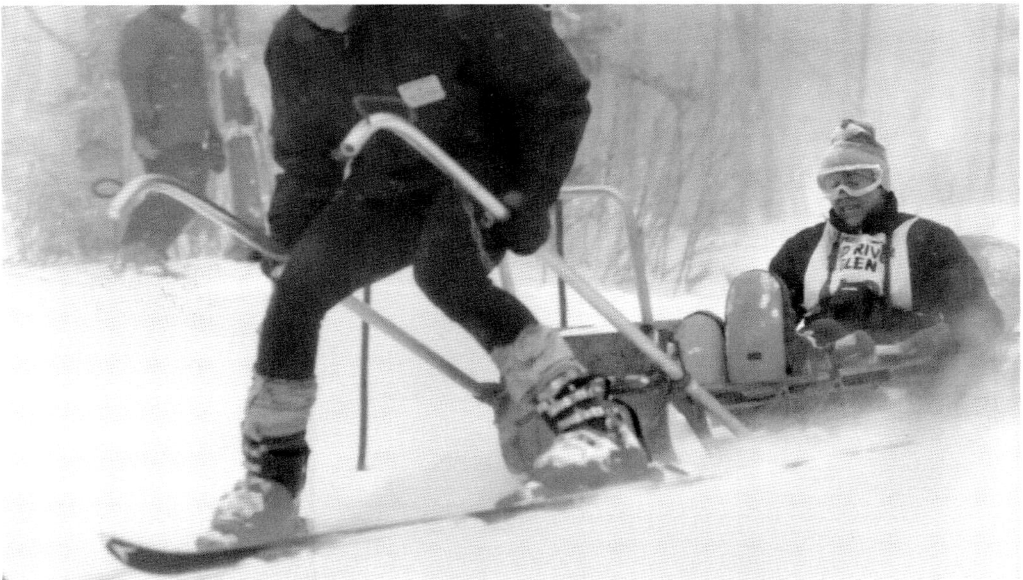

The National Ski Patrol, which was founded by Charles Minot "Minnie" Dole at Stowe in 1938, was soon brought to Mad River Glen by Roland Palmedo. At Mad River, the task of maneuvering a sled weighted with an injured skier requires unimaginable strength and skill on steep trails braced by rocks, ice, trees, and—sometimes—mud. (Courtesy of Mad River Glen.)

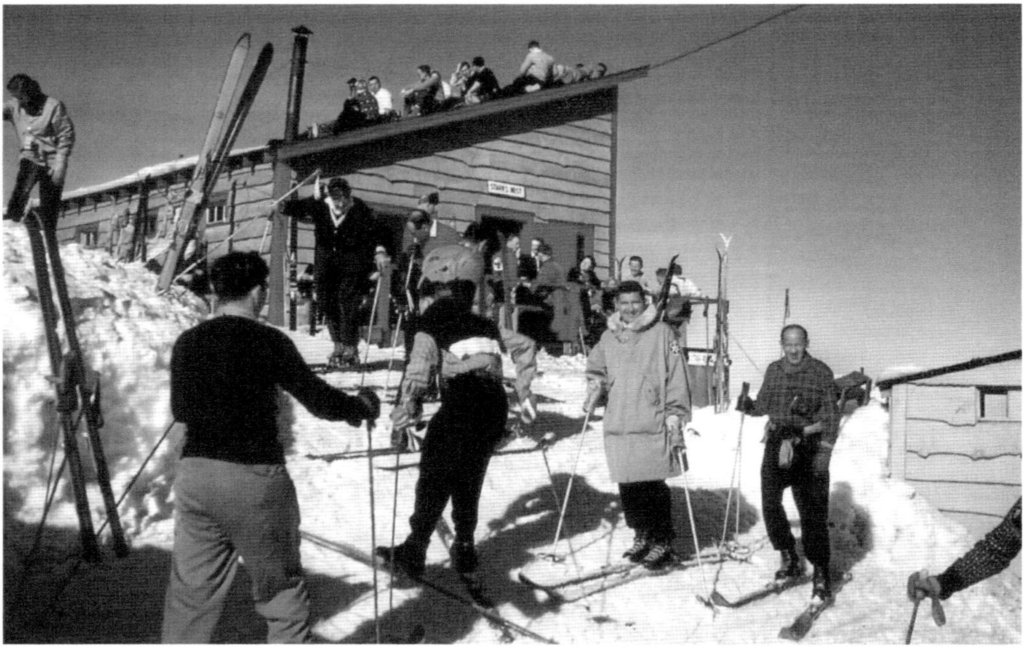

Stark's Nest at the top of the Single Chair lift is also a landmark on Vermont's famous Long Trail, a favorite of hikers, and is at the very top of Stark's Mountain, which was named after Revolutionary War Gen. John Stark. Not to be left out is Molly Stark Mountain, named after John's wife, to the north of John's peak. The shed shown here was renovated in 2000–2001. (Courtesy of Mad River Glen.)

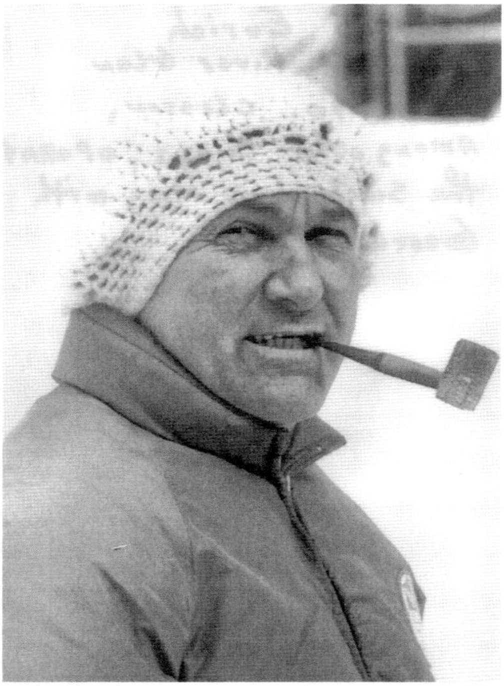

From the beginning, Clesson Eurich was one of three mainstay lift operators, along with George Neil and Bill Peatman, who sent the Single Chair on its way up the mountain. Many employees enjoyed lifelong careers at Mad River Glen. (Courtesy of Mad River Glen.)

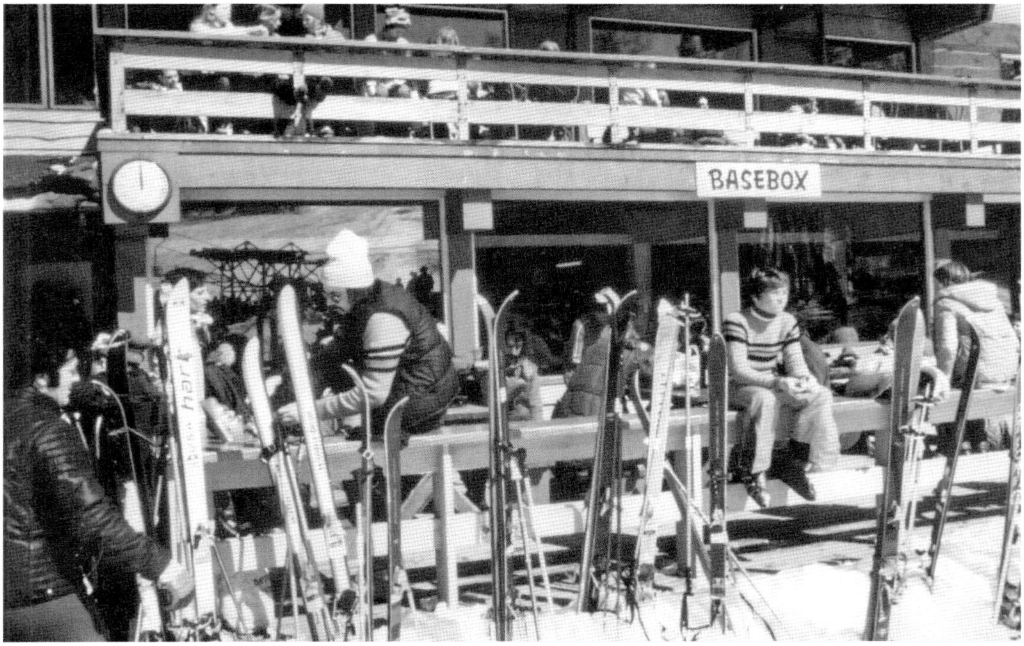

Little more than a decade after opening day in 1948, the core support of skiers at Mad River Glen seemed solidified. The season of 1960–1961 marked one of the busiest periods of the resort's history. The first ski shop was completed, the first Tucker Snow Cat was purchased, and the General Stark Pub was added to the Basebox. (Courtesy of Mad River Glen.)

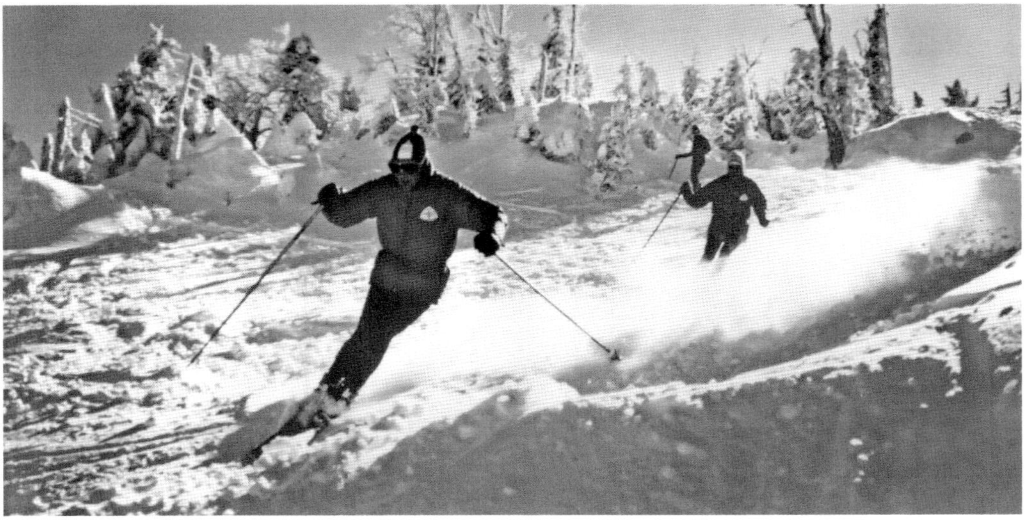

Skiing styles have changed dramatically since Rudi Maier—who, in 1966, took over from Bud Phillips as ski school director at Mad River Glen—handled these moguls near the summit of Stark Mountain on a frosty, bright day. Gone are the locked ankles demonstrated by Maier. An early brochure hailed the smooth skiing style with a report that "the Glen is known for its excellent and beautiful skiers." (Courtesy of Mad River Glen.)

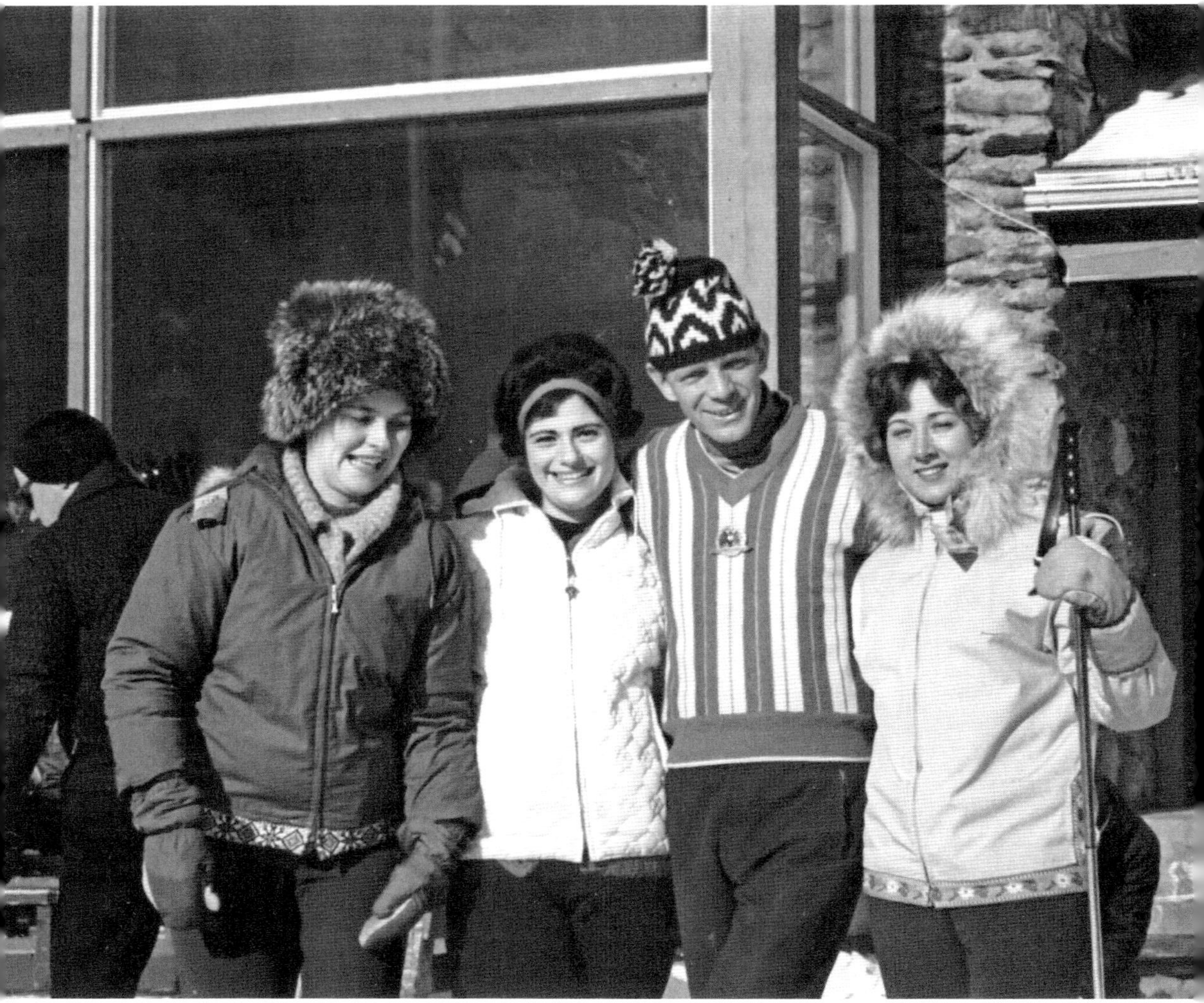

As word spread of the uniqueness of Mad River Glen—its interesting and tough terrain and the old New England ambience of the surrounding villages and the valley—the initial isolation vanished, and the mountain's popularity grew, as attested to by these guests from United Nations headquarters in New York, shown in 1964 with ski instructor Otto Egger. Representatives from Hungary, Japan, Yugoslavia, Kuwait, Pakistan, Spain, and the Sudan visited the valley and Mad River. The international invasion sometimes stood in stark contrast to the pre-skiing days in the remote valley. In 1947 there were only 25 houses in Fayston, and it took 16 years for that number to triple. Expansion came after 1956, when the McCullough Turnpike was extended over the Appalachian Gap and down the other side to Bristol. (Courtesy of Mad River Glen.)

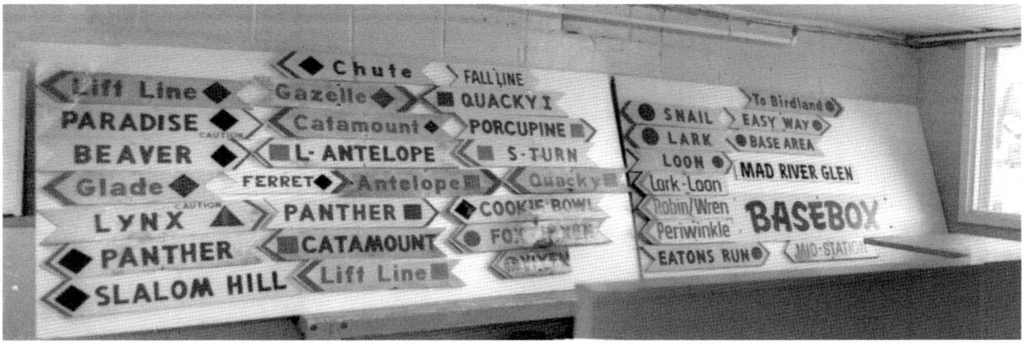

Giving names to ski trails is a lot easier than building them. Mad River Glen, in the beginning, had Charlie Lord as its general manager to thank for recognizing pitch and direction, felling trees, and bringing other engineering skills to the mountain. He originally helped develop Stowe at Mount Mansfield, and at one time he served both mountains. (Courtesy of Mad River Glen.)

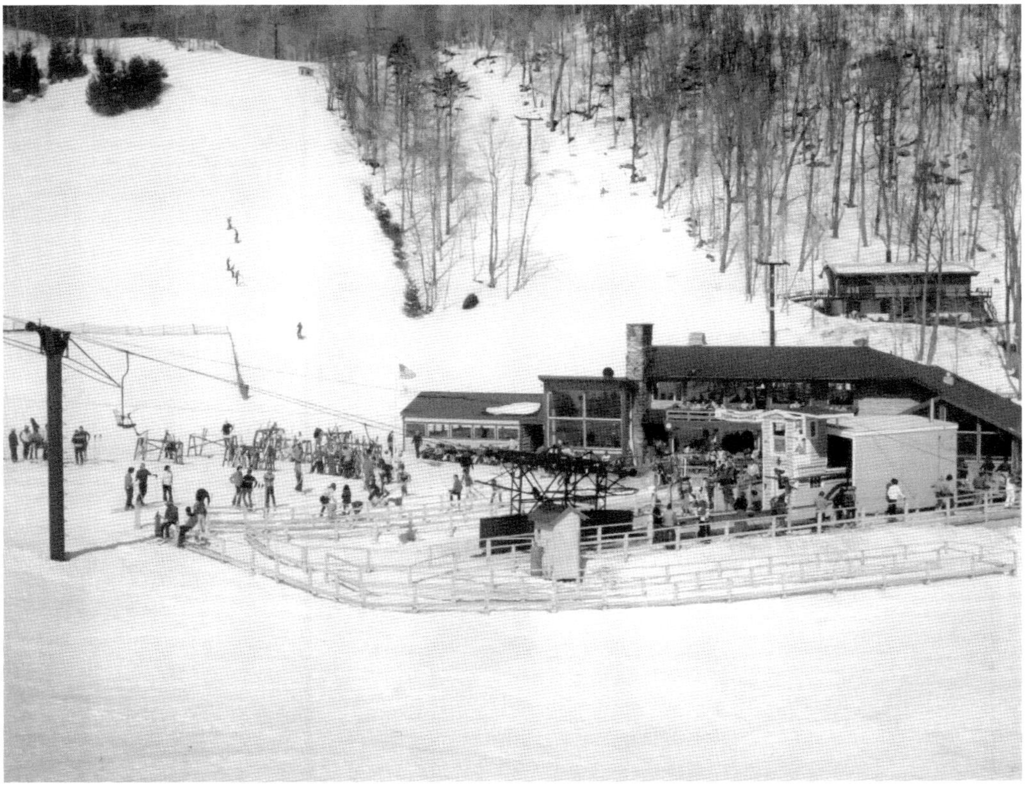

As the popularity of Mad River grew, the area surrounding the Basebox was developed—but not into large condo units and hotels. Housing in keeping with the low-key approach instilled by Palmedo, like a cluster of private chalets and seven ski clubs: Hartford, Amateur Ski Club of New York, Montclair, North Jersey Whiz Skiers, Garden City, Ramapo Mountain, and White Plains. (Courtesy of Mad River Glen.)

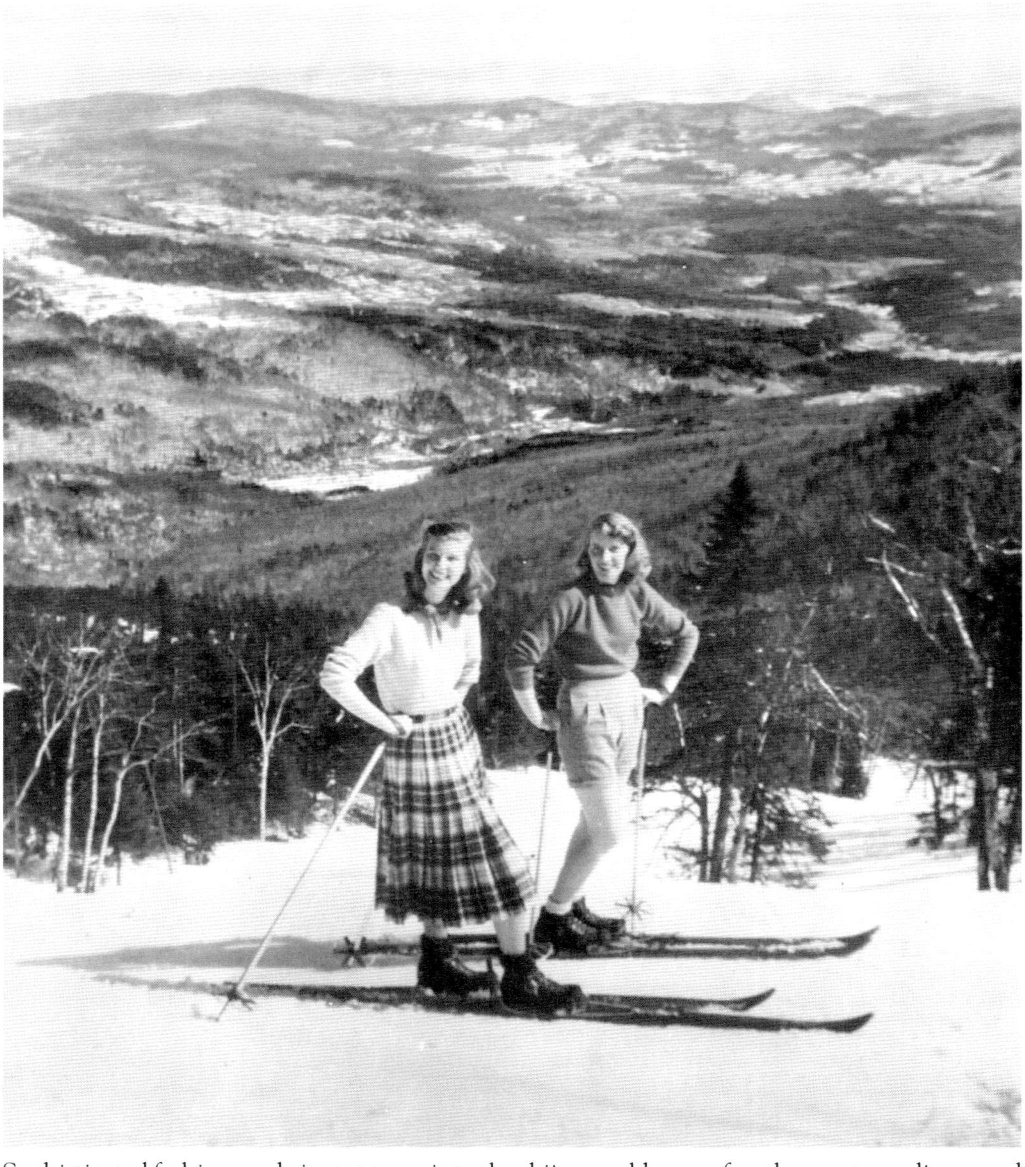

Sophisticated fashion made its entrance into the skiing world soon after the sport was discovered by high society. Having taken a weekend train from New York City to Vermont, and even to Mad River Glen, these two young ladies pose against the beautiful backdrop of the valley. Today, high style is the exception at Mad River. Flannel, wool, and puffy jackets top the sartorial chart. When skiing became fashionable to city folk who made visits to Vermont a "must do" on the social circuit, Mad River Glen was somewhat of an exception, most likely due to the demands of the mountain's trails. Ripped pants were common in the early days as skiers learned to dodge the trees and rocks. Even the less difficult trails at Mad River took part in the challenge. Though of an easier pitch, they still followed the natural contours of the mountain, which could be on the rough side. (Courtesy of Mad River Glen.)

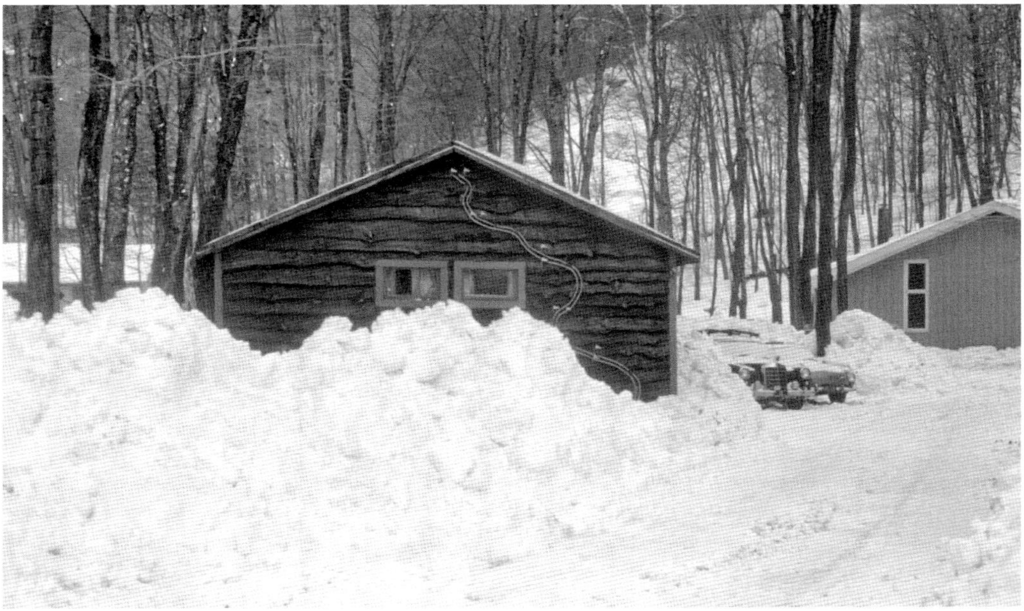

Bountiful dumps of snowfall in 1965–1966 led to Mad River Glen's best season since the resort opened 17 years before, with the 133 total days of operation beating the old record of 130 days during the 1958–1959 season. (Courtesy of Mad River Glen.)

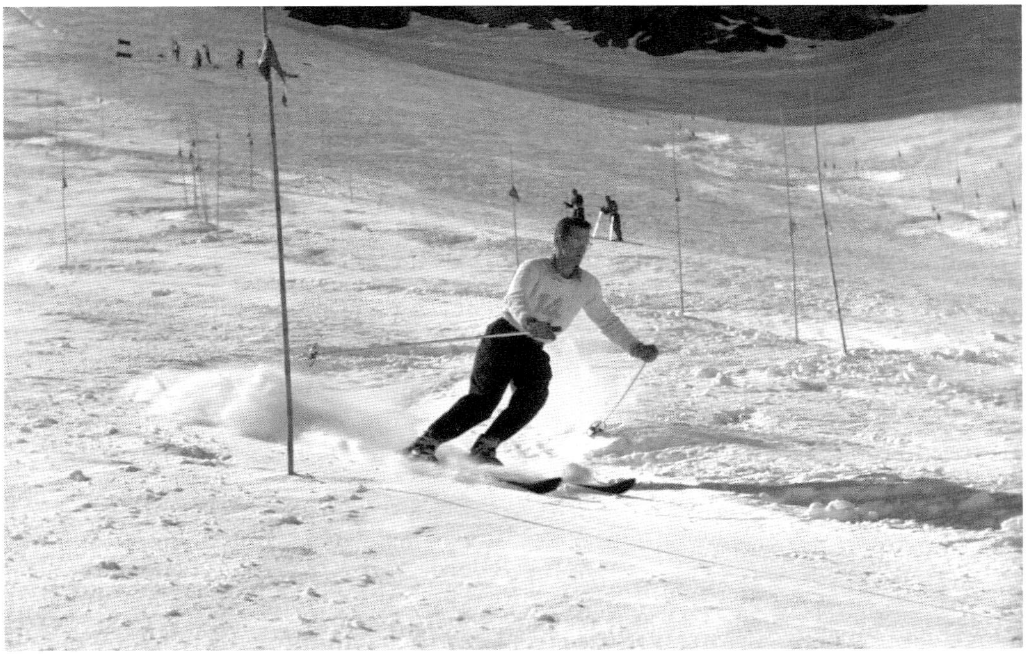

There have been many racing programs at Mad River Glen, ranging from national and invitational races down to the amateur Inter Club Race and Family Tournament, the Chipmunk Race for little people, and the all-ages No Stop, No Fall contest. (Courtesy of Mad River Glen.)

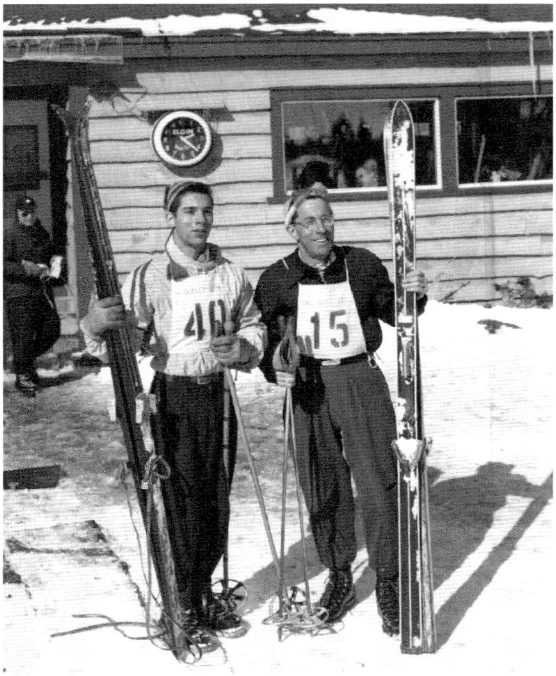

Ed Eaton, right, helped supervise many of the races held over the years at Mad River Glen. Ed and his son, Ken, posed after taking gold in the annual Father and Son Race, which was no just-for-fun event but a serious undertaking of speed that embraced several generations. (Courtesy of Kelly Murphy Wood.)

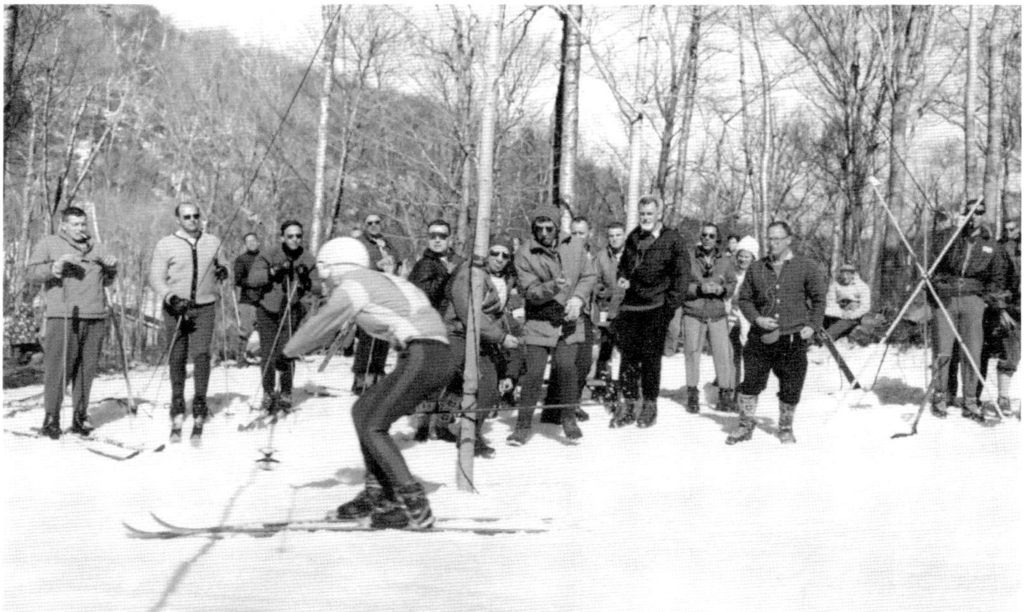

On March 25, 1956, the first New England Kandahar race was held at Mad River. The naming of the race has a long and twisted history, beginning with the battle of Kandahar in Afghanistan, where in 1880, a British general, Frederick Sleigh Roberts, distinguished himself against Afghan troops, earning him the title Lord Roberts of Kandahar. The popular Roberts put up a trophy in 1903 for the first in a series of ski races in Europe. (Courtesy of Mad River Glen.)

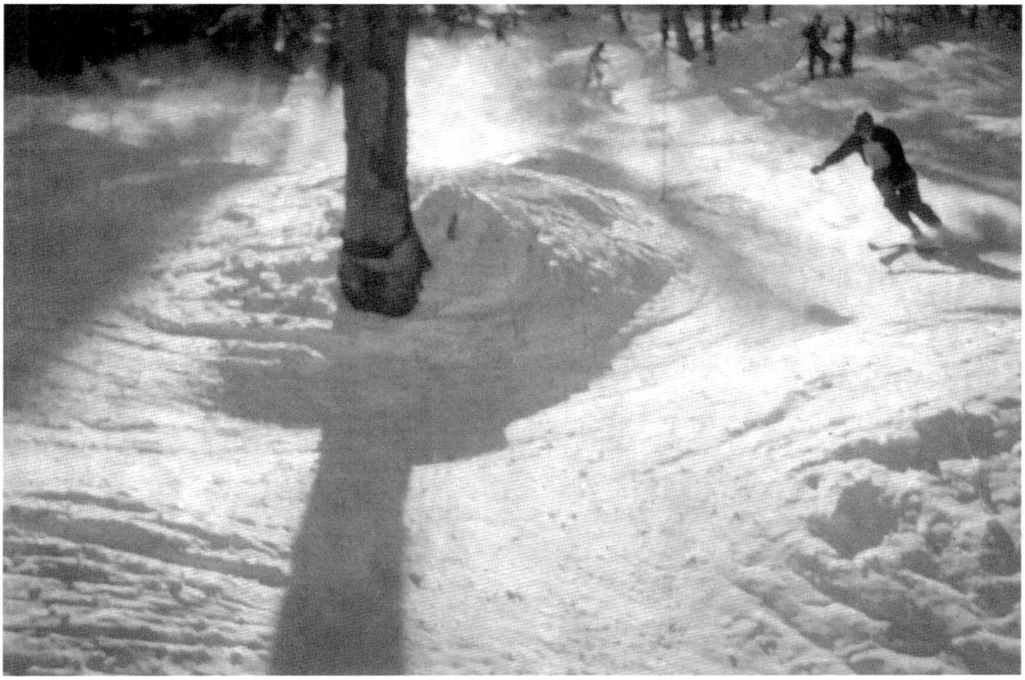

Trees may be viewed as an obstacle to some skiers, but to Mad River Glen habitués, the trees create the roundabouts of tummy-tumbling dips and swoops that make a day of skiing worthwhile. (Courtesy of Mad River Glen.)

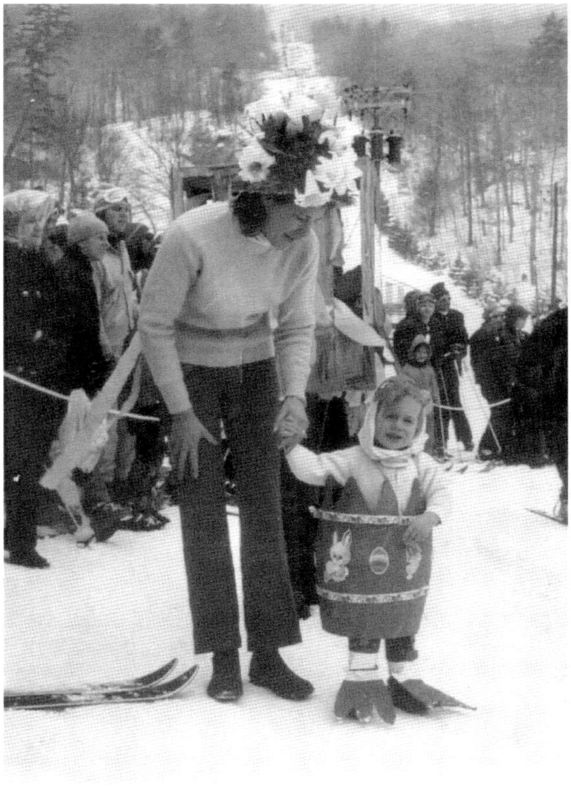

Shucking off the wool caps and ski jackets when the weather teases into spring culminates in a joyous, annual Easter parade, celebrated at Mad River Glen for 60 years. Here Nancy Spencer Smith shows off her Easter bonnet, and little Spencer Leon poses as a Tiffany egg. (Courtesy of Mad River Glen.)

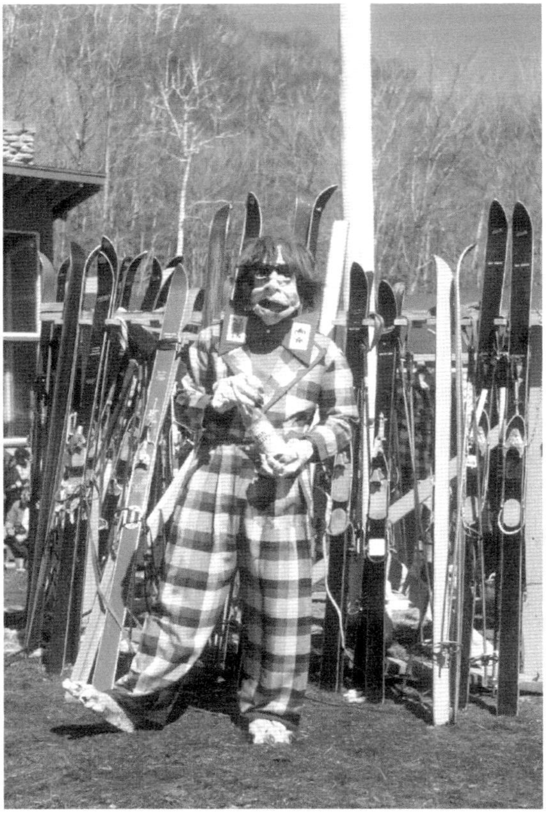

Easter at Mad River Glen usually featured the dual celebrations of a Sunrise Service followed by a parade marking the leap from winter into the realities of the Mud Season, a day for both solemnity and partying with hopefully a few more runs of skiing. Though there is no snow under the clown's feet at left, the skis in the racks indicate that the lifts are humming and somewhere up there is enough snow to make tracks. In the bottom photo, tree skiing is a skill not yet mastered by this participant in one of the annual Easter Day celebrations outside the Bandbox. (Both courtesy of Mad River Glen.)

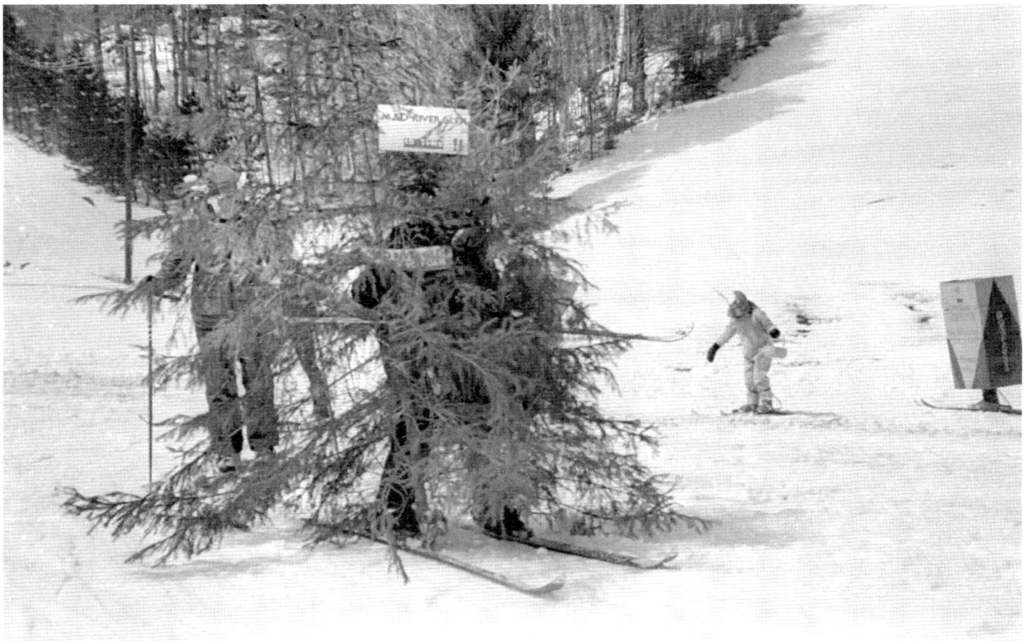

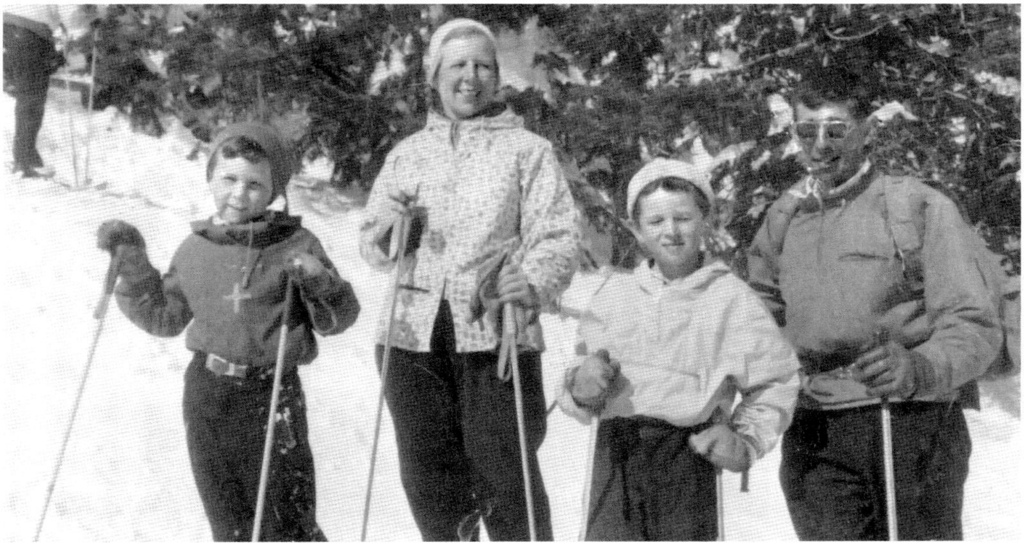

The daily routines of the Clark family were intertwined with Mad River Glen in the aspects of livelihood, social life, sports, and recreation. The family ski lodge, operated by parents Nancy and Allen, pictured here, was just down the road. Their sons Tom (left) and Dave, when not in school, practically lived at Mad River. Tom and his wife Leigh spent more than three decades on the ski patrol and as a ski instructor, respectively. Allen died in 1997 and Nancy in 2003. The Clarks' Ski Lodge is now the Mountain Side Lodge. (Courtesy of Kelly Murphy Wood.)

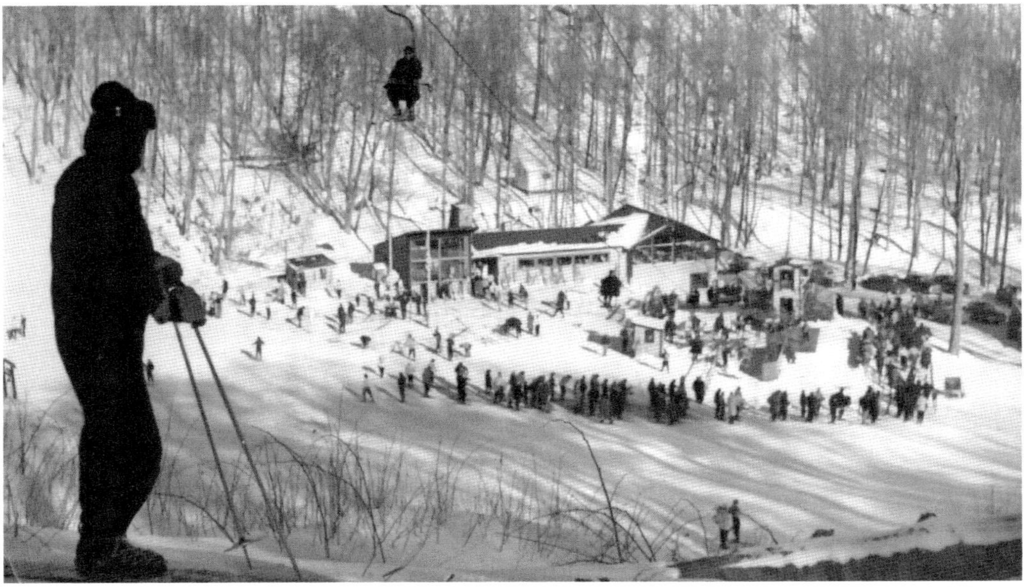

When the cooperative finally decided to rebuild the Single Chair, not much trouble was had attracting financing. More than 1,300 individuals donated, and Mad River skiers themselves raised more than $1.7 million. Major contributors were honored by brass plaques placed on the towers. (Courtesy of Kelly Murphy Wood.)

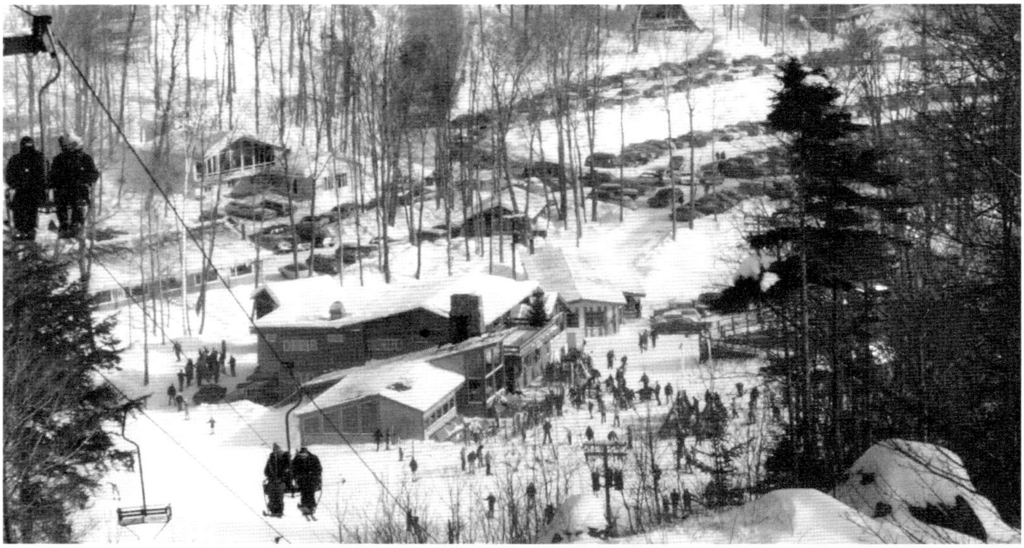

Riding up the Sunnyside Double, Mad River Glen skiers have their choice of several novice and expert trails, like Panther and Partridge. In 1998, the 50th anniversary of the mountain resort, the double chair was replaced with a new one. (Courtesy of Mad River Glen.)

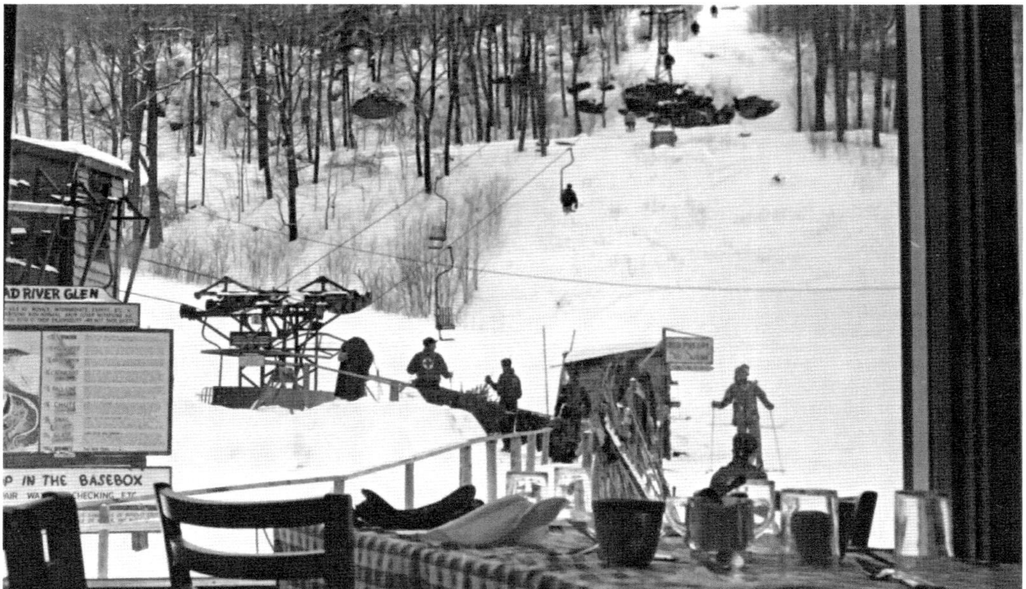

One of the best years enjoyed by skiers at Mad River was 1958–1959. Up to 4 feet of snow had fallen at the base of the mountain by Christmas. One snowstorm in March of 1959 dumped 22 inches of snow within 48 hours. In the winters spanning 1992–1994, 30 feet fell on the mountain during each of those years. A heavy snowfall and cold temperatures dropping on the northward, wind-protected slopes of Mad River adds up to many days of powder, affirming the wisdom of Roland Palmedo and Charley Lord. (Courtesy of Kelly Murphy Wood.)

On Mad River Glen's 40th birthday in 1989, several devotees gathered. Among them were, from left to right, Dave Cripen, Ted Iwerson, Serge ?, Hugh McIntyre, Patty Latte, Betsy Pratt, Ellie McIntyre, and Barbara Ireland. Betsy Pratt took over control of the mountain upon the death of her husband, Truxton, who had bought the resort in 1972. She stayed the course of keeping the mountain somewhat different by not giving into the temptation to turn it into a purely moneymaking enterprise. (Photograph by Sandy Macys.)

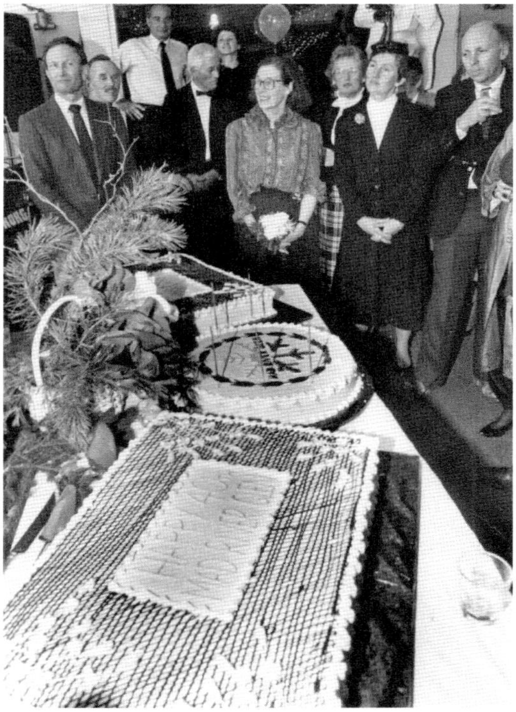

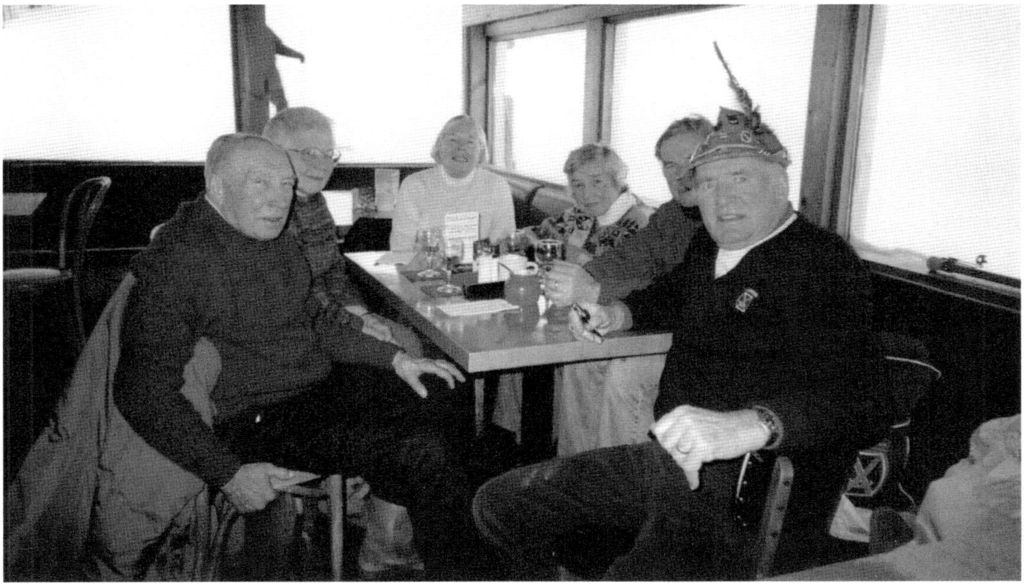

Decades of valley history are shown here seated in the General Stark Pub. Clockwise, from left, are Ken Quackenbush, former general manager and president in the ski area's formative years; Nancy Clark, who, with her husband, ran the Clark's Ski Lodge until 1973; Ann Williams; Fran Quackenbush, Ken's wife; Arthur Williams; and Sewall Williams, Arthur's brother. Ann, Arthur, and Sewall were proprietors of the Ulla Lodge. (Courtesy of Vermont Ski Museum.)

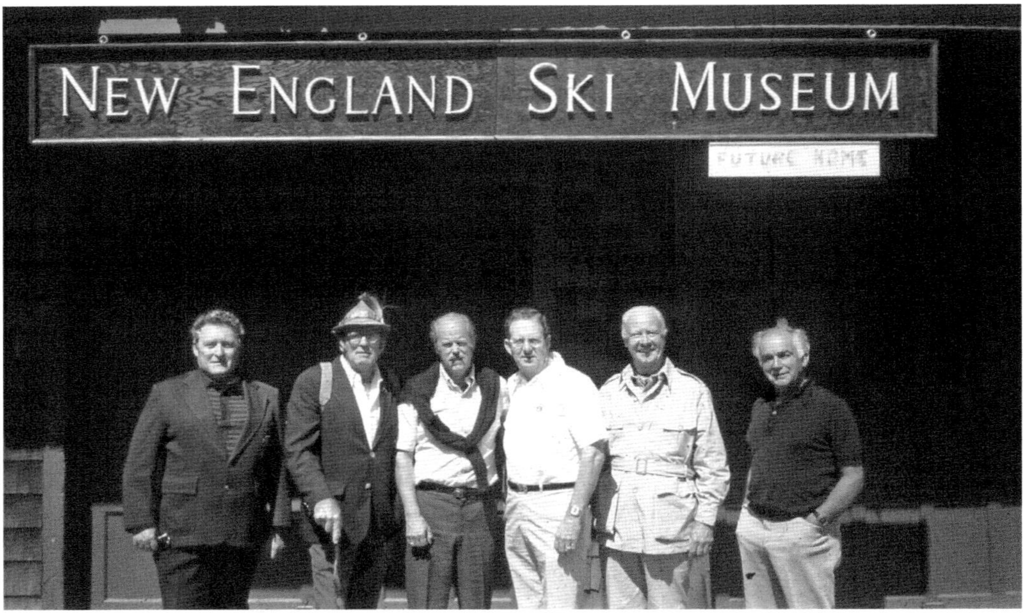

Veterans of the U.S. Army's 10th Mountain Division were honored by the New England Ski Museum. They are, from left to right, Andy Hastings, Sewall Williams, Newcom Eldredge, Mac MacKenzie, Vinnie Kehoe, and Arthur March. More 10th Mountain Division veterans appeared with Betsy Pratt, the owner and operator of Mad River. Pictured below, from left to right, are Tom Duff, Dick Leo, Sewall Williams, Betsy Pratt, Henry Perkins, Bill Hoople, Bob Traynor, and Don Linscott. Betsy succeeded her husband, Truxton Pratt, as owner of Mad River in 1975. In 1995, she sold the mountain to the Mad River Glen Cooperative after fighting off several would-be commercial buyers for months. Her goal was to keep control of Mad River in the hands of the loyal people who skied there. (Courtesy of Sewall Williams.)

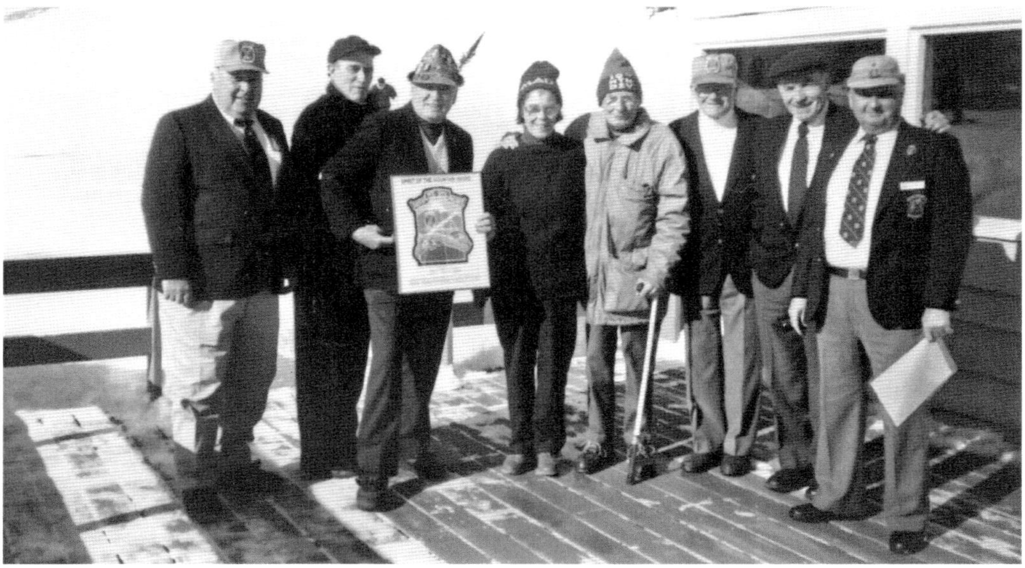

Sewall Williams was stationed at Camp Hale in Colorado when the 10th Mountain Division was organized and trained during World War II. Williams was one of 260 Vermonters in the division, which was organized by C. Minot "Minnie" Dole, who also founded the National Ski Patrol. The division served heroically in World War II, particularly in the mountains of Italy. (Courtesy of Sewall Williams.)

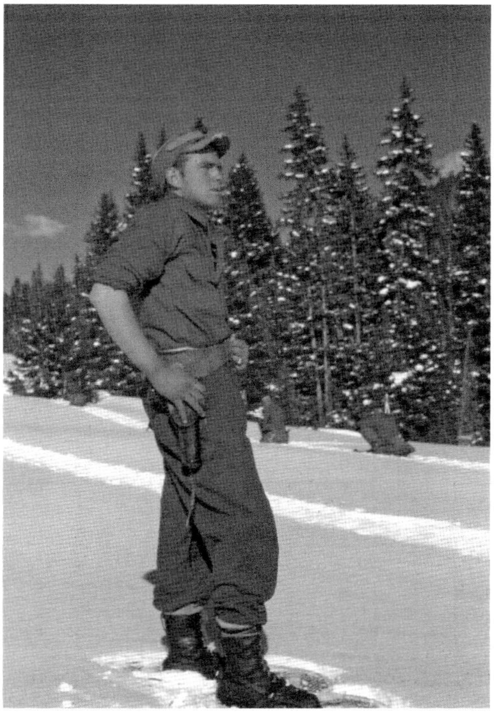

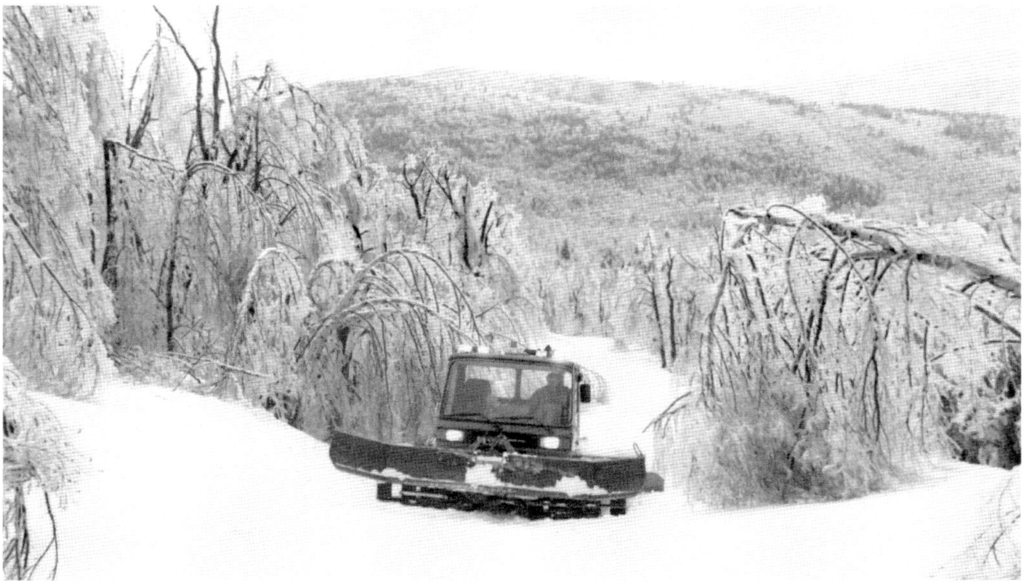

Rebounding from the Great Ice Storm of 1998 was just a matter of grooming for ski resorts, but throughout New England and, in particular, Quebec, the weather phenomenon was devastating. More than 30 people died, mostly from hypothermia, while four million people lost power, some of them for several weeks. The ecological damage hit birch trees very hard, bending tree tops to the ground, where they remain bowed in supplication to this day. (Courtesy of the *Valley Reporter*.)

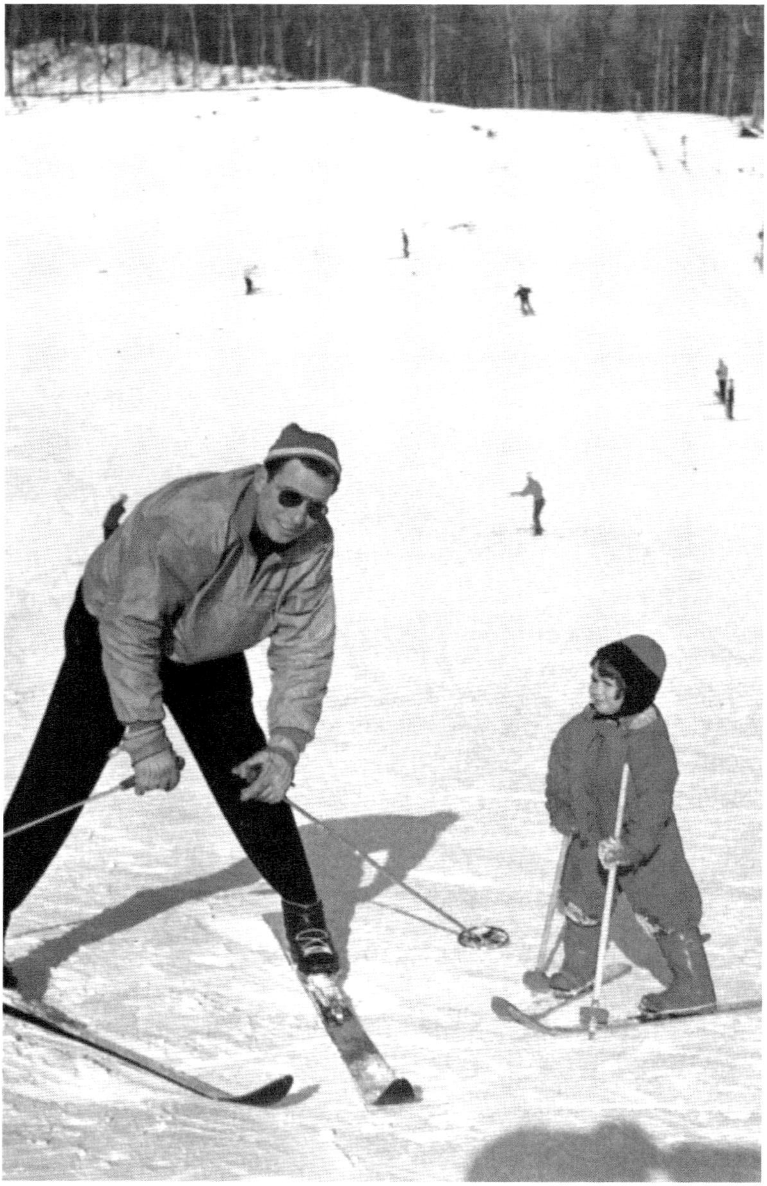

Ski instructor Frank Weston towers over little Debbie Day, daughter of Frank and Ann Day, during Debbie's lesson in 1954. Debbie was three years old at the time. Her parents owned the Knoll Farm and were responsible for installing rope tows east of Knoll Farm, as well as another one at the Alpen Inn on Route 100. They were also among the farmhouse owners who opened their doors to the newly arrived tourists. Old farmhouses, like those owned by the Clark and Perkins families, were turned into ski lodges without any noticeable changes in the overall architecture. Bunk beds were installed, and visitors seemed not to mind sharing a single bathroom. And, in the evening, they shared in home-cooked meals, followed by convivial socialization with other strangers around a fireplace. (Photograph by Roland Palmedo, courtesy of Ann Day.)

2

MASCARA MY EYE

Looking at it from close up, investing all your money in a ski resort is about the dumbest thing a capitalist can do. When the demand is high and your supply (of snow) is low, an orange grove looks better and better.

But Damon Gadd not only moved forward, he leaped into Sugarbush. His helper was Jack Murphy, a typical veteran of the 10th Mountain Division, whose risk takers are legendary. Together, they brought to their isolated valley in Vermont a destination resort that swelled with the good life.

Magazines started sending reporters and photographers to Vermont to publicize a place that was quickly dubbed "Mascara Mountain" for the jet-set crowd who found a winter alternative to the South of France.

But it is easy to brush away jokes when the Lodges and Kennedys of Boston are dropping big bucks at your place, along with other glittering people who scheme to get written up in Cholly Knickerbocker's gossip column in the Hearst papers.

What was overlooked in the beginning was certainly noticed after the Broadway swells were long gone, and that is that Sugarbush was, perhaps, the best overall ski mountain in the East, with an eventual 111 trails spaced nicely over six big peaks. The place continued to grow, with a succession of owners taking on more risk. Glen Ellen to the north was added to the mix, bringing in 34 trails and stretching the vertical to nearly 3,000 feet.

Then along came the biggest dreamer of all. He was Les Otten, who spent $24 million on new lifts and snowmaking, including the longest lift in America, called Slide Brook. What was a very nice ride between Lincoln Peak and Mount Ellen was written up as folly. Today Summit Ventures—headed by the troika of Win Smith, Bob Ackland, and Adam Greshin—has tempered its investment boldness with necessary caution, building first a huge condo-hotel and gradually thereafter the base buildings that complement the grandeur of the mountain.

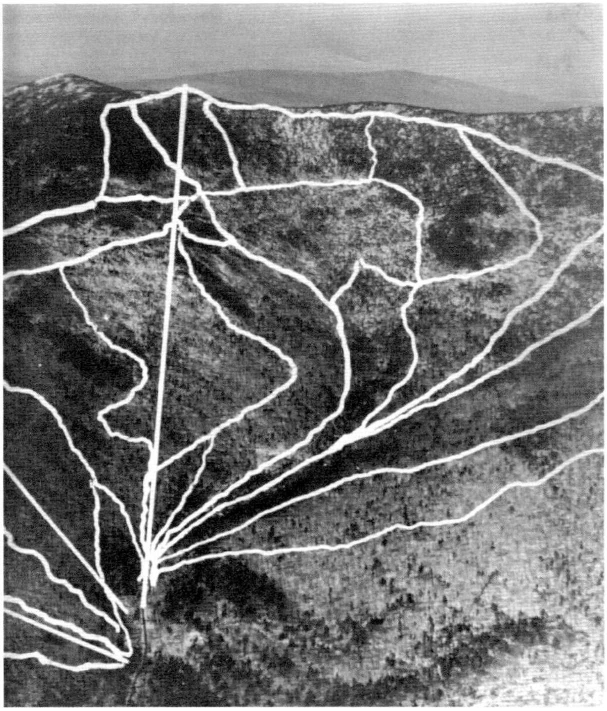

The original trails at Sugarbush were marked on this aerial photograph of Lincoln Peak. The straight line on the left is the 9,300-foot, Italian-built Carlevario Savio gondola lift based at the Valley House. The gondola line was quickly rebuilt after a fire in the summit motor shed in 1974. The lift to the top was abandoned in 1983 and replaced with the Super Bravo and Heaven's Gate lifts. (Courtesy of Kelly Murphy Wood.)

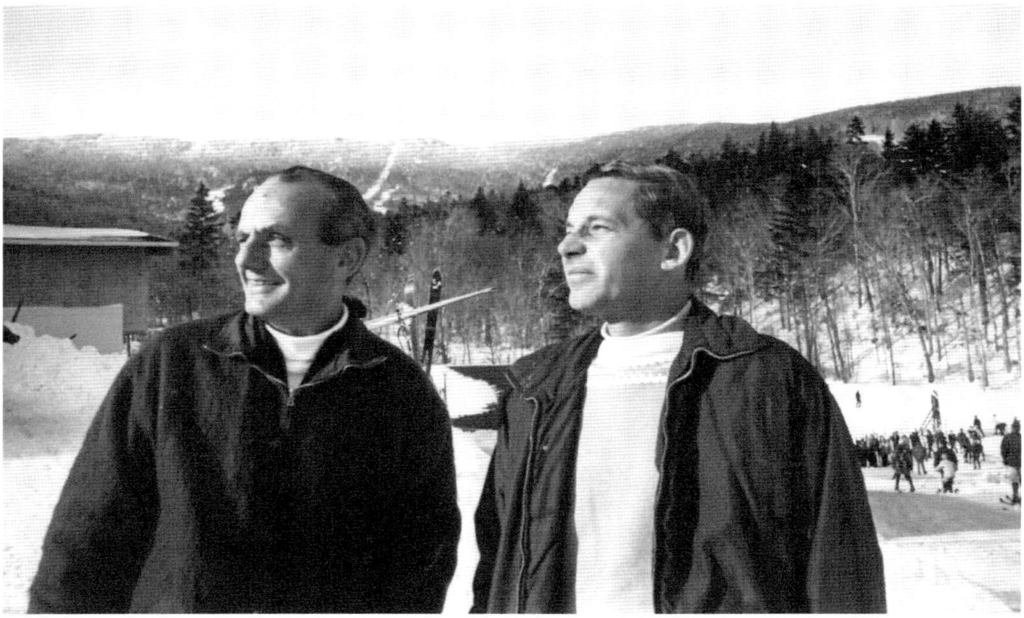

Looking into the distance are the two insightful men who made it happen, Jack Murphy (left) and Damon Gadd. The resort, from the beginning, focused on creature comforts that attracted the rich and famous, but when it came to naming the place, something Vermonty was chosen, honoring maple syrup; thus, "Sugarbush." (Courtesy of Kelly Murphy Wood.)

Almost lost in the hoopla over a Vermont ski resort that had top-of-the-line comforts, like the gondola seen here in the background, was the fact that Sugarbush's terrain offered skiing that was as good as it gets, with powder days like the one pictured that rivaled anything the Rockies could offer. (Courtesy of Charlie Brown Productions.)

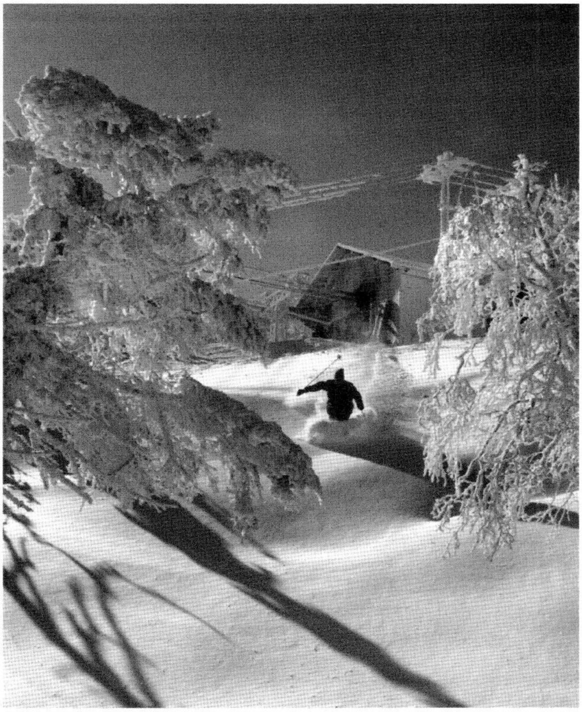

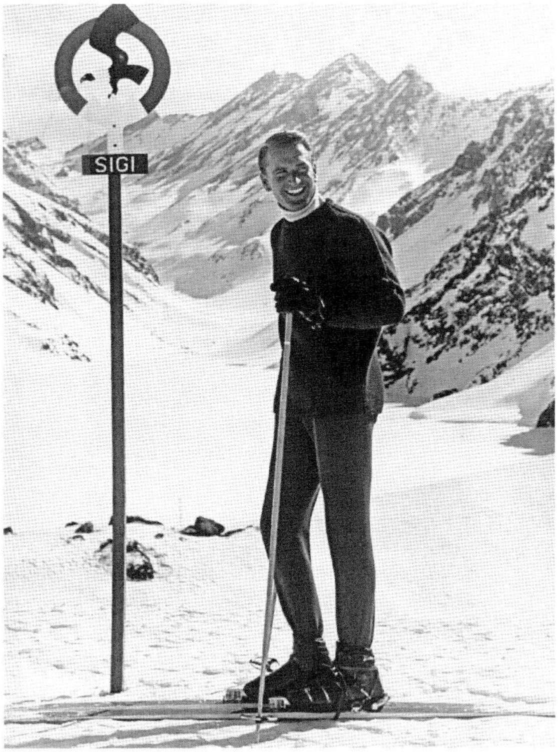

Sigi Grottendorffer, originally from Salzburg, Austria, was Sugarbush's ski school director from 1969 to 1987. He earned the sobriquet "ski meister" by training hundreds of instructors, who in turn trained thousands of students. He never stopped training in order to ski better; for instance, putting on his socks while standing on one leg: "Try it, it's not easy." (Courtesy of Vermont Ski Museum.)

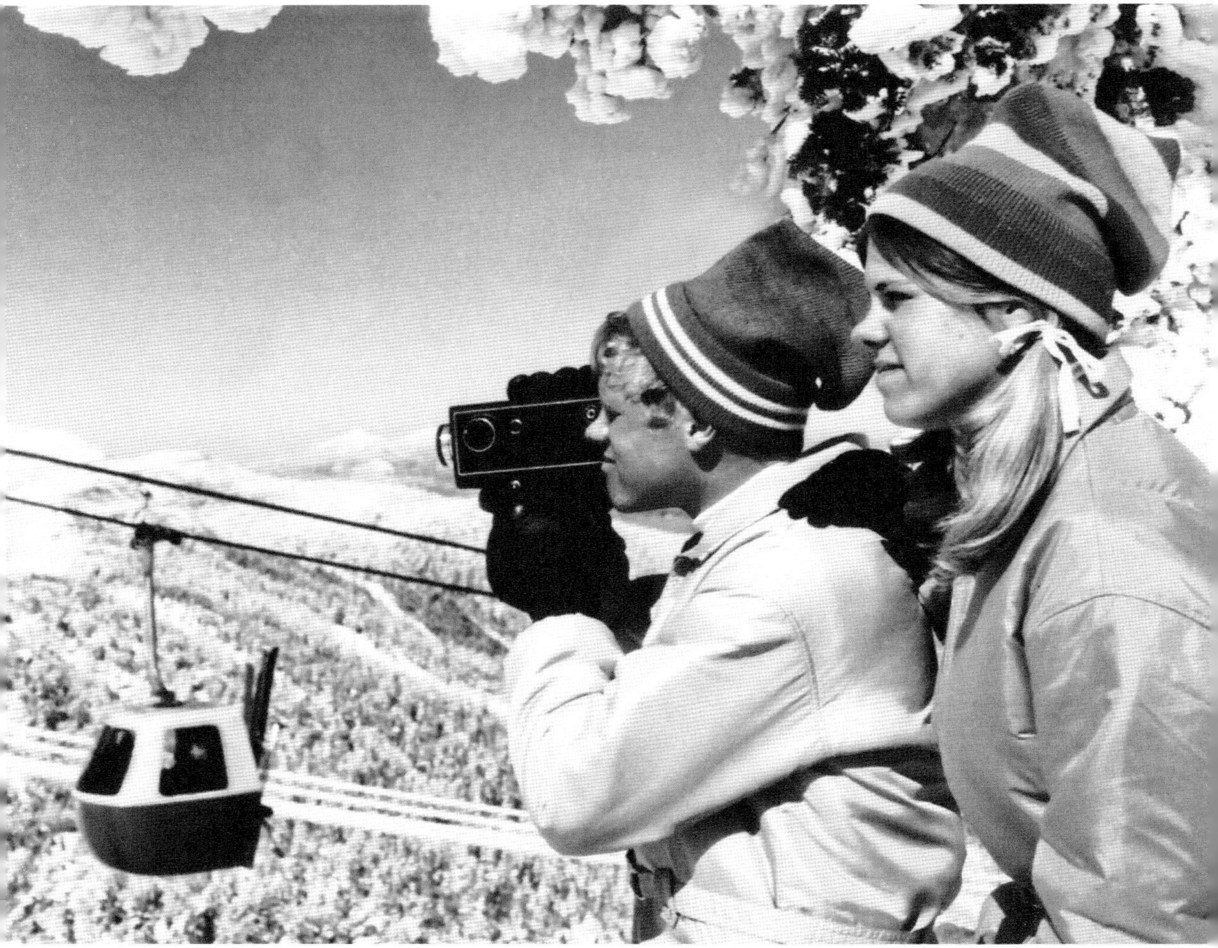

The novelty of the Sugarbush gondola attracted media attention worldwide, with photos in glossy magazines and newspapers inciting an influx of luxury-seeking jet set adventurers. In this photo, as the Gondola climbs to the summit of Lincoln Peak, the man with the camera is looking west toward Lake Champlain and the Adirondacks of New York. After ARA Services bought the resort from Roy Cohen in 1983, the gondola was replaced by the two triple chairs, Super Bravo and Heaven's Gate, thus increasing the uphill capacity of that part of the lift system from 450 persons per hour to 1,800 pph. After being dismantled, most of the egg-shaped gondola carriages disappeared, but many were purchased by aficionados. A few can be seen scattered throughout the Mad River Valley at homes and businesses. (Courtesy of Sugarbush.)

Ginny Oliver and Mike Searsdorph were regular visitors at Sugarbush and fit in with the wide variety of skiing types to visit the mountain. Ski shop owner Sig Buchmayr summed it up: "There is an interesting melange of real skiers, society types, ski bums, and ordinary people." (Courtesy of Charlie Brown Productions.)

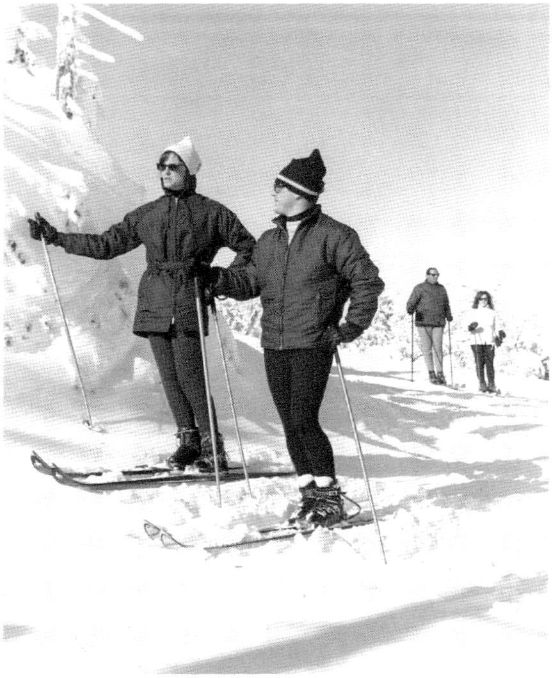

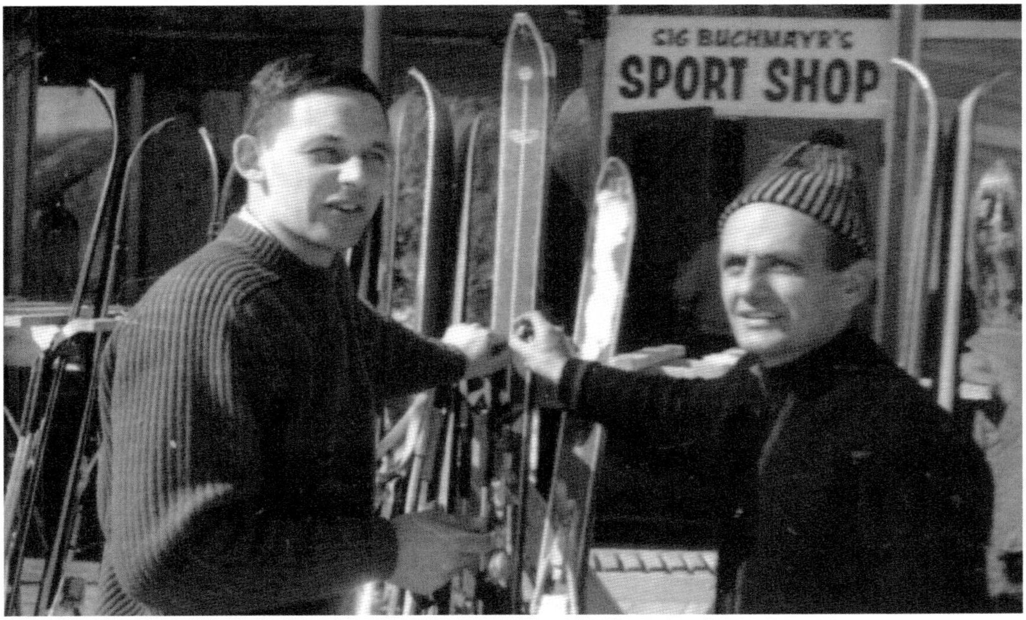

Damon Gadd (left) and Jack Murphy were old friends at Mad River Glen, where Damon and his wife Sara enjoyed skiing and Murphy was the general manager. They sensed Lincoln Peak and the valley's potential to be a great ski mountain—but one with guest amenities in contrast with the spartan atmosphere of Mad River. The Gadds and Murphy opened Sugarbush in 1958. (Courtesy of Charlie Brown Productions.)

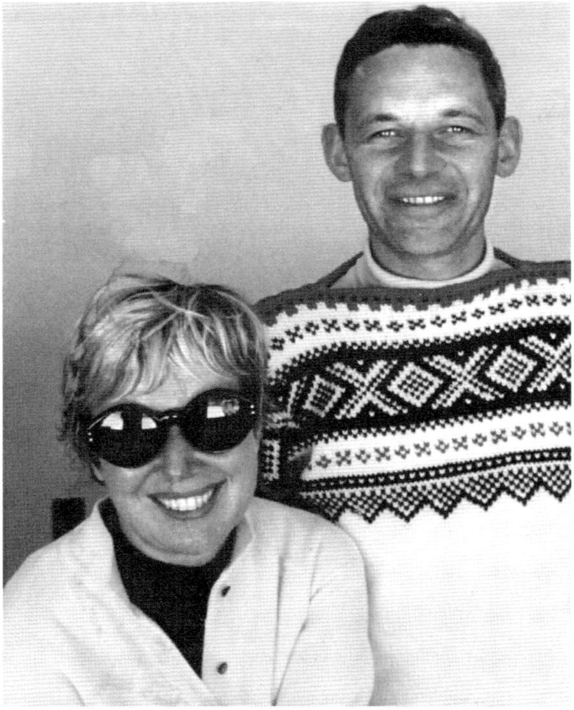

When Damon and Sara Gadd, pictured here, opened Sugarbush in 1958, the ticket price was $5.50. Gadd was a native of New York City and was the son of a New York developer. He graduated from Yale University in 1949 and went to Hawaii, where he helped to set up the state's visitors' bureau. The Gadds settled in Vermont in 1954. (Courtesy of Henri Borel.)

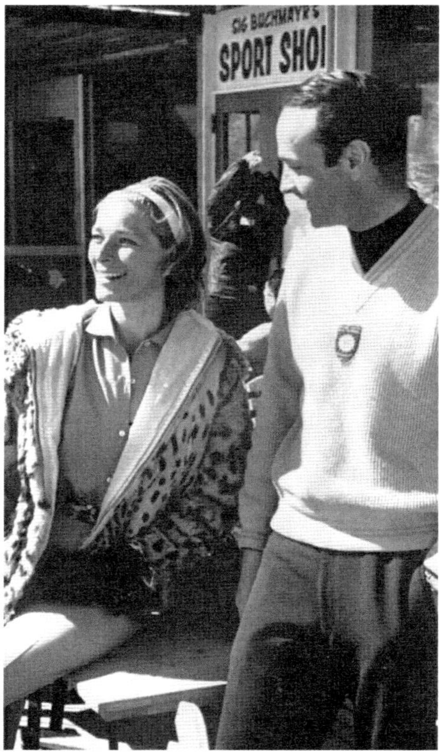

New York socialite Nan Kempner and ski school director Peter Estin were among the fashionable set of cafe society regulars who put Sugarbush on the oh-so-chic map soon after it opened. Many of the show business stars and jet-set crowd came by bus, the Sugarbush Special, which left New York City at 5:00 p.m. on Fridays. (Courtesy of Kelly Murphy Wood.)

Jack Murphy had two enlistments in World War II. In the photograph at right, he demonstrates perfect form, his body perpendicular to the slope at Camp Hale in Colorado, where he taught 10th Mountain Division soldiers how to ski with balance while carrying heavy backpacks and rifles. Below, he is ready to take to the air as an Army Air Corps pilot. Returning to civilian life, he worked at Mad River Glen where he met Damon Gadd. The two then embarked on a dream that created Sugarbush. They operated the resort with the assistance of Lixi Fortna until Roy Cohen purchased it in 1977. Making a reservation in the beginning was as easy as asking the telephone operator to connect to Waitsfield 50. (Courtesy of Kelly Murphy Wood.)

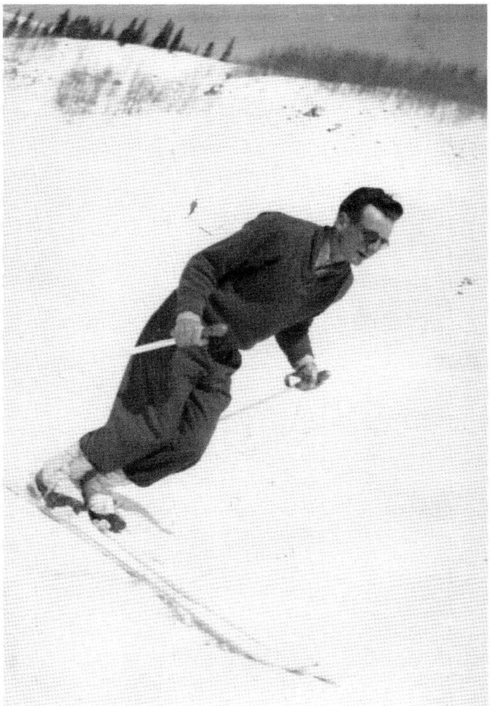

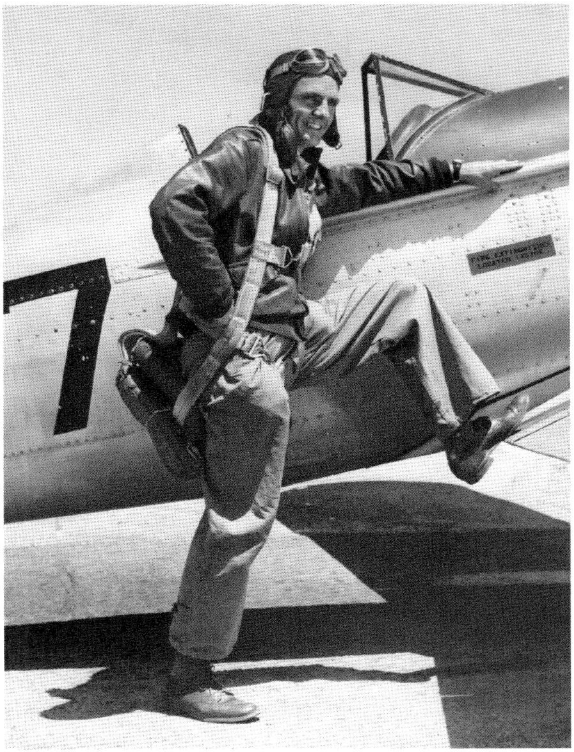

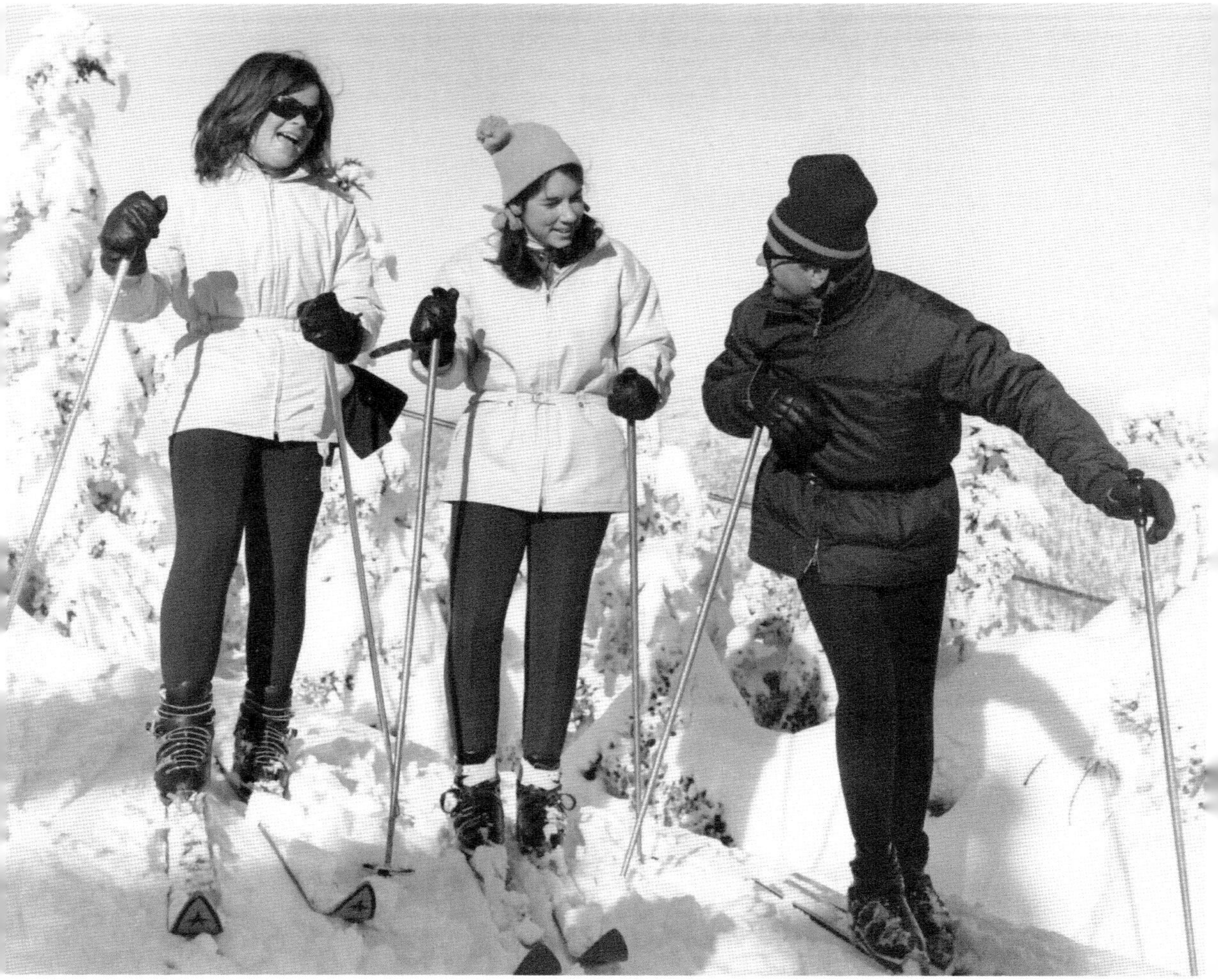

Sigi Grottendorffer, seen here near the summit with two pupils, directed Sugarbush's ski school for 18 years during some of the resort's major expansions. At Sugarbush, he pioneered a workshop on centered skiing, eschewing the Austrian influence in favor of principles resembling Oriental martial arts, using the central region of the body as both the physical center and the center of consciousness. They were techniques that helped skiers be more relaxed and balanced. Grottendorffer was one of the first of several Austrian ski instructors to move to New England and make Vermont their home. Another famous one was Sepp Ruschp, who headed the ski school at Stowe. In 1964, the owners of Sugarbush lured a Norwegian, 1952 Olympic gold and silver medalist, Stein Eriksen, away from Colorado's Aspen Highlands ski area to direct the Sugarbush ski school. (Courtesy of Charlie Brown Productions.)

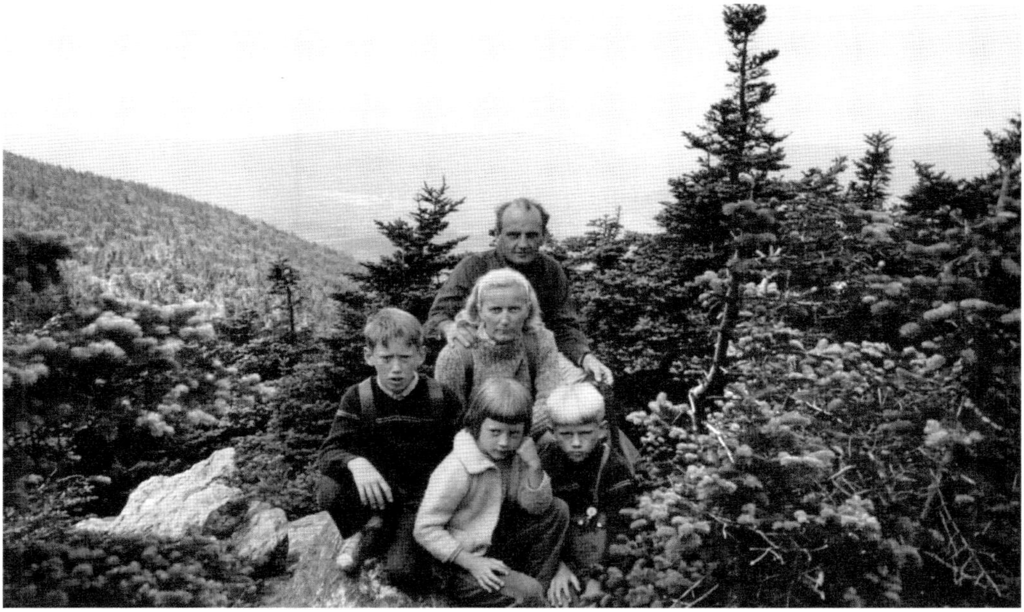

Sports Illustrated came to Sugarbush in 1965 and took this photograph of cofounder Jack Murphy and his wife Audrey, with children Mike, Kelly, and Chris resting from a hike near the summit. (Photograph by Bruce Davidson, courtesy of Kelly Murphy Wood.)

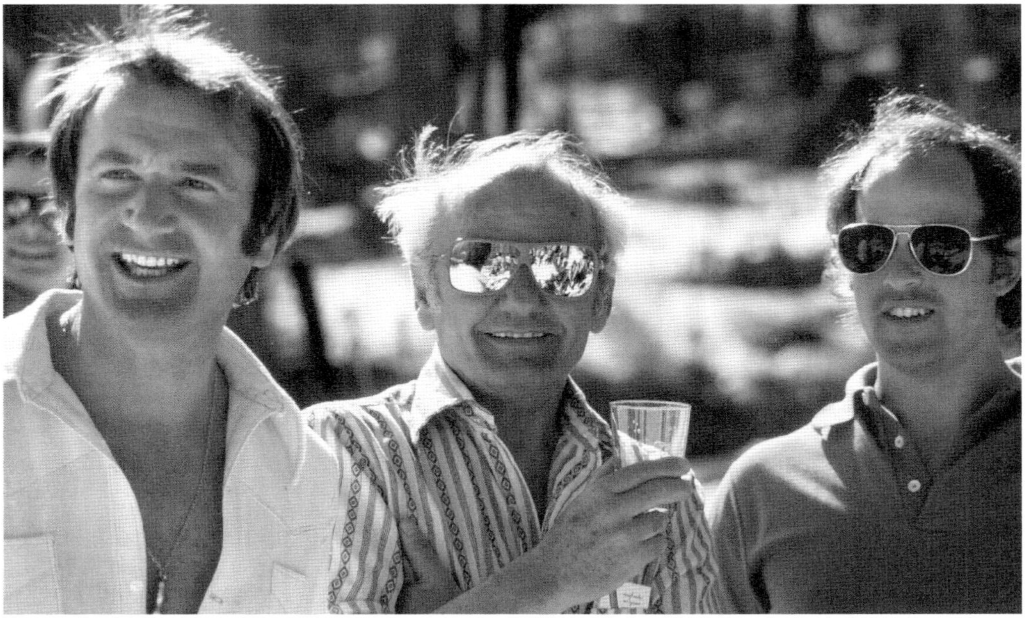

Happy faces on a warm sunny day in April 1977, perhaps reflecting on a successful winter for these three executives, from left to right, Sigi Grottendorfer, director of the Sugarbush ski school; Jack Murphy, who, with the Gadds, got the place going; and Chan Weller, marketing and public relations manager. (Courtesy of Charlie Brown Productions.)

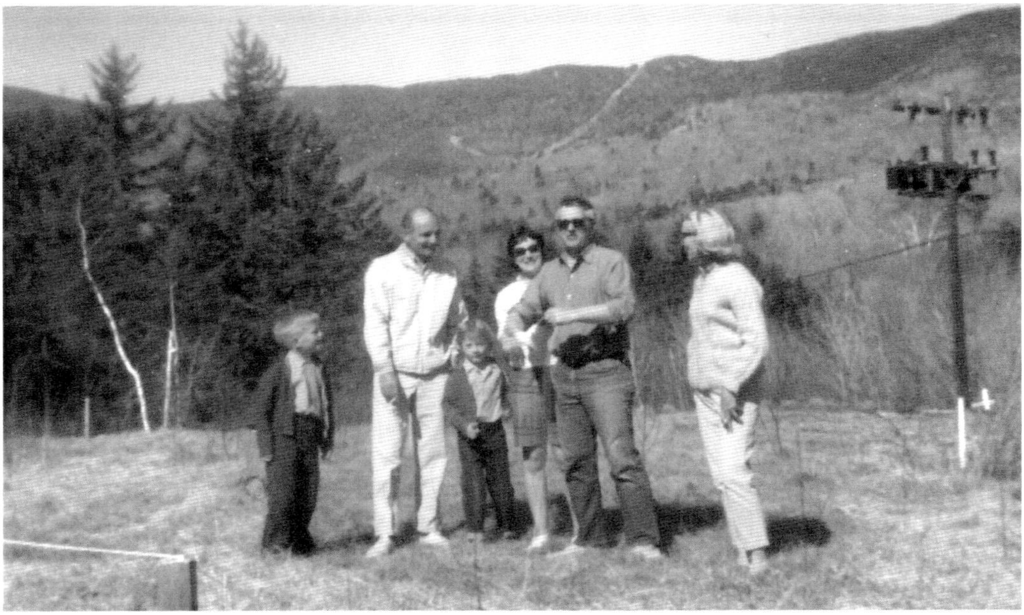

The Murphys and the Fortnas enjoy a day in the sun at Sugarbush. From left to right are Chris, Jack, and Kelly Murphy; Lixi and Trodd Fortna; and Audrey Murphy. The Fortnas built the Golden Horse Lodge on the access road. The building now houses the Sugarbush Administration offices. (Courtesy of Kelly Murphy Wood.)

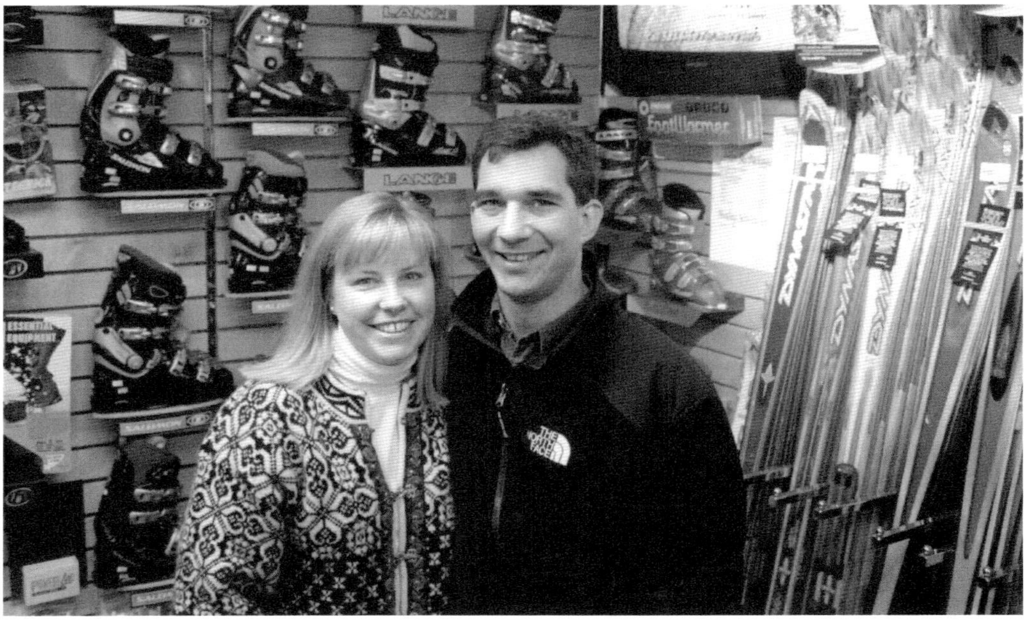

Bill and Jennifer Curley bought the Inverness Ski Shop on Route 100 in Irasville in 1996. The oldest ski shop in the valley, it burned in 1997 and was immediately rebuilt. The store was originally owned by Ned Hamilton, followed by Walter Ruff. (Courtesy of *Valley Reporter*.)

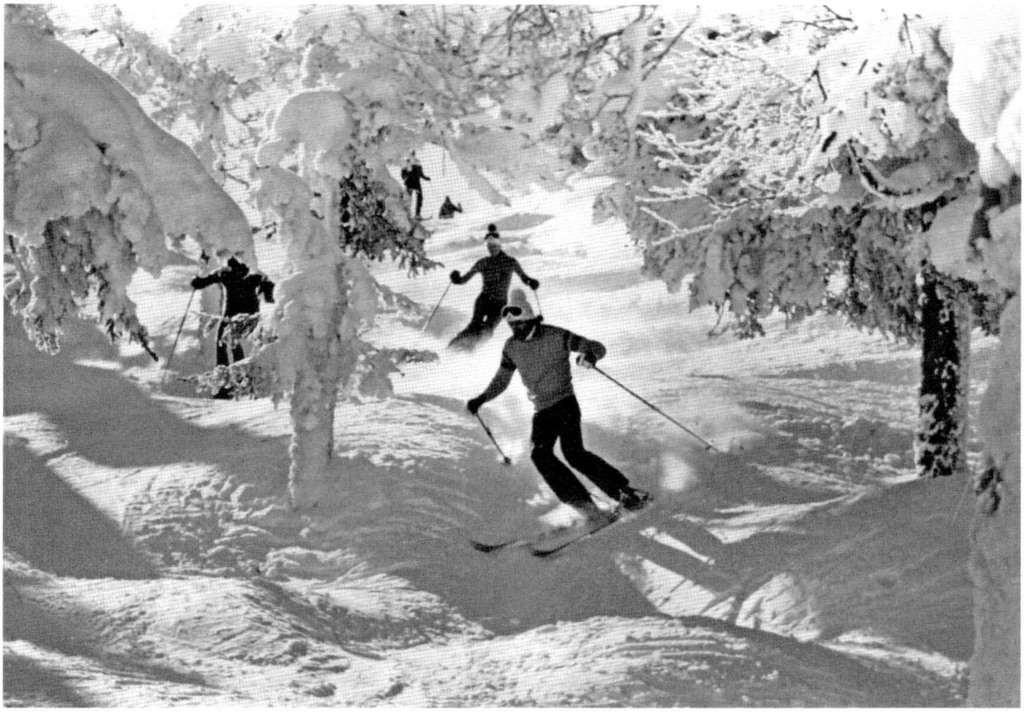

Skiing in the woods is a longtime tradition that, at first, was not totally legal at Sugarbush. Henri Borel tells of an episode in the 1960s when he and some fellow poachers were caught racing out of bounds by Stein Eriksen, the ski school director, who, instead of chastising the trespassers and chasing them home, asked if he could join them. (Courtesy of Ski Vermont.)

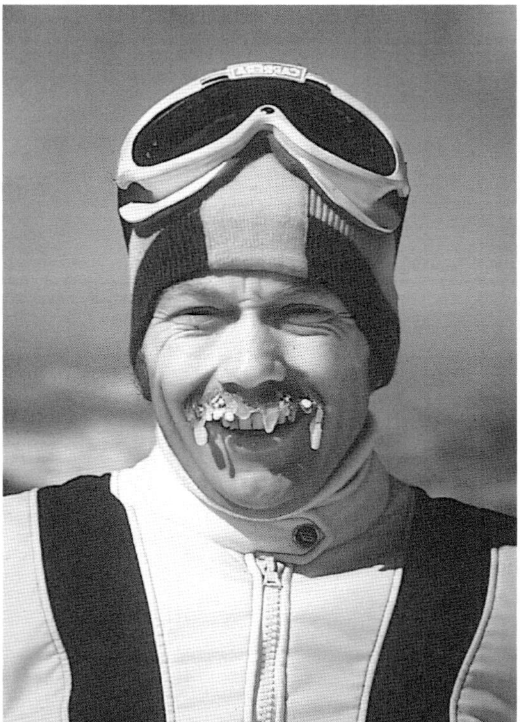

No, this is not a model posing for a "Got Milk?" commercial. It is Hartnut Helmstreet, assistant ski school director, on a happy frigid day in which ice crystals will secure themselves to anything that is slightly moist. Cold is gold to a ski resort like Sugarbush, which thrives on powder borne by below freezing temperatures. (Courtesy of Sugarbush.)

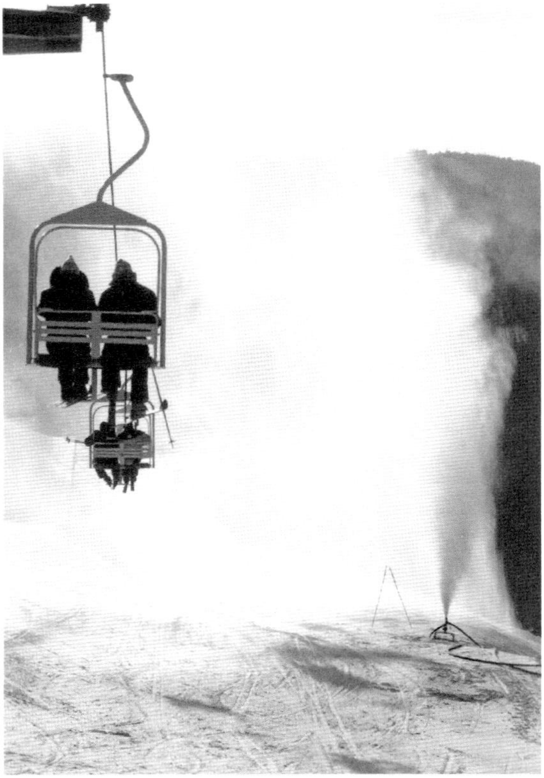

Skiers on the old double chair climbing to the Castlerock area pass through a cloud of artificial snow being shot from a gun. When Les Otten's American Ski Company purchased the area in 1995, snowmaking capacity was increased by 300 percent, with the necessary water pumped up from a new 63-million-gallon retention pond off Route 100 near the Kingsbury Iron Bridge. (Courtesy of Sugarbush.)

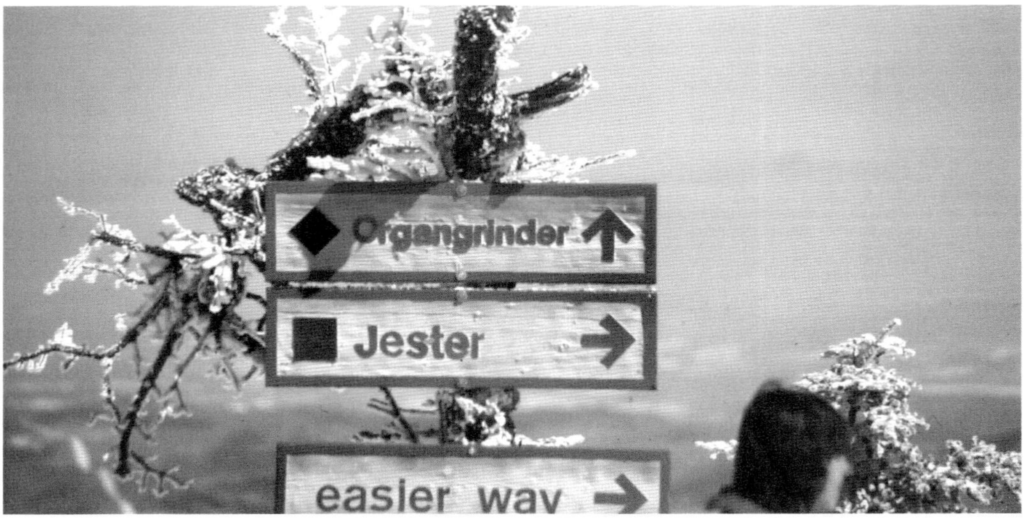

The top of the Heaven's Gate triple chairlift drops skiers off at the summit of the 3,975-foot Lincoln Peak, thus beginning a vertical drop of 2,400 feet to the mountain's base on either Jester, a relatively easy sidewinder; Organgrinder, a straight shot black diamond; or, for expert skiers, Ripcord or Paradise. The view is east toward New Hampshire, which offers a scene of the White Mountains on a clear day. (Courtesy of Sugarbush.)

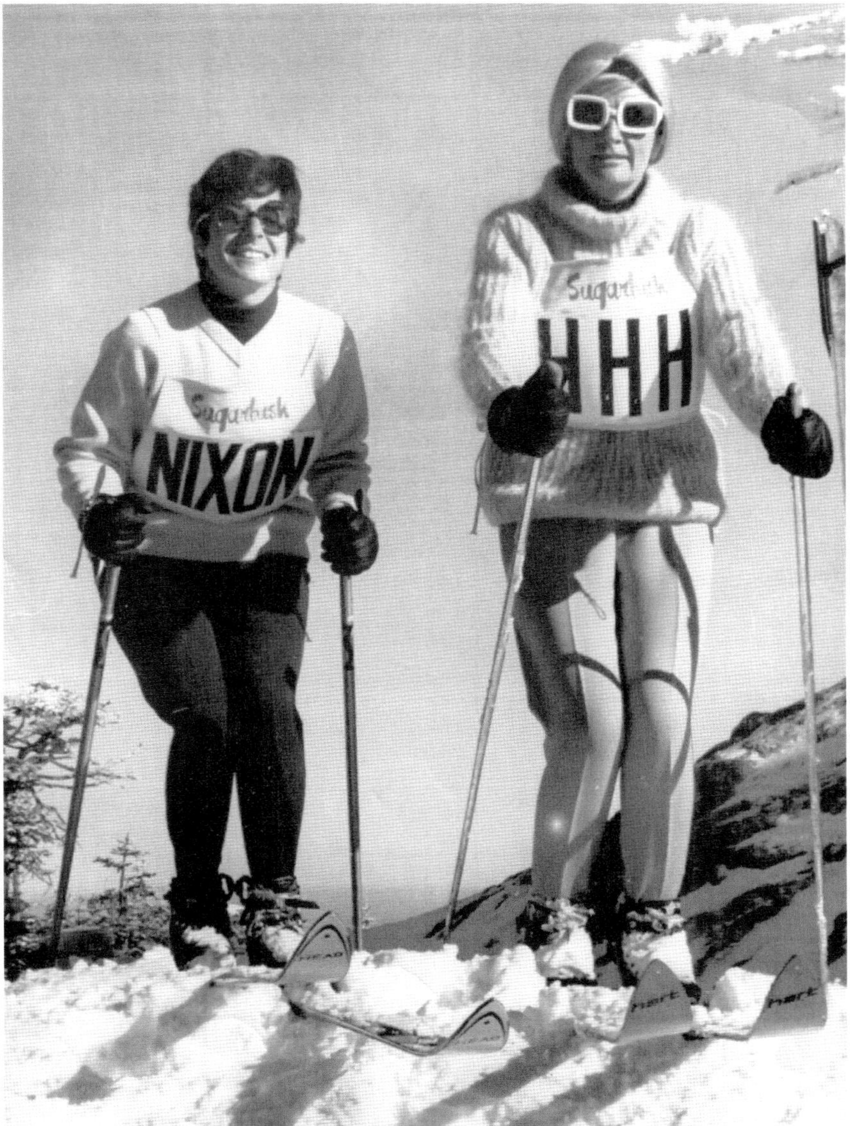

Ginny Roth (left) and Hanne Williams, supporting their respective favorites in the 1968 presidential election (Republican Richard Nixon and Democrat Hubert Humphrey), contemplate a race to the bottom at Sugarbush. It is unknown who won, but Nixon won the political contest. Vermont's politics have always leaned toward the eclectic, at least since the 1960s when an influx of hippies moved to the mountains to enjoy what the state's bountiful nature had to offer. They stayed, had children, and changed the course of politics in Vermont from conservative to liberal. The start of the century left a stew of ideologies that runs the gamut from Progressive to Tea Party Conservative, with a lot of independents in between. Most of these ideologies are reflected during Warren's annual Fourth of July parade, with floats, banners, and costumes sounding off on a variety of political issues. (Courtesy of Vermont Ski Museum.)

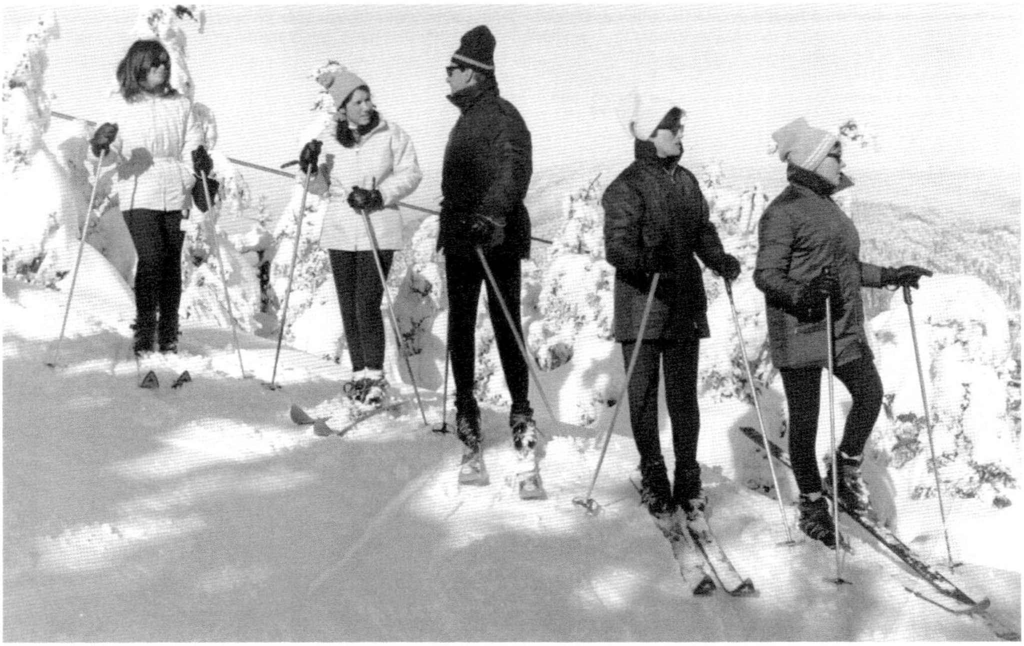

Ski fashions through the years ran from svelte to practical. Soon after New Year's Day in 1958, a week after Sugarbush opened to glittering reviews, *Sports Illustrated* wrote, "On this big holiday weekend, the skiers were as sleek and colorful as the gondola cars, providing a preview of the season's new ski clothes. Odds-on parka favorites were of quilted nylon. With form-fitting stretch pants . . . they confirmed the best sporting look of the season." (Courtesy of Sugarbush.)

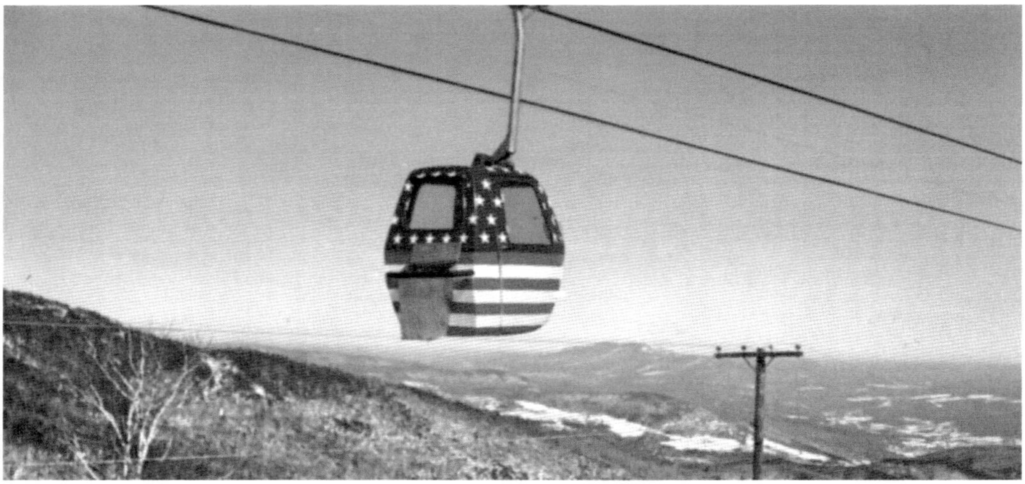

The gaily painted Carlevario Savio gondolas at Sugarbush were as much an icon among Eastern ski resorts as was Mad River Glen's distinguished Single Chair. The gondola became especially popular after a contest for artists to submit fancy, colorful designs for the Easter egg–shaped carriages. Four thousand entries were submitted from 38 states and five foreign countries. (Courtesy of Vermont Ski Museum.)

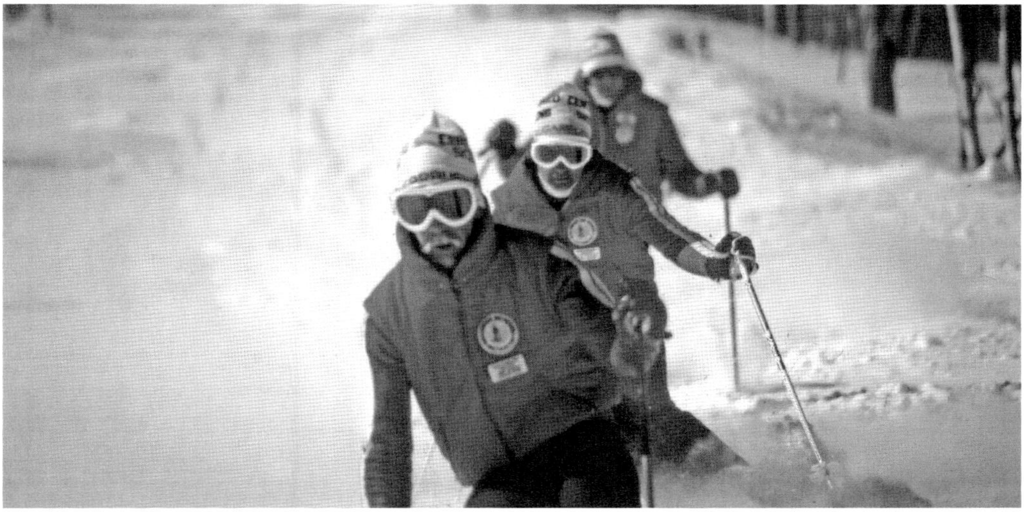

Peter Estin, a socialite turned skier, started a ski school at Sugarbush with mostly Austrian instructors, who taught the newly popular *wedeln* ("tail wagging") reverse-shoulder technique. Beginners were also taught the turning technique known as stem christie, where the uphill ski is stemmed away from being parallel with the other ski. It diminished in popularity in the late 1960s when parallel turns came into greater use. (Courtesy of Sugarbush.)

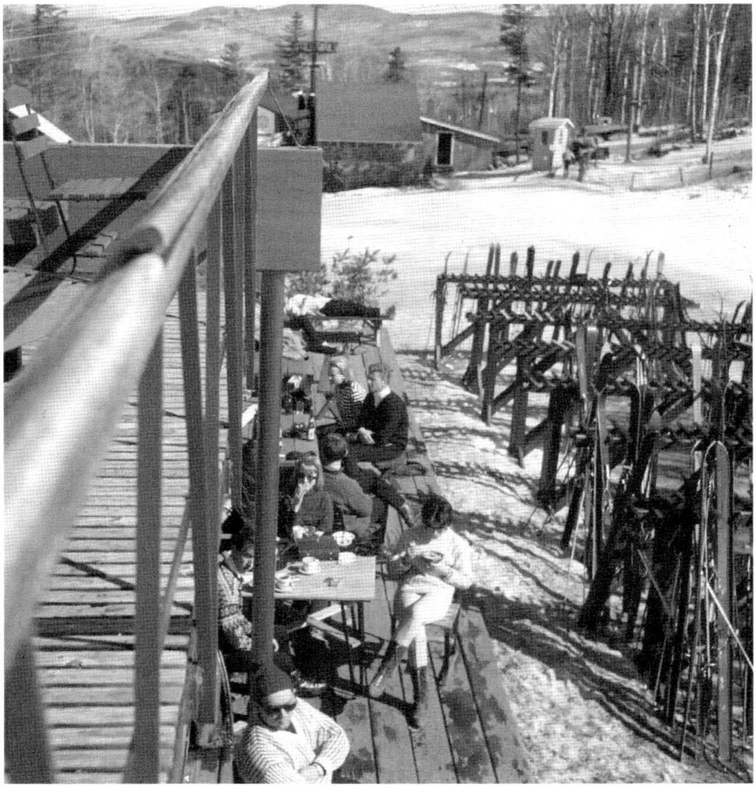

A sign of a good weekend are the racks of skis outside the Valley House, which a year after Sugarbush opened could boast only three lifts: the three-passenger gondola that ran from the lodge pictured up to the summit, the T-bar in the distance that would be replaced later by the Spring Fling chair, and Castlerock, a to-the-summit lift that serves some of the gnarliest expert trails in New England. (Photography by Sewall Williams.)

Taking in the sun on a warm day outside the Valley House, from left to right, are Martha Carpenter, wife of architect Harlow Carpenter who built the Bundy Gallery in Waitsfield; Ann Williams, who with her husband Sewall and brother-in-law Arthur Williams owned the Ulla Lodge on Route 17; Virginia Ward; and Cassie Steinway. (Photograph by Sewall Williams.)

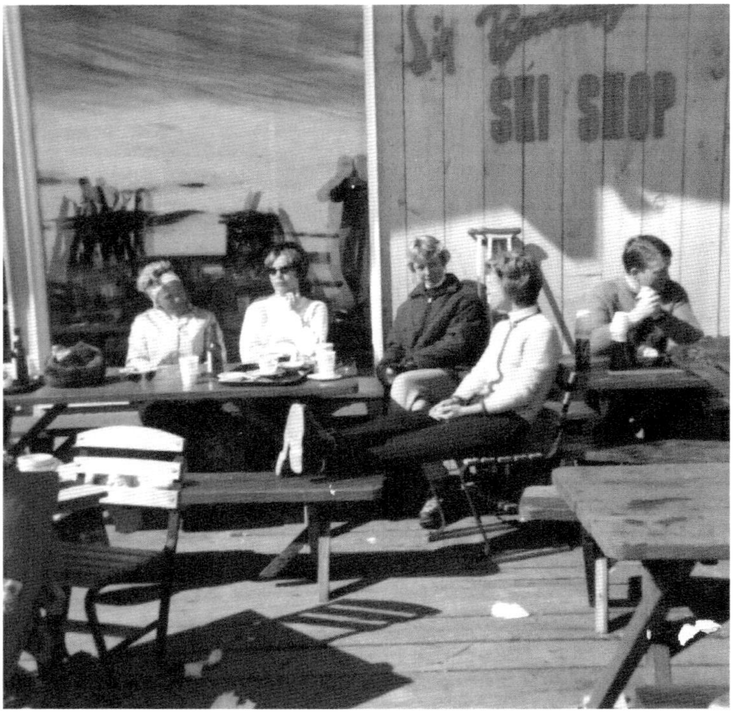

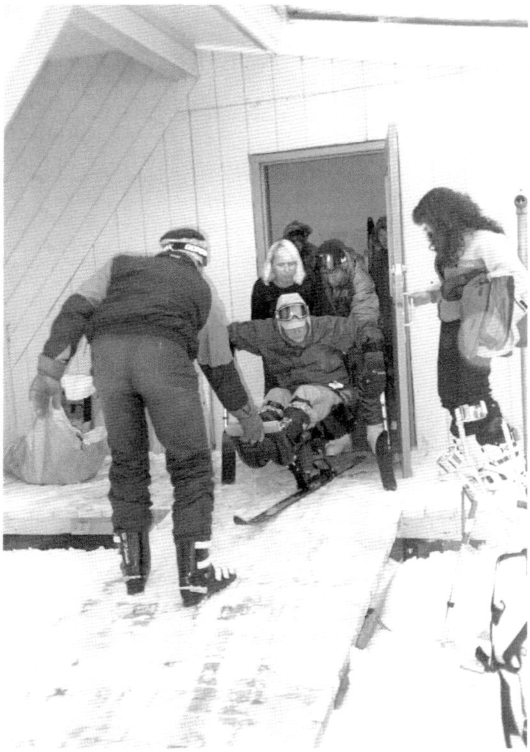

Vermont Adaptive Ski and Sports is an organization devoted to empowering individuals with disabilities. Volunteers, such as these helping a disabled skier at Sugarbush, devote several hours each year to help physically challenged persons enjoy the outdoors. More than 400 volunteers serve clients at Sugarbush, Bolton Valley, and Killington. (Courtesy of *Valley Reporter*.)

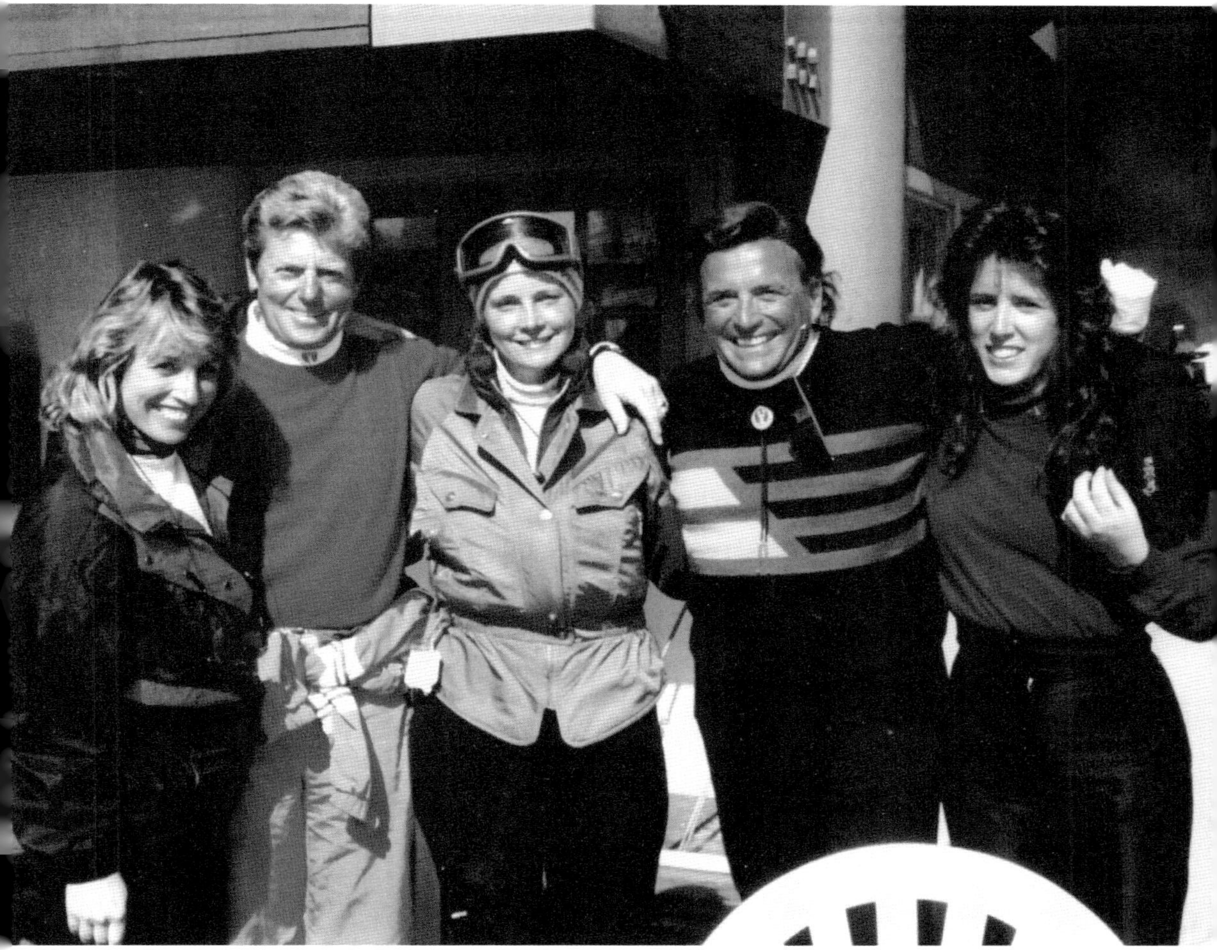

Ski instructors Stein Eriksen (second from left), head of the Sugarbush Ski School, and Frank Covino (the pair familiarly known as "Frank and Stein") are shown here with three unidentified women. The two were an off-piste duo who attracted skiers to Sugarbush with original media presentations that were syndicated in 45 newspapers in the mid-1960s and presented at ski shows in large cities in the United States. Covino directs the Frank Covino Academy of Art, delivering world famous seminars on classical art. He has written several books on classical art, including *How to Paint Like the Old Masters*. He is also the author of the *Digest Book of Downhill Skiing*. The Mad River Valley enjoys a most eclectic group of talents—including artists, painters, writers, musicians, photographers, inventors, computer programmers, and professional athletes—as permanent residents. (Courtesy of Charlie Brown Productions.)

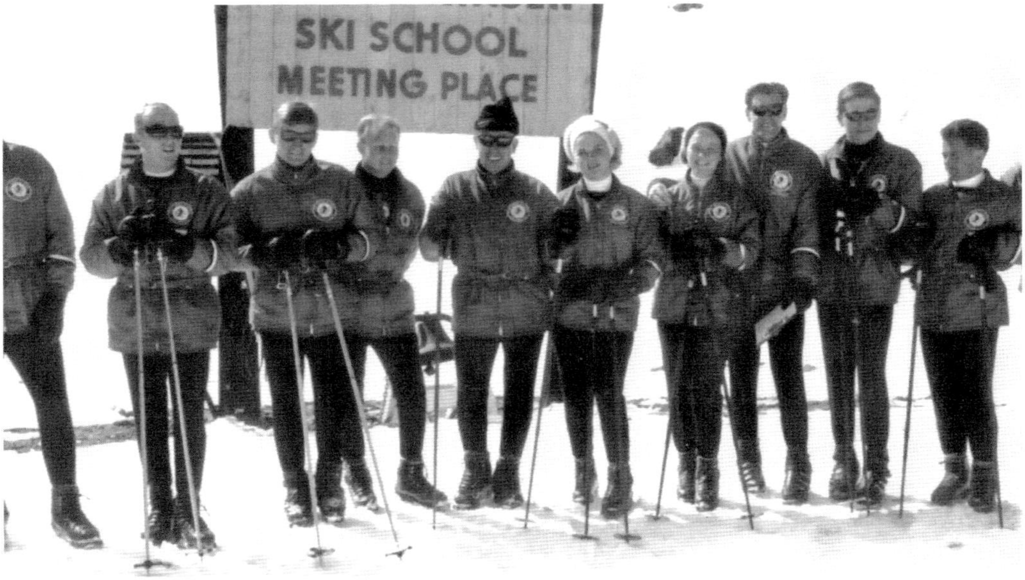

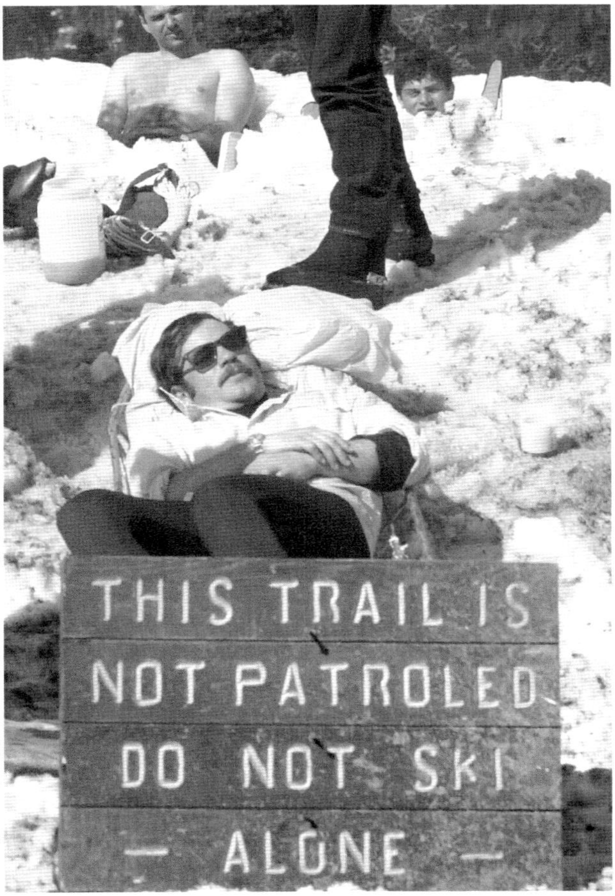

Instructors in Stein Eriksen's ski school are ready for work on a cold day in the mid-1960s. Eriksen was lured away from Aspen in Colorado by Damon Gadd in 1964. He stayed in Vermont for five years before returning to Snowmass in Colorado. Eriksen was honored by the New England Ski Museum with the Spirit of Skiing Award in 2007. (Courtesy of Charlie Brown Productions.)

Doug Mayer, Stu Richards, and Paul Revenna contemplate whether they should ski alone, ski together, or take the rest of the day off and worship the sun in this 1969 photograph at Sugarbush. (Courtesy of Charlie Brown Productions.)

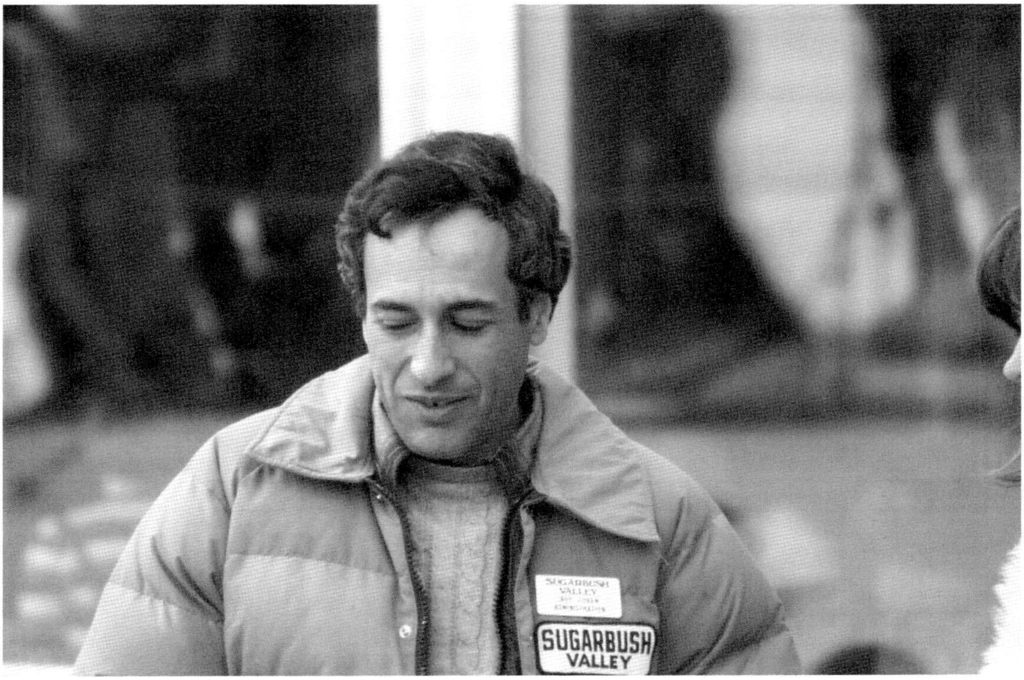

Roy Cohen, who purchased the mountain from the Gadds in 1977, created the biggest expansion of Sugarbush with the acquisition of Glen Ellen, 2 miles to the north of Lincoln Peak. Adding 34 trails and four lifts, the vertical drop also improved to 2,600 feet from the top of Mount Ellen's 4,083 total feet, which is the third highest in Vermont. (Courtesy of Charlie Brown Productions.)

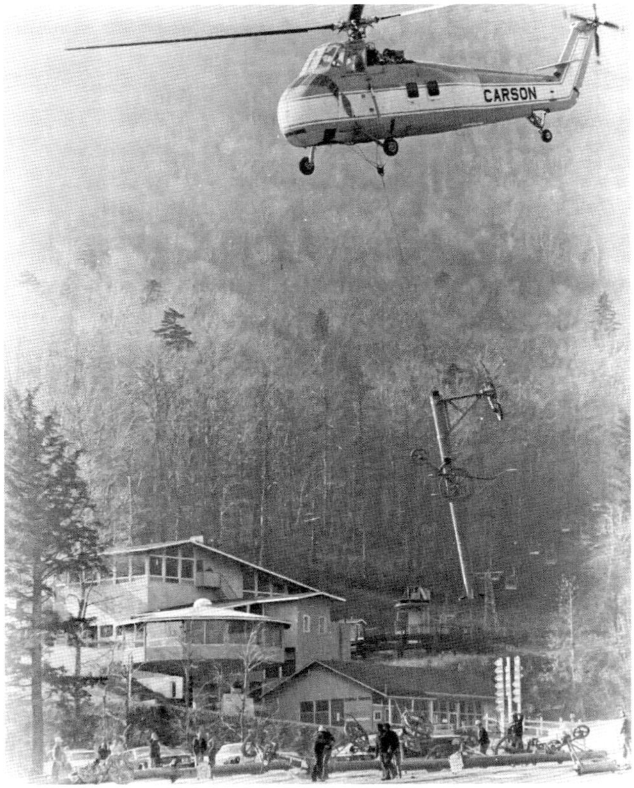

A piece of a lift tower rises over Sugarbush's Valley House on its way up the mountain during one of the resort's many expansions. Using industrial helicopters, several towers could be fitted to their concrete pads in a single day. (Courtesy of Sugarbush.)

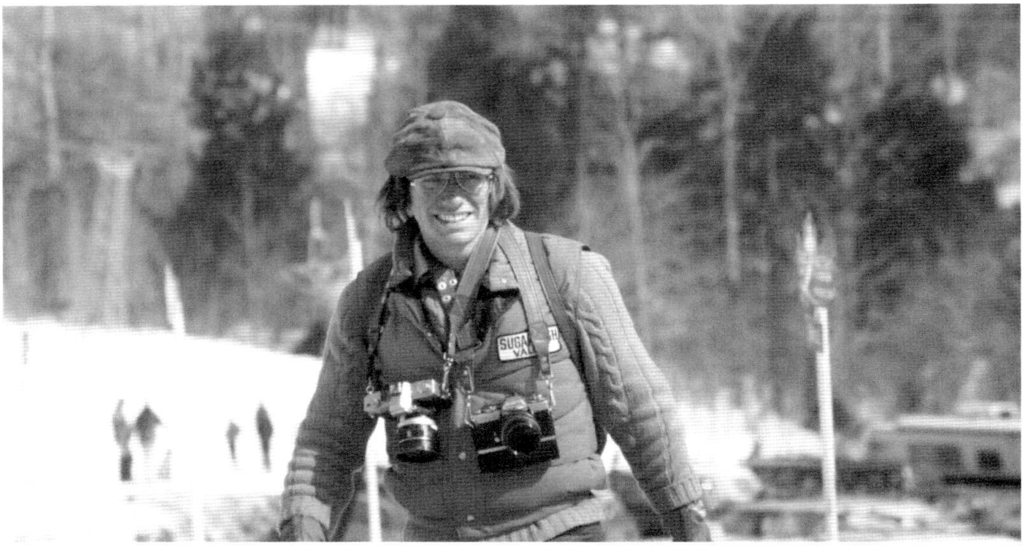

Renaissance man Sparky Potter, draped in cameras in this photograph taken in March 1978, was a serious photographer and ski patroller for many years before settling down and becoming a renowned woodwork artist. His company, Wood and Wood, co-owned with his wife Peggy, fashioned many signs around the valley and for customers worldwide. Their daughter Grace has extended the family fame into the world of rock music as a highly successful performer. (Courtesy of Charlie Brown Productions.)

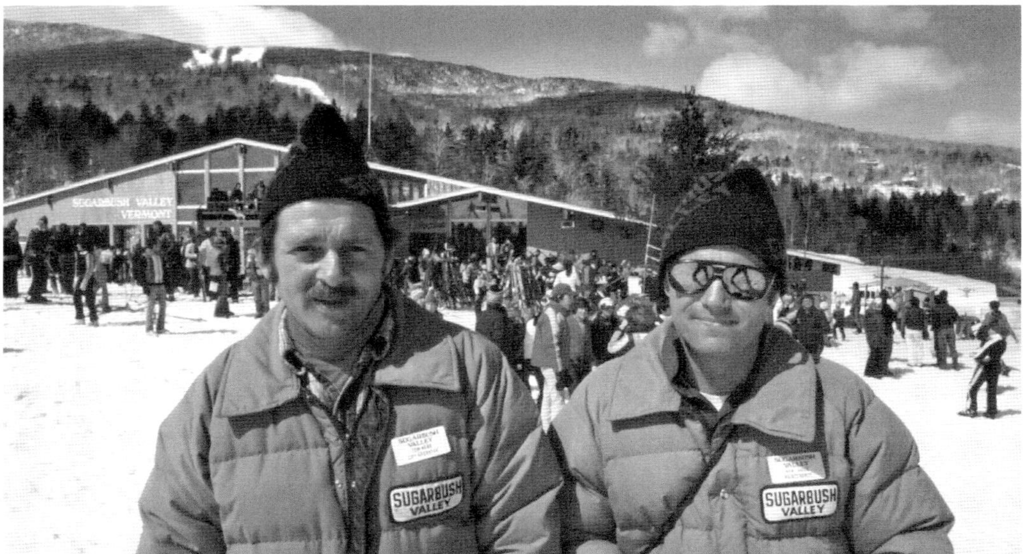

Tom Kerr (left) and Ken Irish were lift supervisors when this photograph was taken in 1978. They had taken on additional duties with the inclusion of the four lifts at Mount Ellen the previous year. The design and location of the lift system at Sugarbush meant far fewer long lift lines than at other resorts in Vermont. (Courtesy of Charlie Brown Productions.)

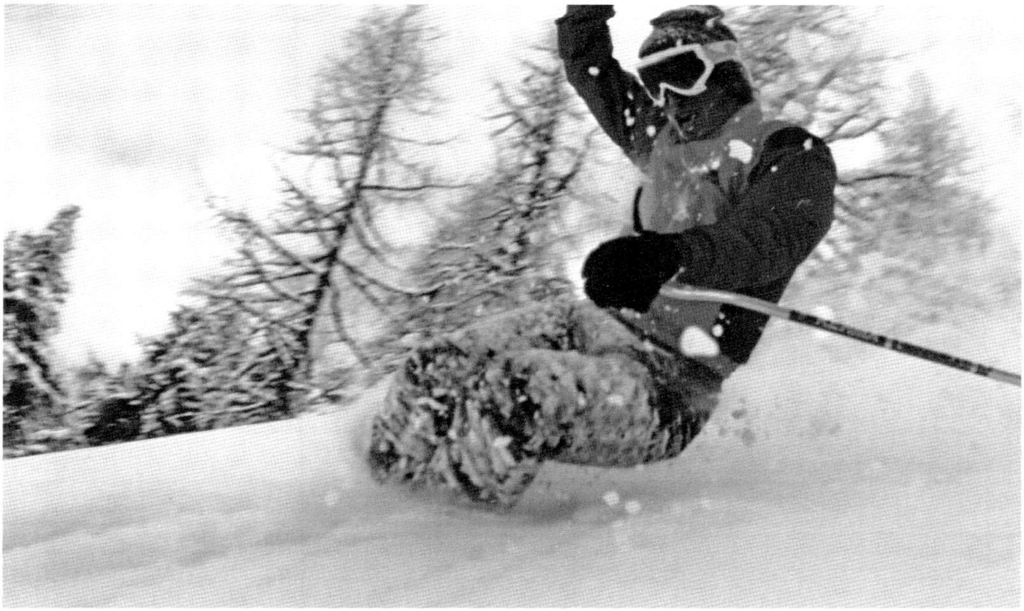

Alan Buridge of Beverly, Massachusetts, enjoys a powder day at Sugarbush in the 1970s. Sugarbush was bought by Roy Cohen, who directed a major expansion of the mountain, including the purchase of Glen Ellen. Still, the largest expansion came under Les Otten and the American Skiing Company, which installed seven new lifts and upgraded snowmaking capacity. (Courtesy of John Egan.)

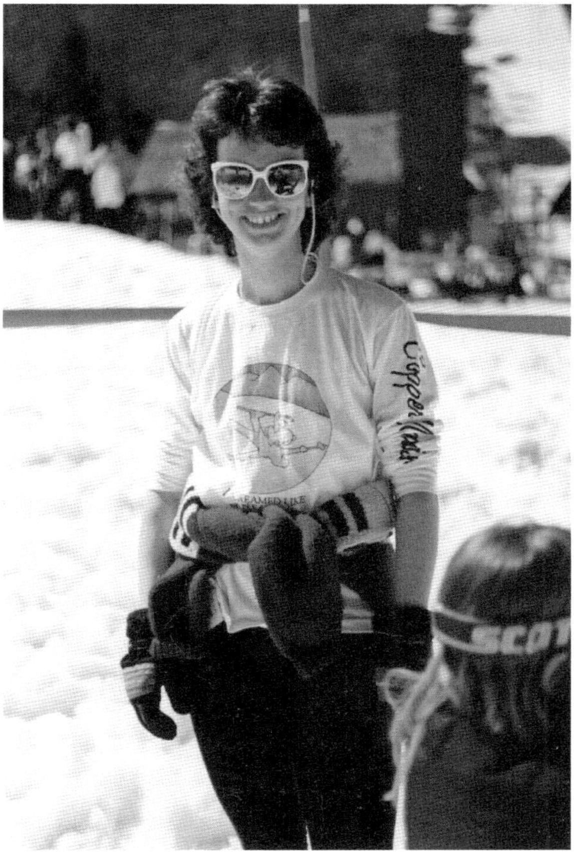

Amy Deutl, pictured here, was typical of the hundreds of ski bums who visited Vermont early on and decided to stay to ski and raise a family. Amy is presently the Moretown town treasurer and her husband, Dave, is employed by the University of Vermont. (Courtesy of John Egan.)

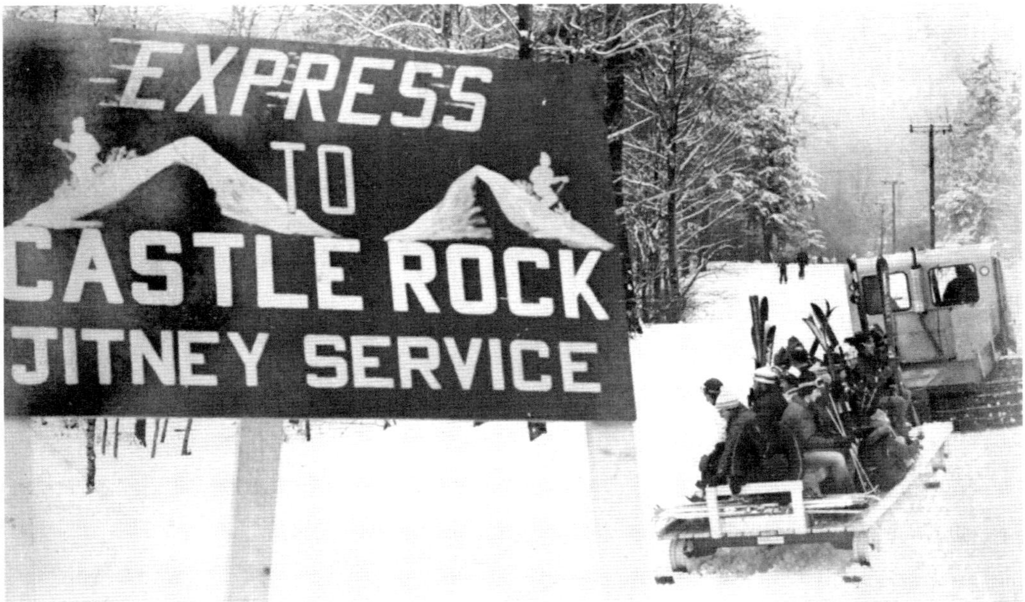

When the motor shack of the gondola was consumed by a fire in 1974, management put to work a snowcat to ferry skiers to the top of Castlerock. Snowcats, which are popular at western resorts, were put into use again by Win Smith in 2008 for Sugarbush's backcountry ventures. (Courtesy of Kelly Murphy Wood.)

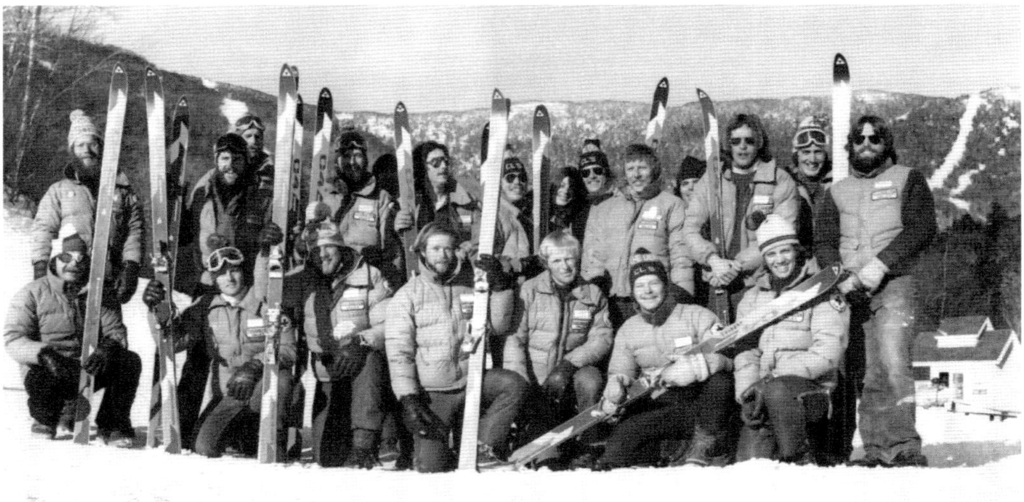

The ski patrol in the 1976–1977 season (the last year of the Gadds' ownership) numbered more than a dozen members. The national organization was started in 1938 in Stowe through the efforts of Charles Minot "Minnie" Dole. Today the patrol's stiff requirements include expertise in Outdoor Emergency Care (OEC), which is equivalent to basic emergency medical technician (EMT) training; outdoor emergency transportation, avalanche training, and mountain travel and rescue. (Courtesy of Kelly Murphy Wood.)

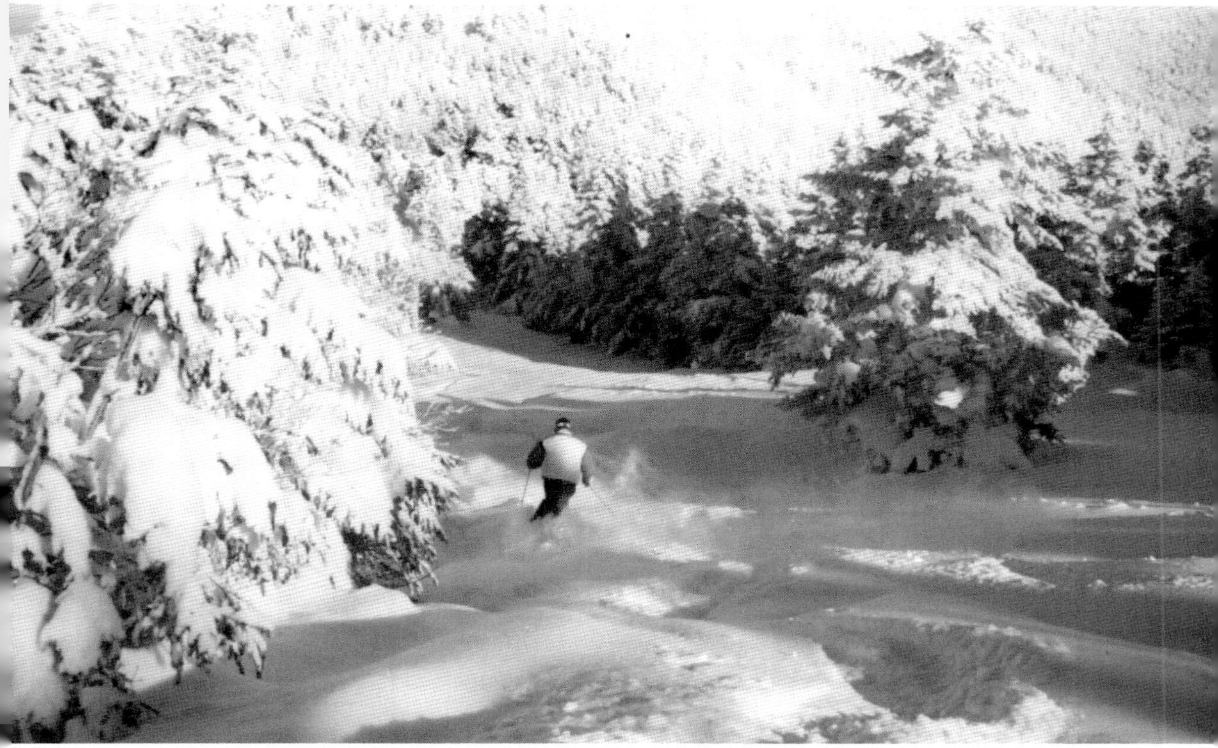

Making perfect turns on Paradise is Mark Woolley, training director of ski instructors at the Sugarbush Ski and Ride School. As a former member of the development team of the Professional Ski Instructors of America (PSIA), Eastern Division, Woolley helps instructors stay tuned to the teaching standards of the PSIA. He first joined the instruction department at Sugarbush in 1979. He is also a former director of the Sugarbush Race Department, and in 1986–1987, he was the assistant director of ski instruction at Portillo, Chile, where several professional ski racing teams from many nations train in the summer months. On the amateur front locally, Woolley is the coach of several children's soccer and lacrosse teams. He played soccer on a scholarship at the University of Virginia, where he graduated with a degree in economics. (Courtesy of Mark Woolley.)

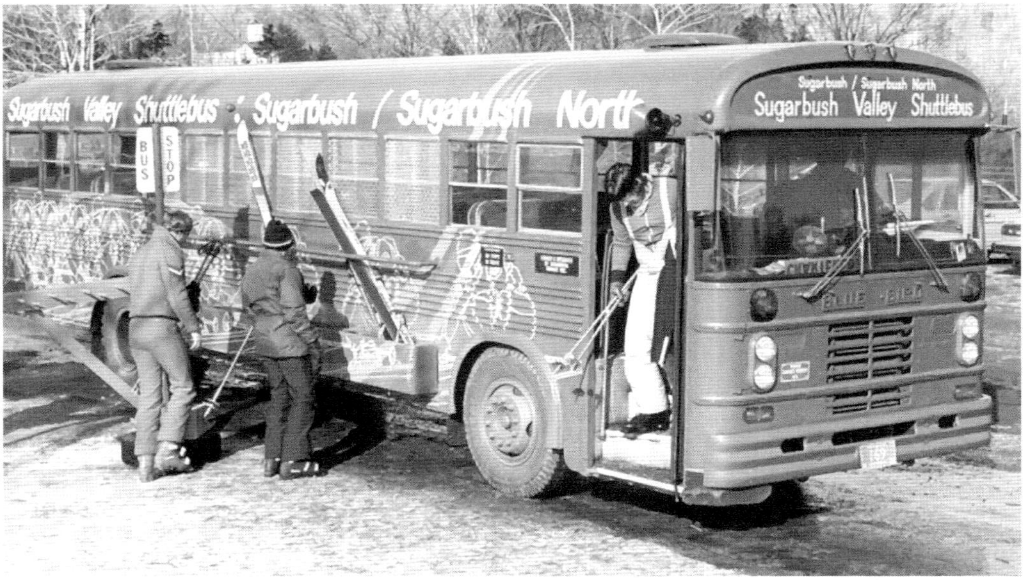

Bound for Mount Ellen, 2 miles north of Lincoln Peak, skiers board the intermountain bus for the 10-minute ride. A woman from England, a nation proud of its trains and buses that run on time, once complained when the Sugarbush bus was five minutes late during a blizzard, saying, "that's unacceptable." (Courtesy of Sugarbush.)

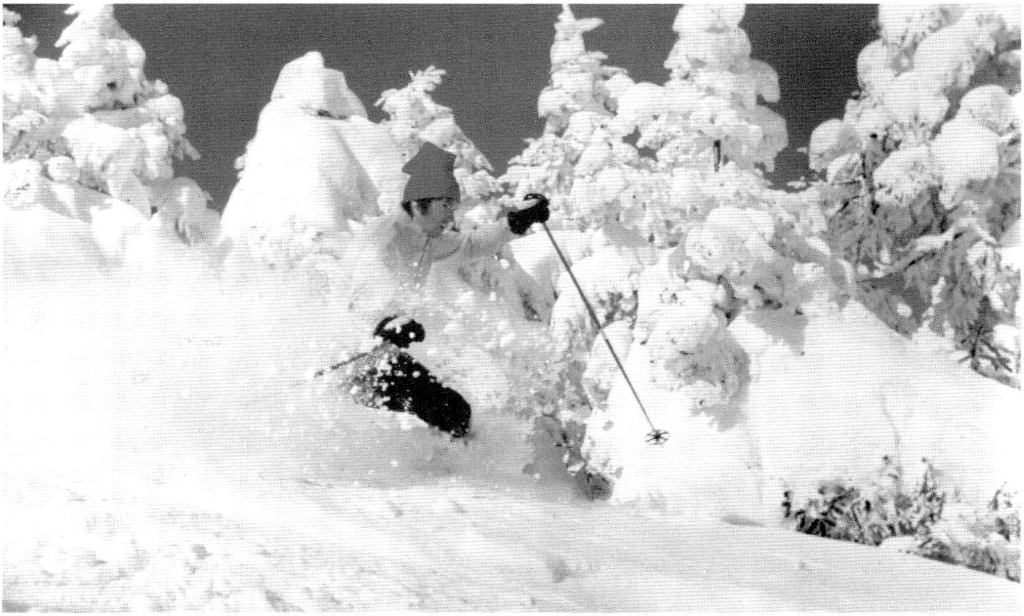

Jonathon Jenkins, shown here busting powder some time in the 1970s on Mount Ellen, succeeded Pierre Stamos as the head of Glen Ellen's ski school. Stamos was one of a few French ski team members brought to Vermont by Walton Eliot, who developed Glen Ellen prior to the resort being sold to Sugarbush after Roy Cohen purchased the neighboring mountain. (Courtesy of Tony Egan.)

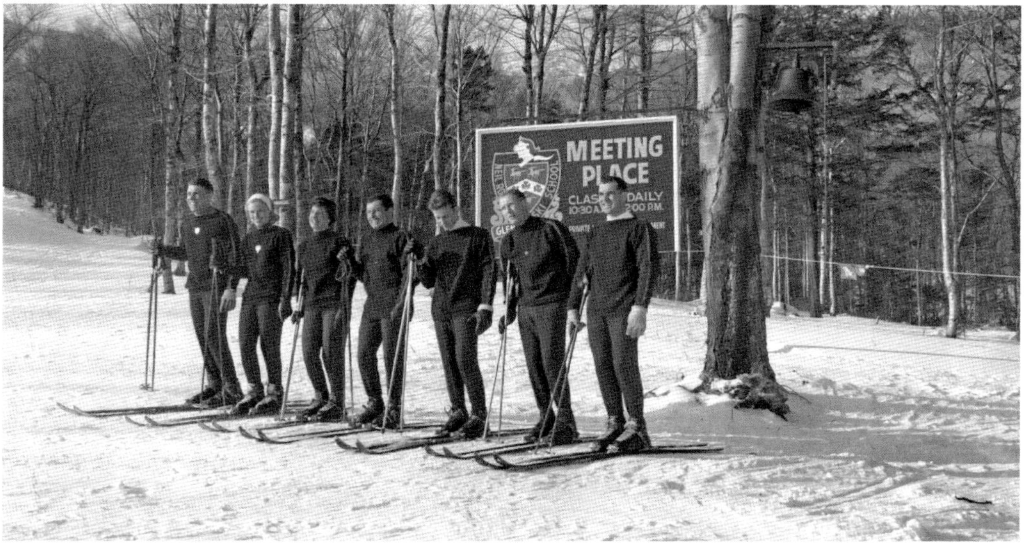

The Glen Ellen Ski School departed from the Austrian and Norwegian influence when Walt Elliot talked Pierre Stamos, who was a teammate of French racing hero Jean Claude Killy, to come to Vermont. Stamos and his fellow French instructors who came with him lived in a farmhouse on Route 100, which later became the Den Restaurant. (Photograph by Sewall Williams.)

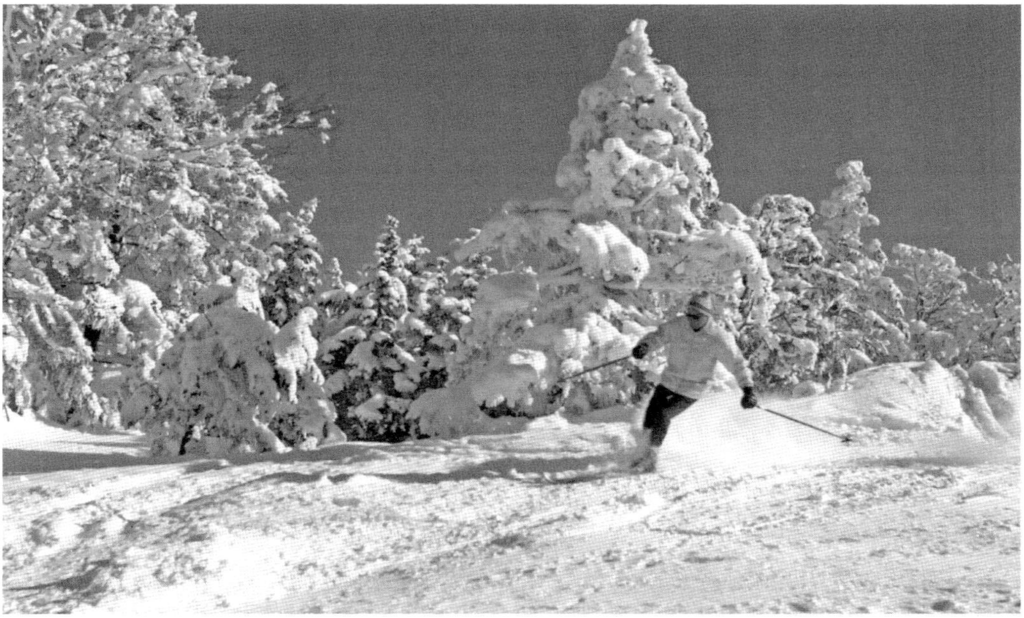

Spencer Field skis Paradise, which looks fairly flat here but evolves into a beautiful double diamond, after taking the Heaven's Gate lift to the summit of Lincoln Peak. Over the years, strong demand by adventurous downhillers pushed resorts to cut trails in the deep and steep woods. Most popular at Sugarbush are Eden, Egan's Woods, Stein's Woods, Gangsta's Grotto, and an intermediate area called Sleeper. (Courtesy of Ski Vermont.)

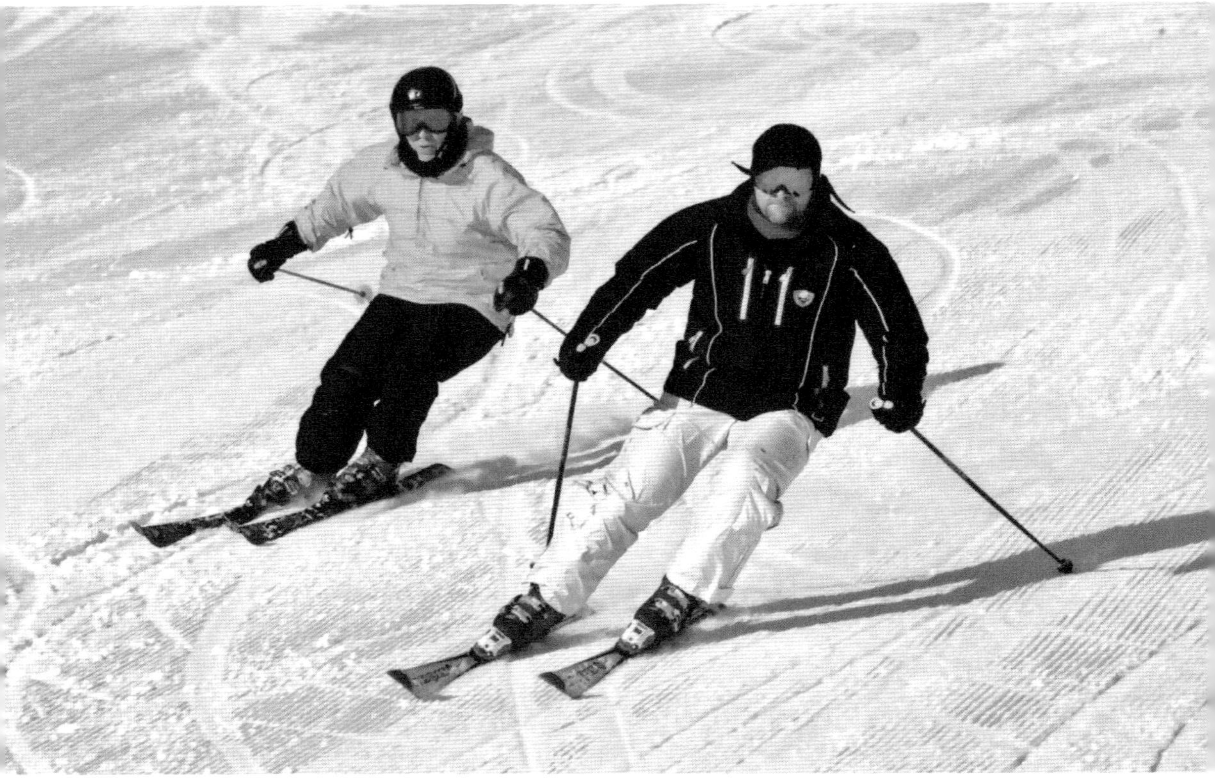

Al Hobart (left), cofounder of the Green Mountain Valley School, wrote *Carving Turns Made Easy*, an instruction book on how to make racing turns in just a few short weeks. Here, he and his pupil, Piero Bonamico, demonstrate the skill on Inverness at Mount Ellen. Bonamico, who designed the instruction book, is the musical director at Green Mountain Valley School and conductor of the Mad River Chorale. Part of the Hobart technique means mastering the lifted ski and matched gorilla turn, beginning with a wide stance on an easy slope. The exaggerated movements while turning put pressure on the outside ski, achieving a better balance. As the pupil progresses, he is taught to plant the inside ski closer to the outside ski. Hobart claims the technique helps to wipe out bad habits early in the lesson. (Courtesy of Al Hobart.)

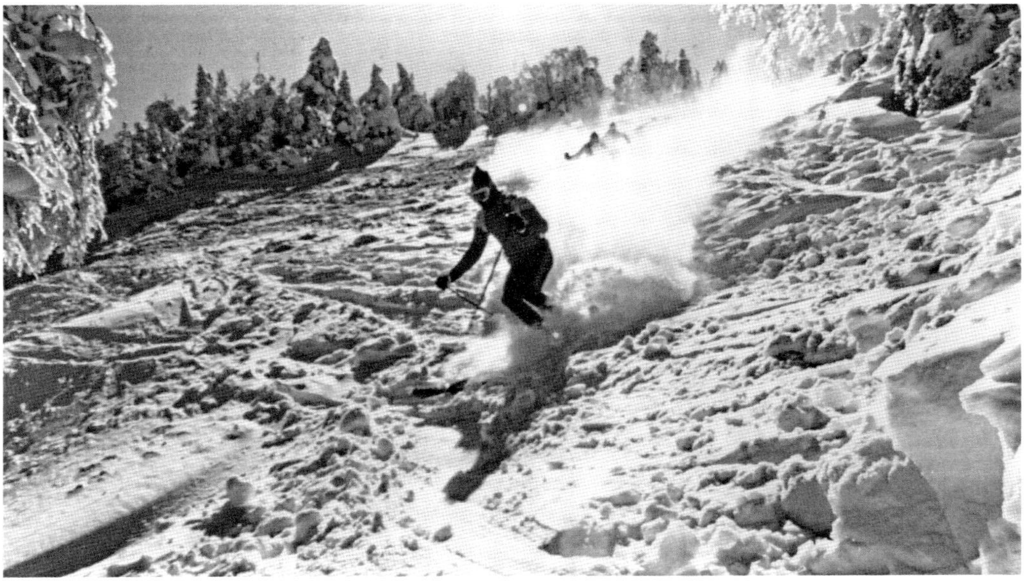

An early season storm brings out the powder hounds, a typical example of a first-class skiing experience that replaced the years when Sugarbush may have been noted more for image rather than substance. The resort has been singled out several times for the variety of its terrain, which has averaged more than 22 feet of snow each year. (Courtesy of Ski Vermont.)

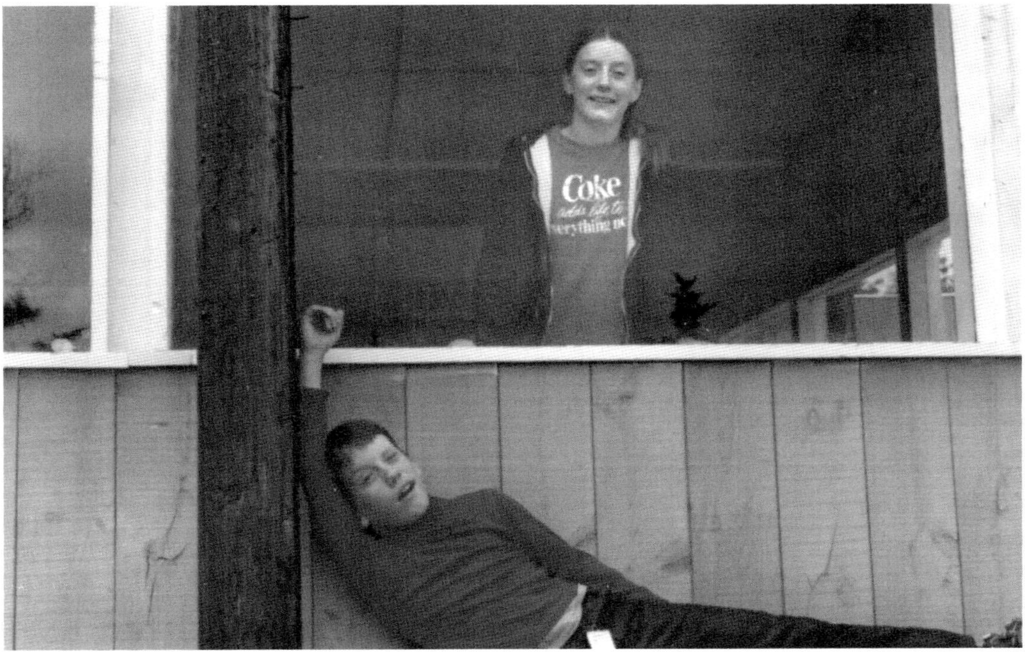

Casey Murphy and his sister Kelly relax on a warm day in April 1978 at Castlerock on Lincoln Peak. The Murphy kids are the children of Jack Murphy, an original co-owner and developer of Sugarbush when it opened in the late 1950s. (Photograph by John Egan.)

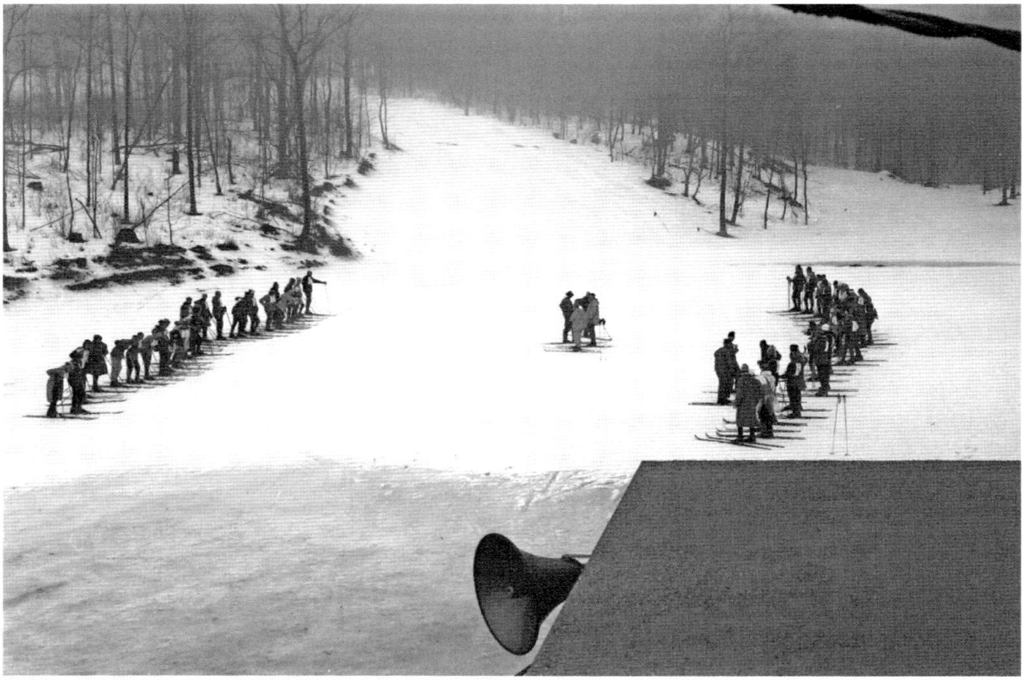

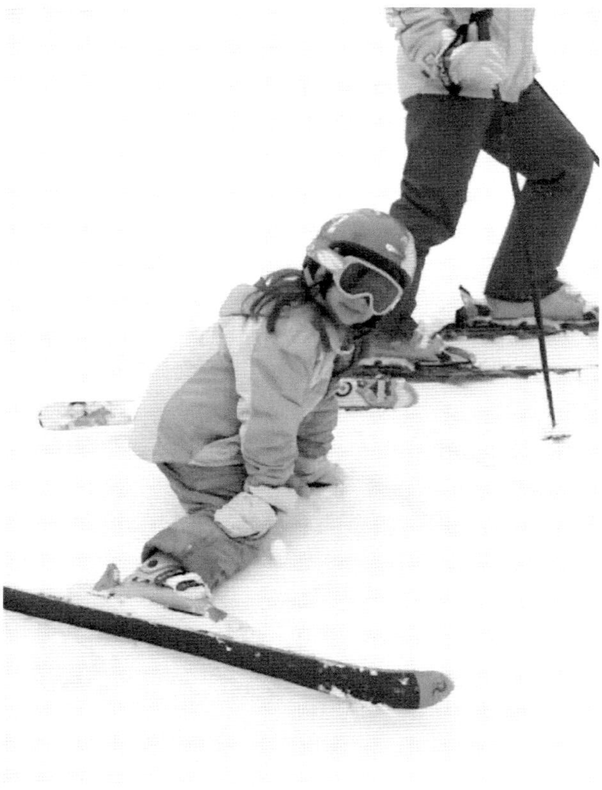

Ski school is in session at the Gate House Lodge. The trail in the center is Sleeper, a lightly gladed intermediate trail with gentle bumps and silver birches. The 111 trails at Sugarbush have given the resort accolades as the Eastern resort with the most variable terrain for experts and beginners. (Photograph by Sewall Williams.)

In his book written after alpine skiing got underway in the valley, Frank Day wrote, "If you can walk you can ski." Both Mad River Glen and Sugarbush agreed with the concept and started up learning programs that began with toddlers, in this case, Ella Cook, six, who seems to have caught an edge but survived. (Photograph by June Cook.)

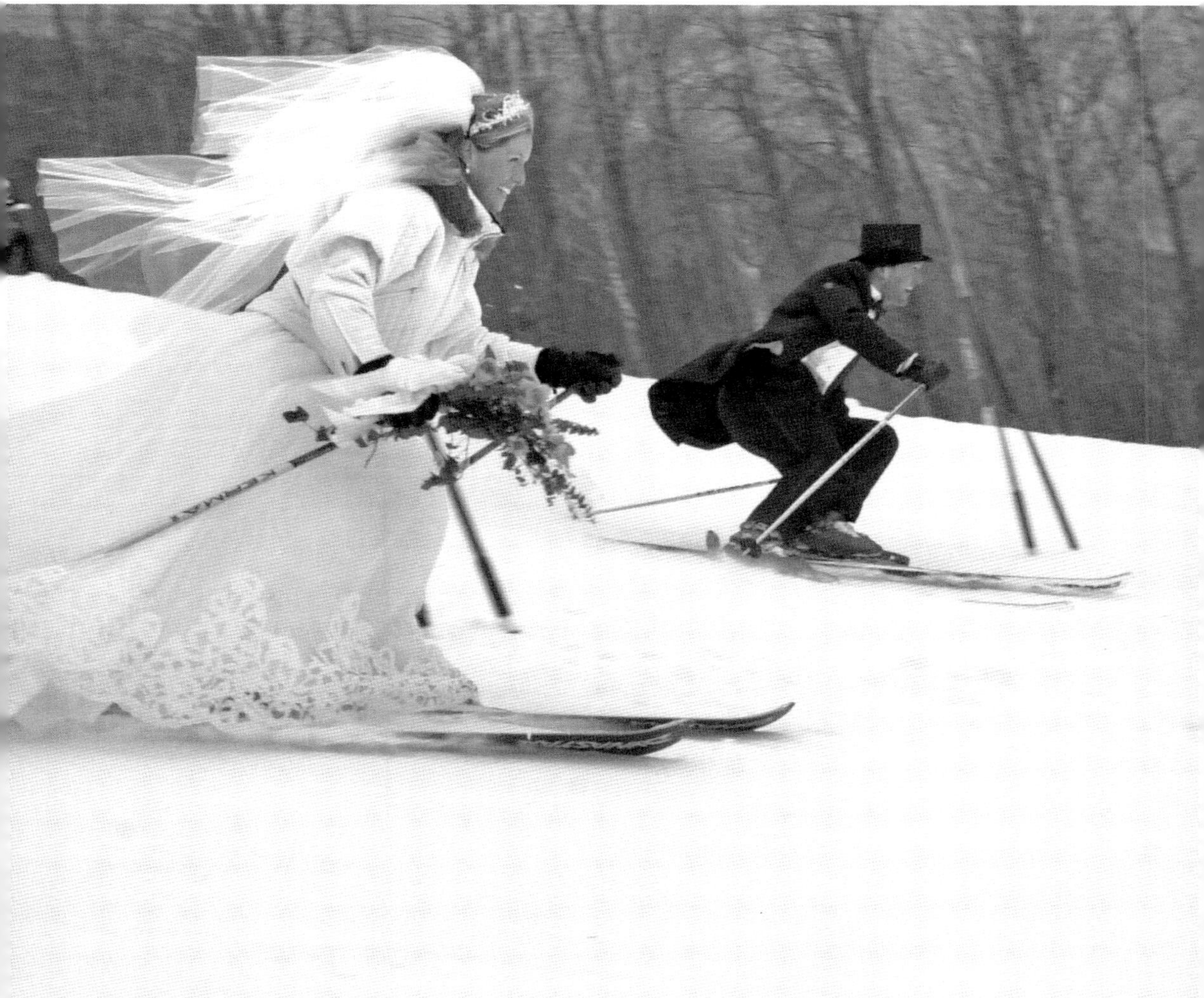

A decent powder day waits for no one, as demonstrated by this gag shot featuring real-life Mr. and Mrs. Doug and Kelley Lewis at Sugarbush. But the photo emphasizes two economic mainstays in the Mad River Valley: weddings and skiing. Sugarbush has hosted more than 25 wedding events in a summer. "Lew" and Kelley host Vermont Spotlight Videos, and in the summer they run ELITEAM summer camps for young athletes. They also do television commentary for major outdoor networks. Doug, a graduate of the Green Mountain Valley School and former member of the U.S. Ski Team, competed in the Winter Olympic games in 1984 and 1988. Kelley was a World Cup downhill racer, a member of the famed Canadian "Crazy Canucks" team. (Photograph by Sandy Macys; courtesy of Sugarbush.)

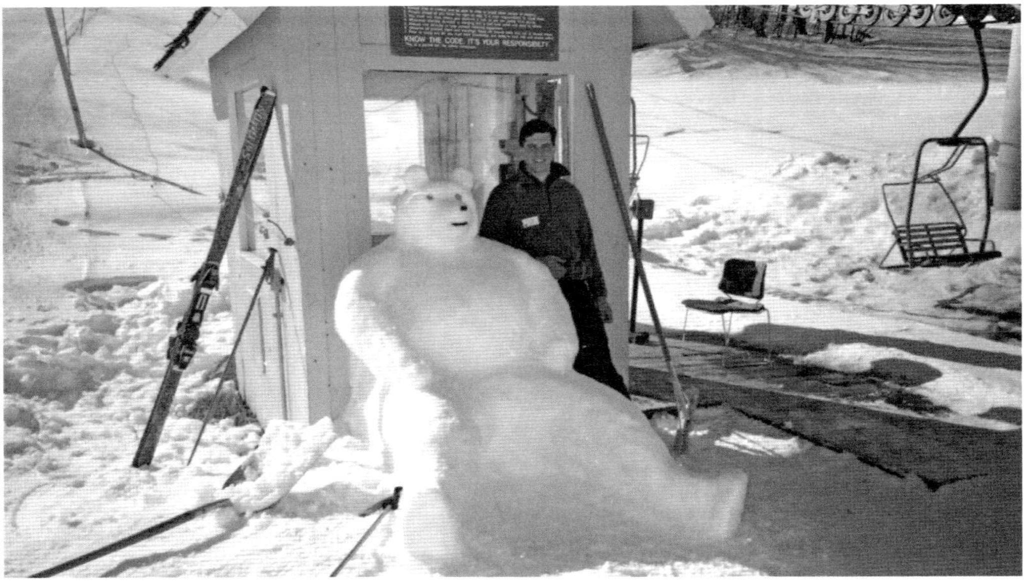

This is a Sugar Bear on Snow, resting comfortably at the foot of the Sunny D lift at Mount Ellen, which serves less difficult trails and also contains a terrain park where both snowboarders and skiers who seek a little more action are bound to land. (Photograph by Ellie Hilferty.)

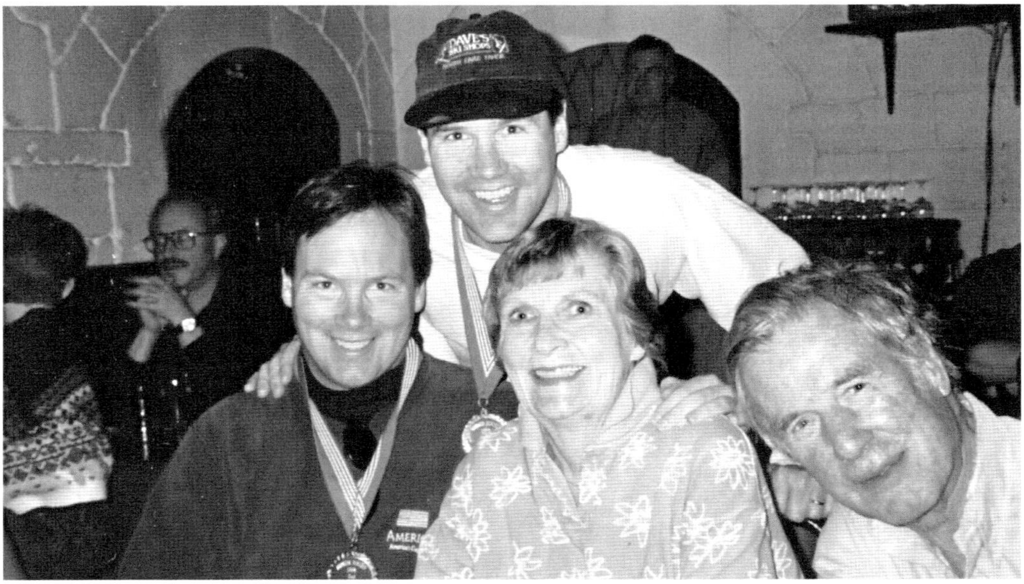

Arthur and Hanne Williams came to the valley in 1957 as teachers sharing space in one-room schools in Moretown and Fayston. Hanne taught the first four grades, and Arthur grades five through eight. In this photograph, their son Nate is standing, and in front of him, from left to right, are their other son John, Hanne, and Arthur. John wears a medal won in the Georges Duboeuf race sponsored by Chez Henri as a fundraiser for the Mad River Community Fund. (Courtesy of Henri Borel.)

The September 1980 cover of *Skiing Magazine* illustrates the thrill of handling Upper FIS at Mount Ellen. Originally designed as a World Cup race course when Glen Ellen's Walt Eliot created the resort, Upper FIS still reigns as a major mogul challenge. (Photograph by Clyde Smith; Courtesy of *Skiing Magazine*.)

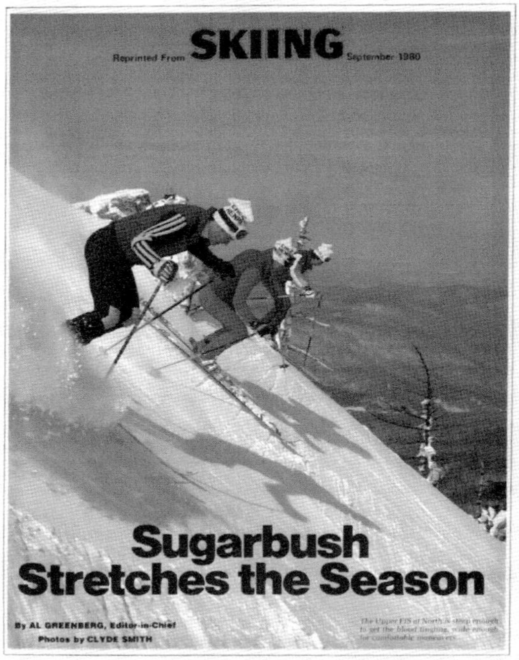

Reprinted From **SKIING** September 1980

Sugarbush Stretches the Season

By AL GREENBERG, Editor-in-Chief
Photos by CLYDE SMITH

The Upper FIS at North is steep enough to get the blood tingling, wide enough for comfortable maneuvers.

COPYRIGHT © 1980 ZIFF-DAVIS PUBLISHING COMPANY. ALL RIGHTS RESERVED.

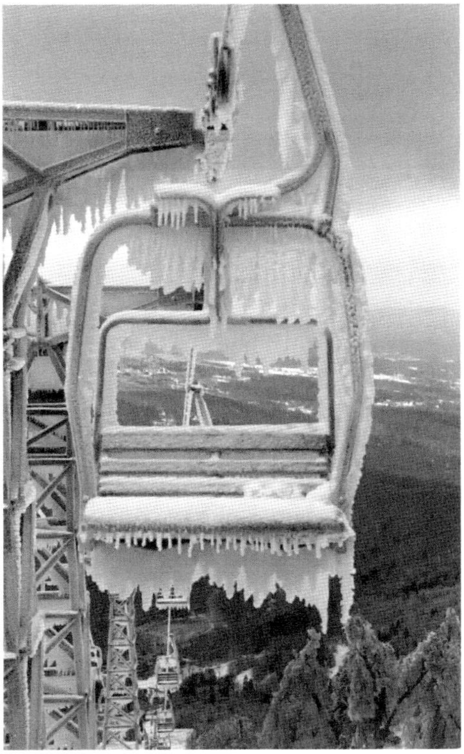

Ghostly and beautiful was the ice pasted to this ski lift at Sugarbush during the January 4, 1998, ice storm. The freezing phenomenon occurs when falling snow melts into rain as it passes from a cold to an above-freezing warmer layer of air. As the rain then falls upon frozen ground and trees, the droplets freeze on contact, creating a thick and sometimes deadly accumulation. (Courtesy of the *Valley Reporter*.)

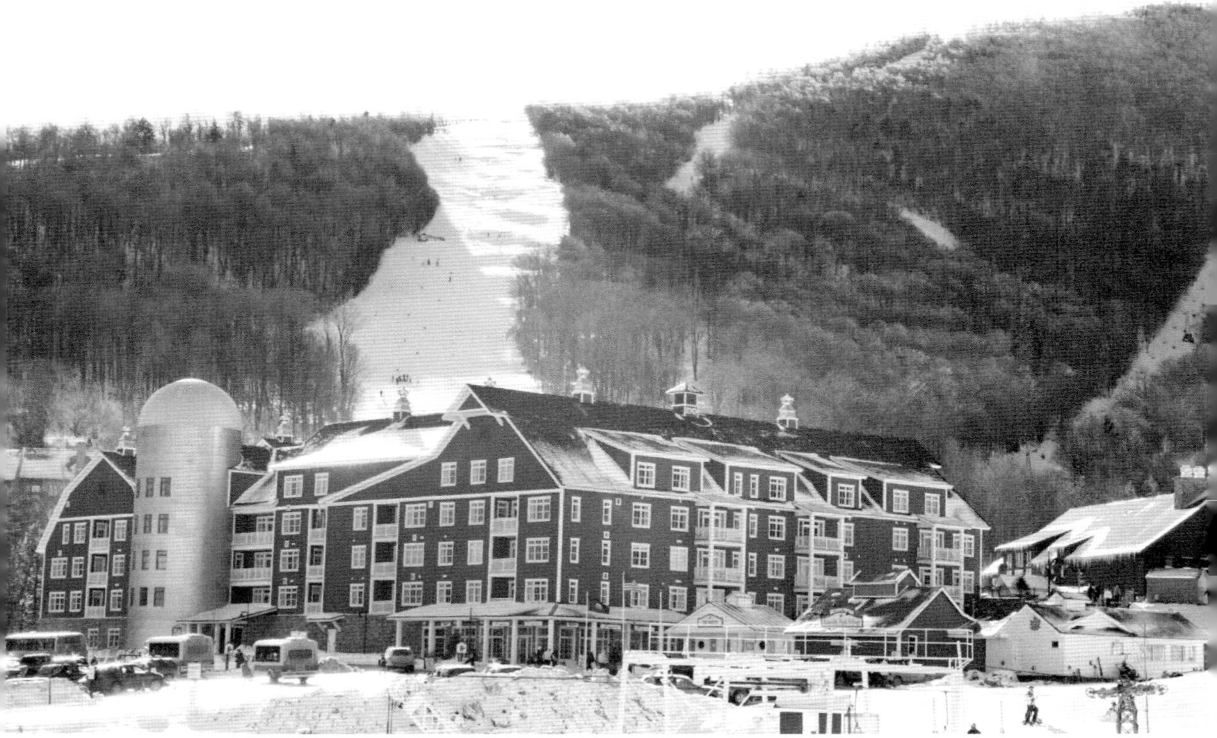

Clay Brook, the centerpiece of Summit Ventures' $60 million expansion in 2006, was the answer to years of complaints that Sugarbush was lacking "pillows" within its boundaries. The 61-unit barn-style hotel also contains Timbers, a fine-dining restaurant. Across the way, the Gate House Lodge was doubled in size. Besides the creation of several condo units on the Sugarbush property, overall development in the Mad River Valley has been sparse. The plus side, however, is that the character of the valley, which in many cases is architecturally rooted in the 19th century, has continued pretty much intact. In the 1960s, there were about 40 lodging establishments in the valley, a number that has not varied much in the past 50 years. (Photograph by Ellie Hilferty.)

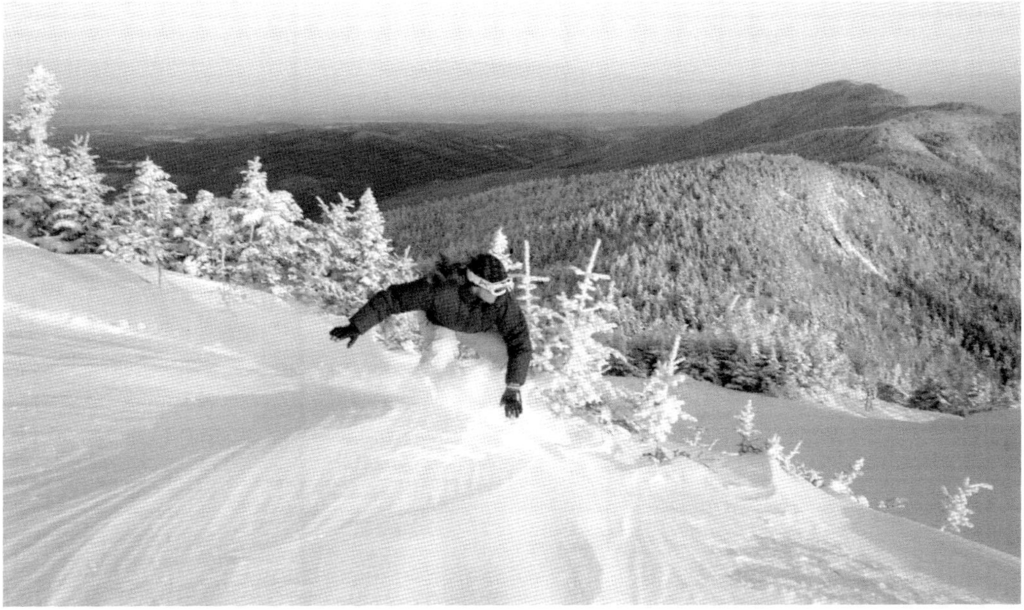

Morning sunlight breaks upon the corduroy (below) as Meredith McFarland makes first tracks for the day at the summit (above). Though experiments with similar equipment go back as far as 1929, snowboard development took off in the late 1960s with the Snurfer, followed by Jake Burton Carpenter's advances in Vermont in the late 1970s. Acceptance came easily among teenagers but reluctantly among adults. With six interconnected peaks, Sugarbush's expansive terrain on more than 100 trails and abundant off-piste areas accommodated the new sport with relative ease. It is estimated that about 97 percent of all ski areas in North America and Europe allow snowboarding, and more than half have jumps, rails, and half-pipes. (Courtesy of Sugarbush.)

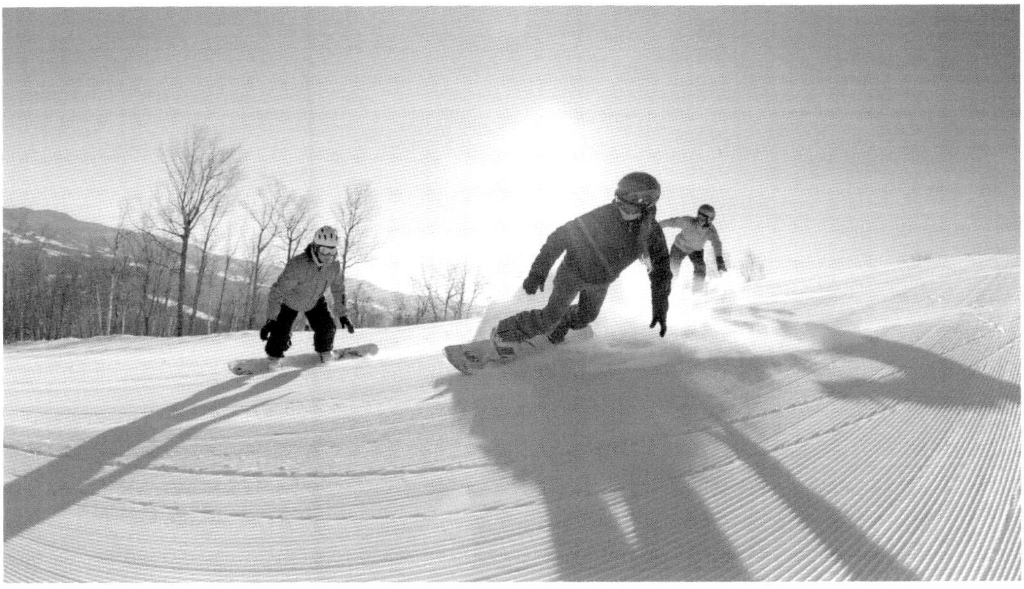

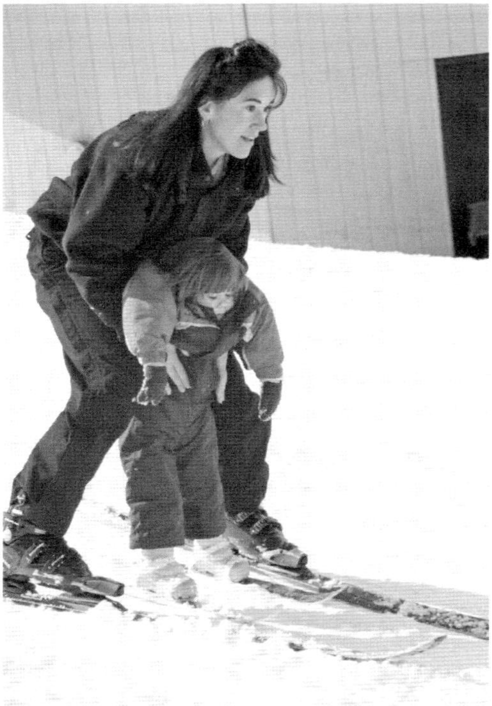

Two-year-old Shannon Cook gets her first ski lesson from mom June, a ski instructor at Sugarbush. A few years later, Shannon, a graduate of the Sugar Bear school, was handling moguls on Stein's Run and tree skiing throughout the resort. In the photograph below, Ginny Roth, originally from Massachusetts, takes in the scenery on a bright sunny day at Sugarbush. She settled in the valley with husband John after talking with Sugarbush founders Damon Gadd and Jack Murphy. "They made it sound so appealing, we moved here" from Aspen, Colorado, in 1960. The Roths have a successful real estate business and gift shop in Warren. (Left, photograph by Ellie Hilferty; below, courtesy of Sugarbush.)

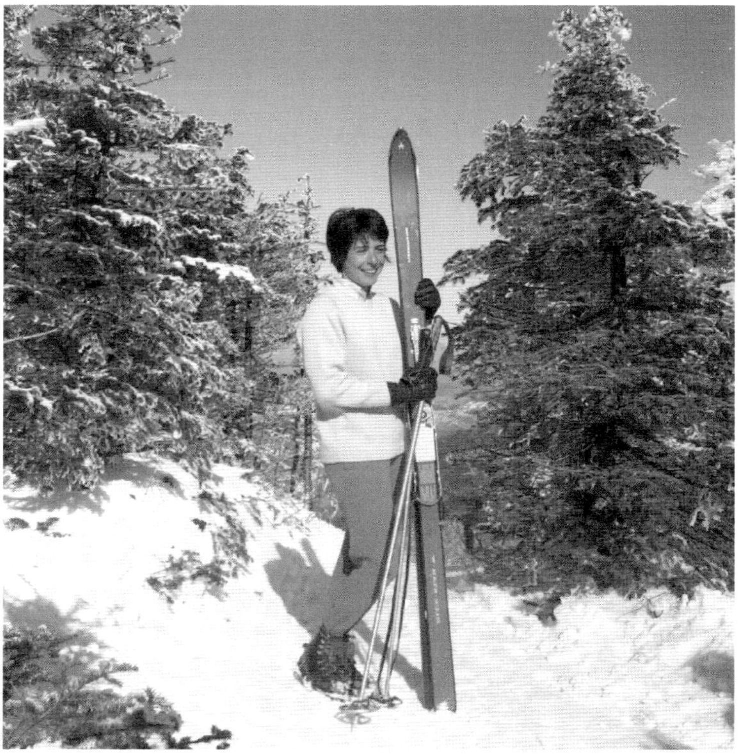

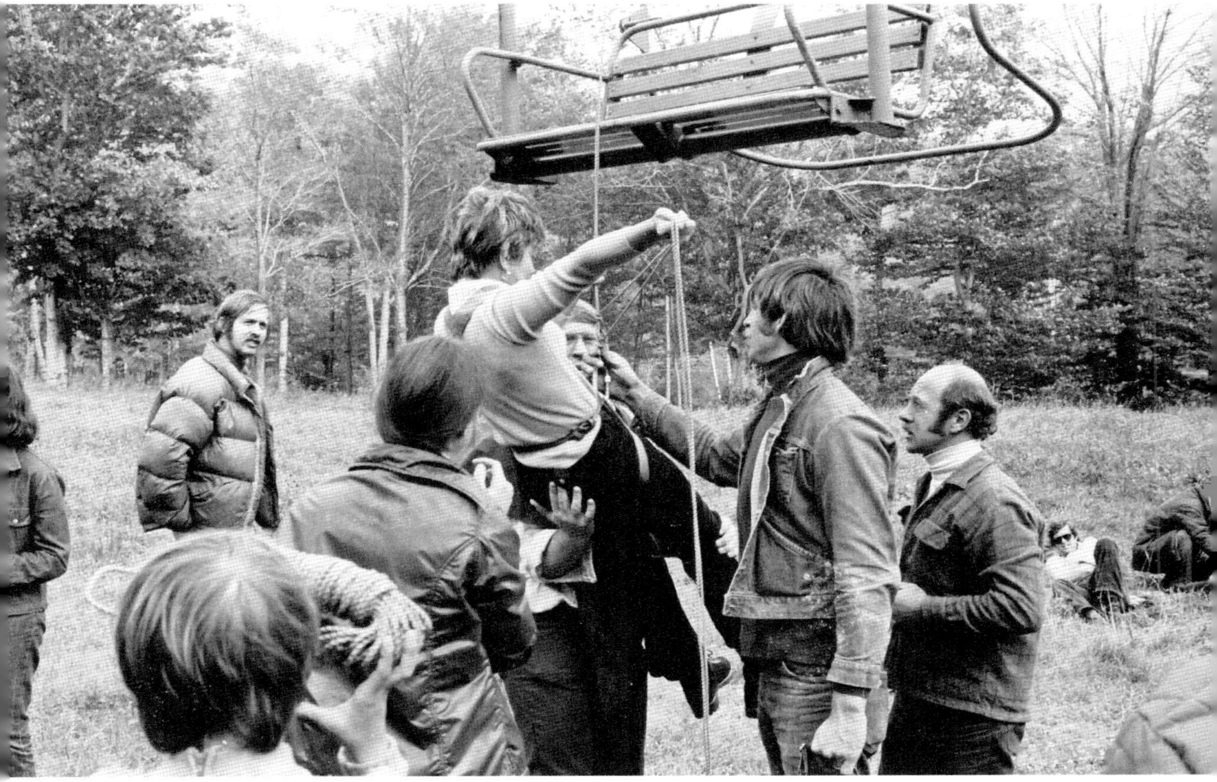

Bill Bozack, right, conducts a lift evacuation drill at Glen Ellen for members of the resort's ski patrol. Bozack, who was the head of Glen Ellen's patrol in the 1970s, was famous for the training clinics that he ran as the National Ski Patrol System's (NSPS's) national professional director. In 1971, Bozack's wife Mary Ann became only the second woman to become certified by the NSPS nationwide. The testing procedures for ski patrollers can be exhausting. In addition to making sure that skiers, who may become stranded when a lift stops running, are able to get safely to the ground, patrollers must learn to handle heavy sleds on steep slopes and be proficient in first aid. The NSPS, founded in 1938, has more than 26,000 members in 600 different patrols throughout the United States and military areas in Europe. (Courtesy of Bill Bozack.)

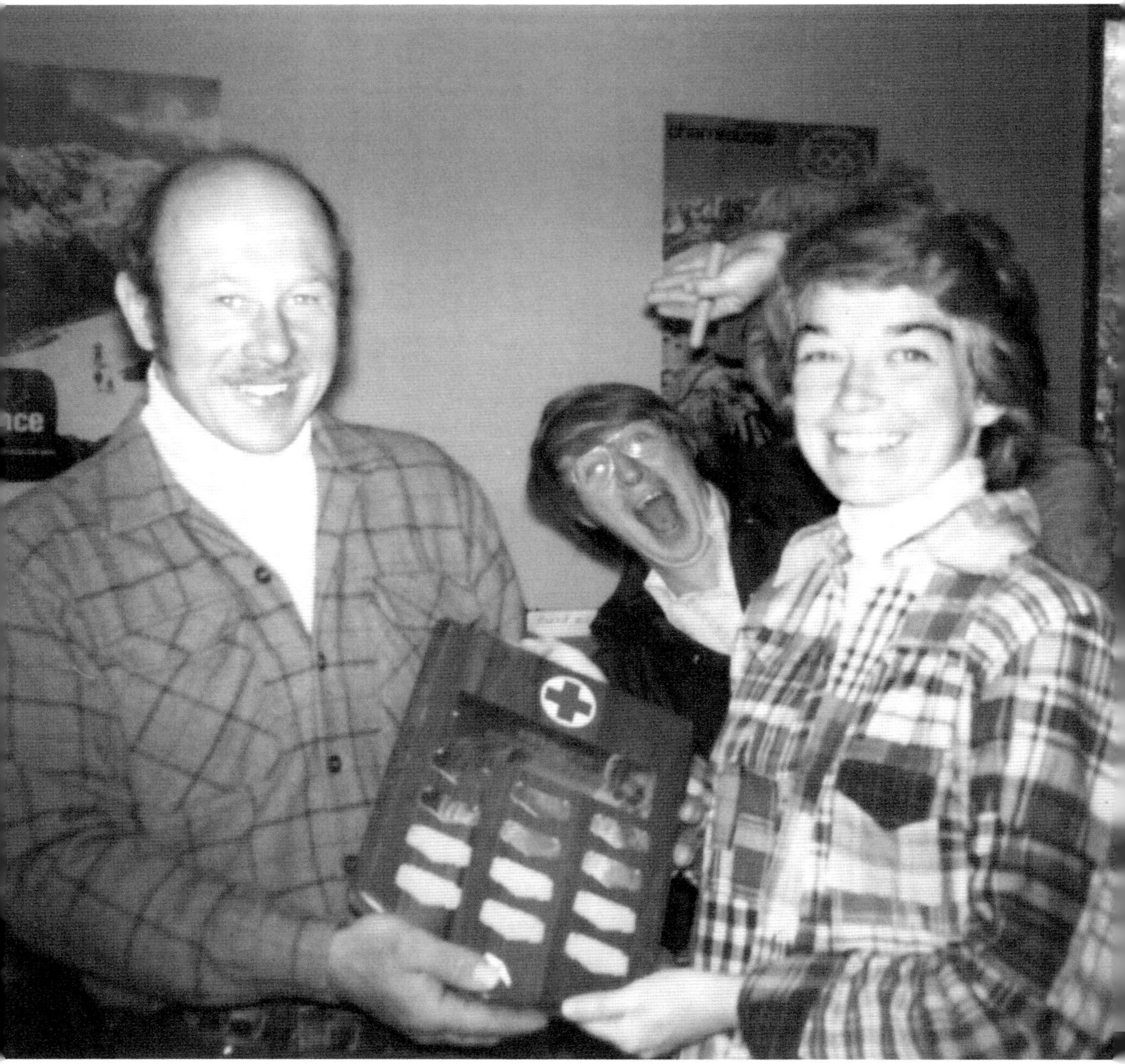

Kandi Clark receives the Bob Ray Award as Patroller of the Year at Glen Ellen for the 1973–1974 season. Presenting the award is Bill Bozack, Glen Ellen patrol leader who was named the National Ski Patrol System (NSPS) Outstanding Professional Ski Patrolman nationwide the year before. The national organization has stretched beyond rescue work on the mountains by helping other organizations in outreach projects. An example is the NSPS alliance with the organization known as PHAT (Protect Head at All Times), a ski helmet advocacy program that is also supported by Vermont Children's Hospital at Fletcher Allen Health Care in Burlington. A study by the U.S. Consumer Product Safety Commission found that nearly 8,000 head injuries each year could be prevented if all skiers and snowboarders wore helmets. (Courtesy of Bill Bozack.)

3

FAME, GLORY, AND FUN

Competition on skis or snowboards comes as easily to valley residents as falling out of bed in the morning—and often that's when it starts. Whether it is the gut-wrenching feat of competing in the Sugarbush triathlon every April or the predawn training to prepare for a slot on the U.S. Ski Team and then World Cup or Olympic competition, the intensity of valley athletes in training is no joke.

This chapter chronicles, in photographs, a remarkable history of performance by valley residents—young and old, professional and amateur. Sometimes lost in the achievements are the coaches, many unpaid, and personnel behind the scenes of victory. They set the pace, set the gates, and bake the cookies.

Whether it is a junk race, where waiters and waitresses carry trays of glasses around the obstacles, or gutsy downhillers turning it loose on Spring Fling, there are always crowds to push the competitors. Then there are those who are always trying to think up another excuse for another race.

The training never stops. In summer, the man or woman on a dirt bike scrambling down a mountain, or on a road bike on Route 100, or in a kayak in the Mad River, is likely to be your competition on the snow in the upcoming winter.

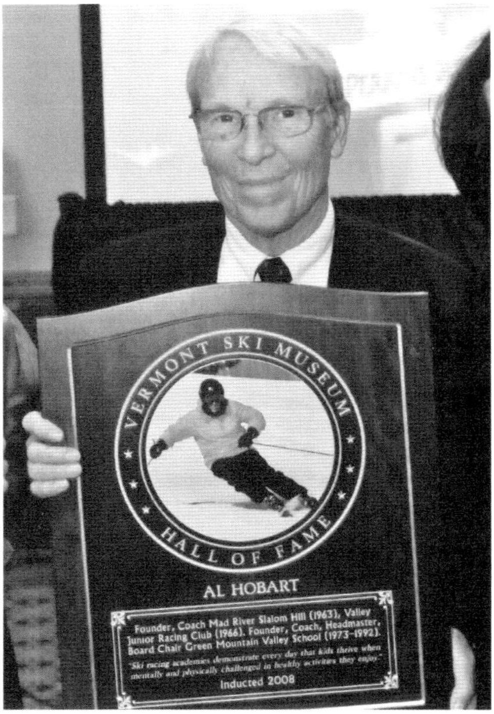

Al Hobart, who cofounded the Green Mountain Valley School and was its headmaster until 1980, was inducted into the Vermont Ski Museum Hall of Fame in 2008. As a ski racer, he won many masters national championships in giant slalom and slalom, but he may be more prominently known as an instructor of ski racers. He founded the Valley Junior Racing Club, which he ran from 1966 to 1972, and was prominent in the instruction of several champions for the U.S. Ski Team. (Courtesy of Al Hobart.)

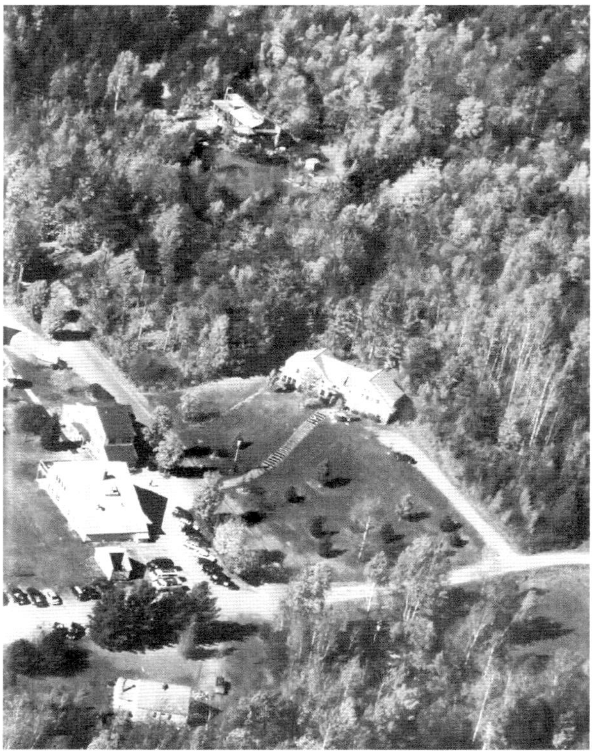

This aerial view reveals the Green Mountain Valley School (GMVS) campus as a leafy retreat on Moulton Road in Fayston. The administration building is at left, and in the center is a building housing classrooms. The present campus was created from a cornfield in 1978. It was moved from a barn located in Moretown on the property of John Schultz, a GMVS cofounder. (Courtesy of Al Hobart.)

A para-ski race at Mad River Glen in 1960 required leaping 2,500 feet down from an airplane, landing on a target in the Catamount Bowl, then racing downhill on skis to the bottom. The winner posted a time of 6:05.3. (Courtesy of Mad River Glen.)

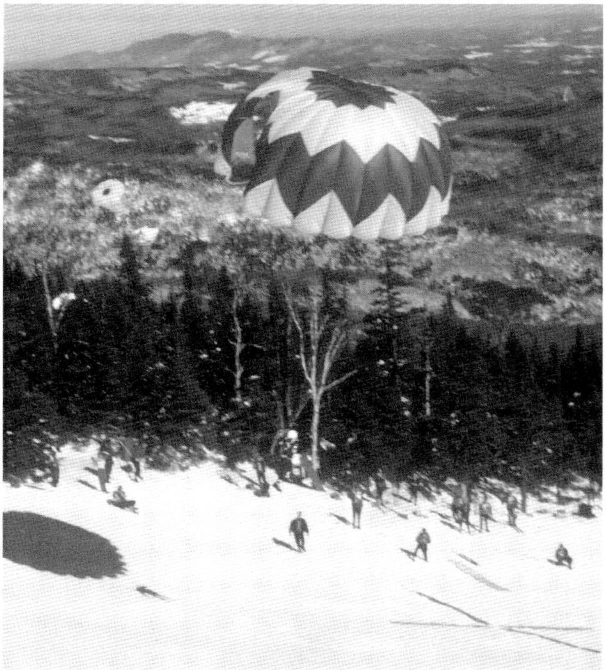

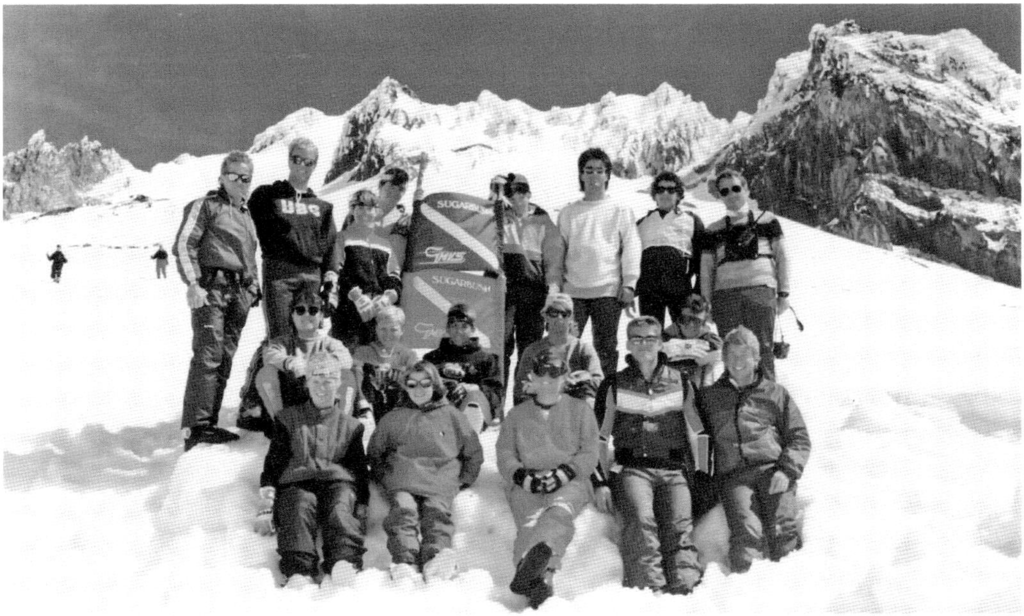

Green Mountain Valley School (GMVS) racers took part in summer training regularly at Mount Hood in Oregon. The mountain near Portland regularly receives 300 inches of snowfall each winter. In 1997, GMVS purchased a facility in Kössen, Austria, in the heart of the Tyrolean Alps. From this home base, it is just 19 miles to Kitzbühel, the site of the difficult Hahnenkamm downhill race, and 60 miles to Innsbruck. (Courtesy of Al Hobart.)

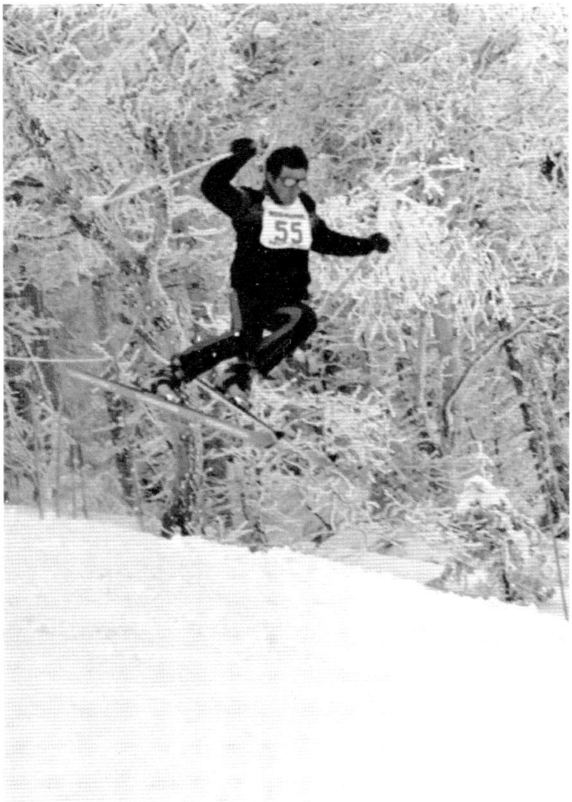

Robert Forenza competes in a mogul competition on Stein's Run in 1979. Sugarbush's other challenging bump course is FIS (Federation Internationale de Ski), designed by Walt Eliot at Glen Ellen for World Cup ski races. (Courtesy of John Egan.)

A weekend program of Green Mountain Valley School that was held in 1984 at Sugarbush included a team led by extreme skier John Egan to a famous off-piste location called The Church. This group shot suggests the thought "follow me, you go first." (Courtesy of John Egan.)

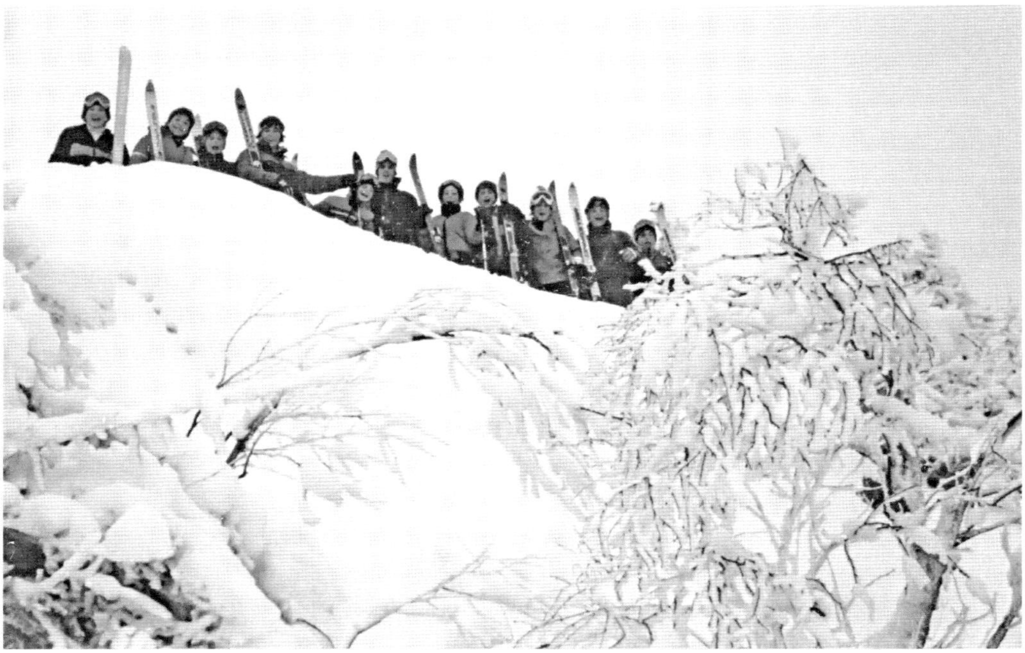

In 1988, noted ski movie filmmaker Warren Miller's crew shot at Sugarbush. The trio pictured consists of Dan Egan, Tom Day, and John Egan flying down FIS at Mount Ellen. The Egan brothers, who have skied all over the world, made regular appearances in Warren Miller films. (Courtesy of John Egan.)

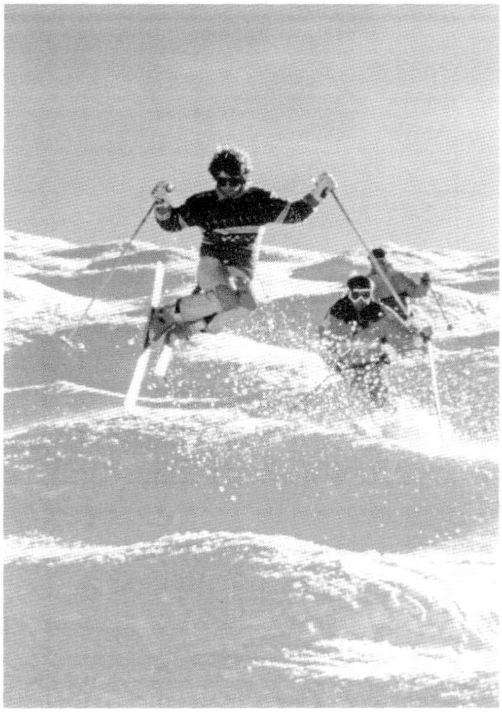

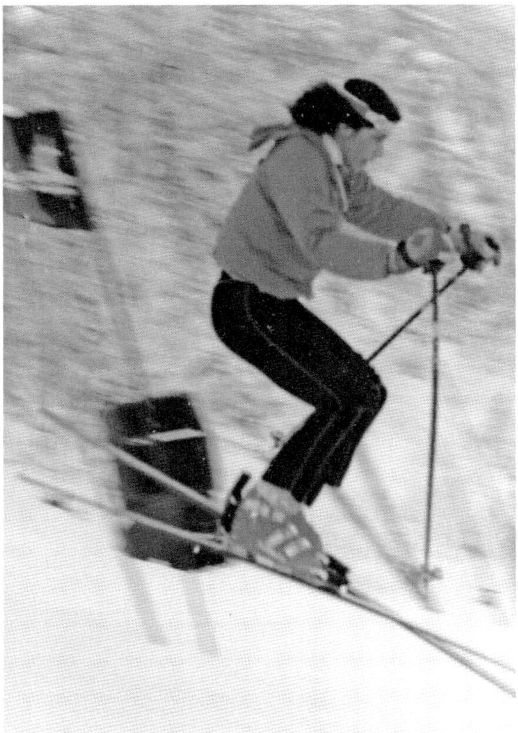

Julie Anderson competes in the 1980 Spring Moguls Championship held annually on FIS at Mount Ellen. The upper part of the black diamond trail joins Rim Run before trailing off on its own, a little used portion that stretches to the bottom of the mountain. (Courtesy of John Egan.)

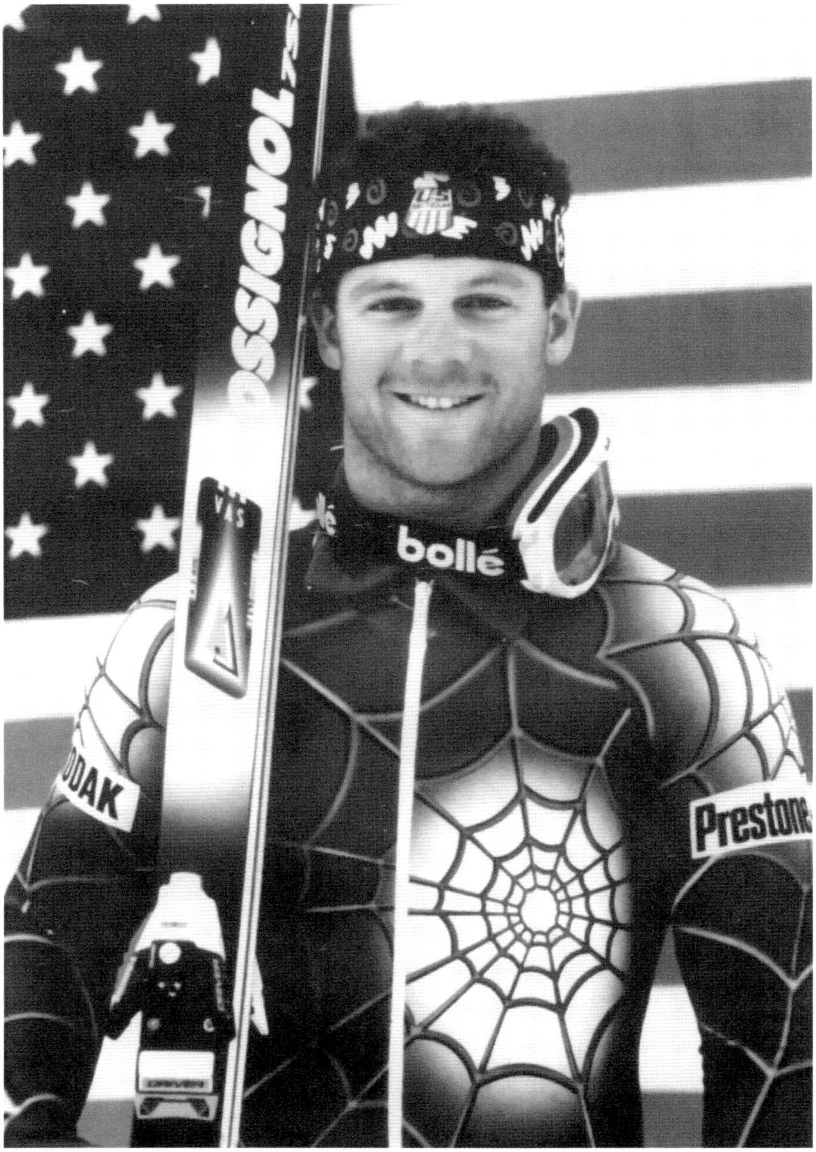

Unless a person is a close relative or friend of Alva Ross Kitt IV, one may remain ignorant that he is the one and the same "A. J. Kitt" of skiing fame. One of the many Green Mountain Valley School graduates who were members of the U.S. Ski Team in the 1990s, Kitt landed on the podium in six World Cup races and finished in the top 10 a total of 21 times. He competed in four Olympics, with his best finish being ninth place in the downhill in 1992. He grew up in the small town of Gates, near Rochester, New York. He was inducted into the U.S. National Ski Hall of Fame in 2004. His parents, Ross and Nancy Kitt, were part-time ski instructors. After retiring from World Cup skiing, he was the traveling NASTAR pacesetter and competed in the Jeep "King of the Mountain" downhill series. He is now a real estate professional in the Columbia River Gorge area of Washington state. (Courtesy of GMVS.)

Fifteen-year-old Green Mountain Valley School student Daron Rhalves carves a turn on Inverness in 1988. Rhalves stood on the World Cup podium 28 times in his 13-year career on the U.S. Ski Team, beginning in 1994. He won three World Championship medals, including a gold in super G in 2001 and a silver and bronze in downhill and giant slalom, respectively, in 2005. (Courtesy of GMVS.)

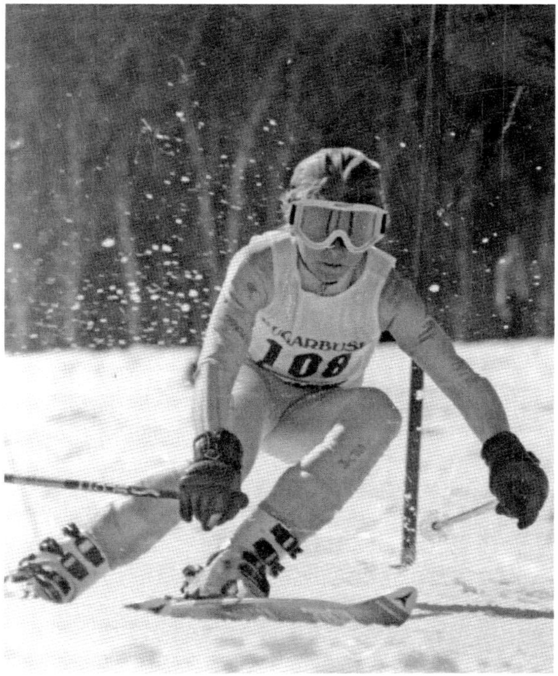

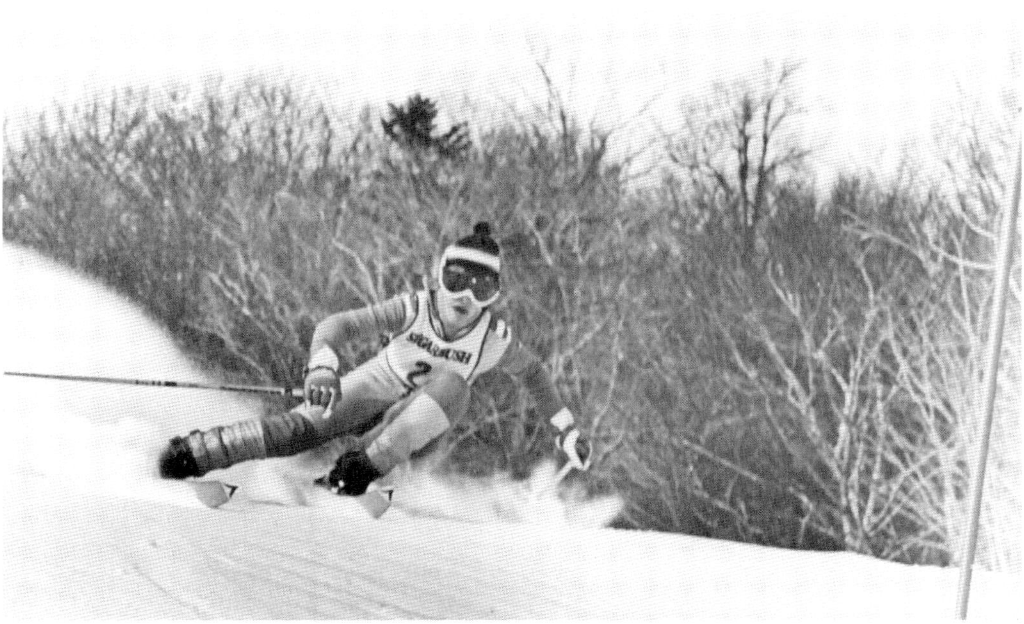

The children of Malcolm and Judy Reiss of Waitsfield made their mark on the Green Mountain Valley School, with five of them attending GMVS over the years. Pictured is daughter Colly, who raced in the 1980s and was a member of the U.S. Ski Team. Others were Toby, Patricia, Adrian, and Sarah, all of whom raced for the University of Vermont. (Photograph by Malcolm Reiss; courtesy of GMVS.)

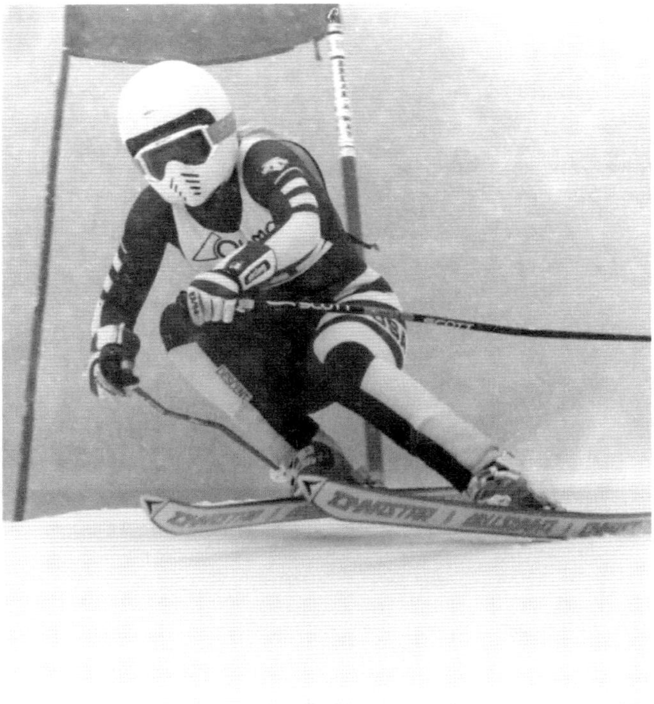

Katie Monahan, shown racing in 1990, was in the 1998 Olympics and was a member of the U.S. Ski Team from 1994 through 2004, with best results in the downhill and super G. (Photograph by Malcolm Reiss; courtesy of GMVS.)

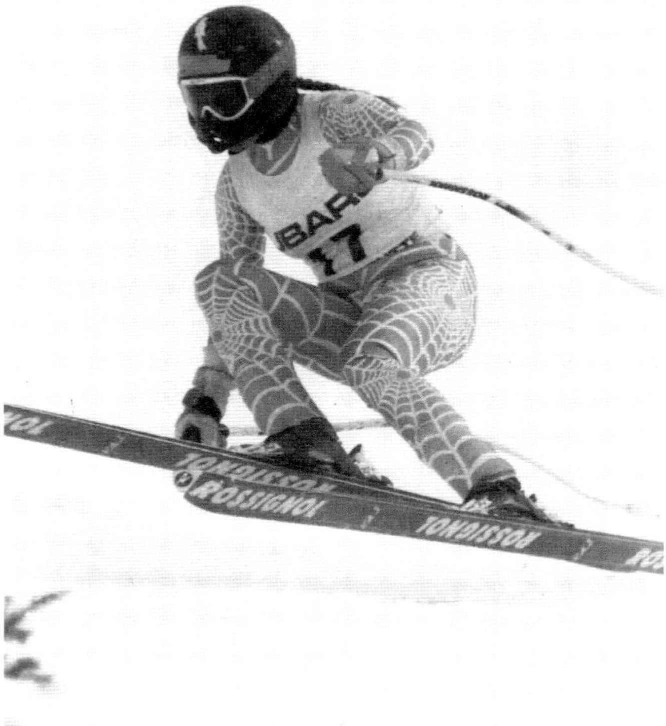

Green Mountain Valley School students Shannon Nobis, pictured here, and her brother Jeremy were U.S. Ski Team members in the 1990s. Shannon finished 10th in the super G in the 1994 Olympics. She hit the podium in one World Cup super G, and had six finishes in the top 10 of the racers in super G. (Courtesy of GMVS.)

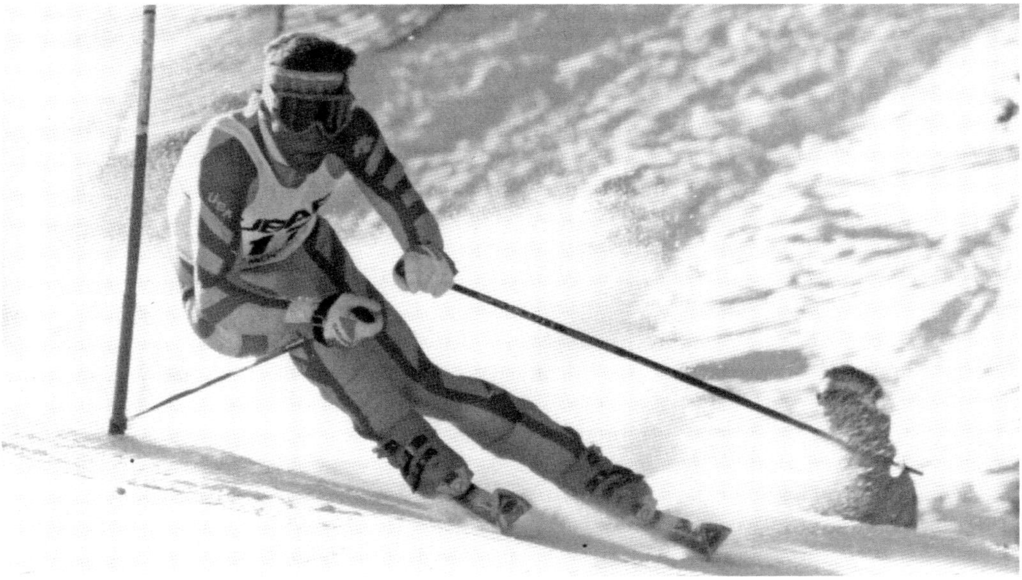

Jeff Olson, shown here racing for Green Mountain Valley School in 1984, was part of a phenomenal combination of GMVS graduates who represented the United States in the 1988 and 1992 Olympics. The others were A. J. Kitt and Doug Lewis. Olson was a three-time National Downhill champion. His professional career over, he skied onto Wall Street and cofounded Well Nourished Worldwide, a company that provides health and nutritional techniques to athletes. (Courtesy of GMVS.)

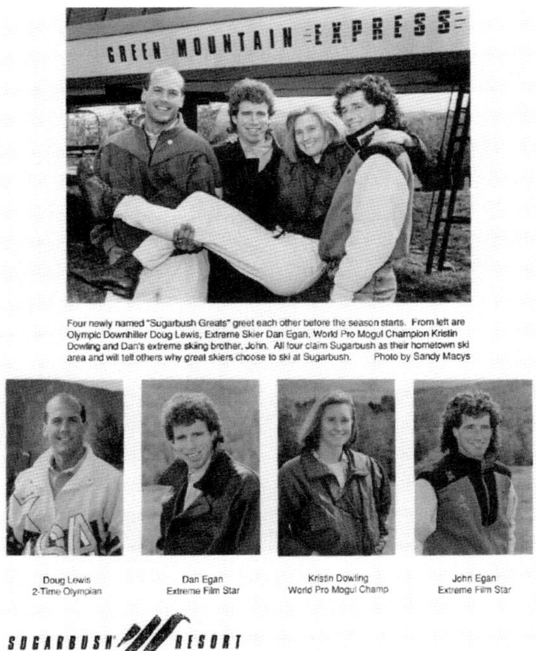

Among the many competitive champions who called the Mad River Valley home base were, from left to right, Olympic and World Cup downhill racer Doug Lewis, extreme skier Dan Egan, World Pro Mogul champ Kristin Dowling, and John Egan, who coupled with brother Dan as extreme and adventure skiing pioneers. (Courtesy of Vermont Ski Museum.)

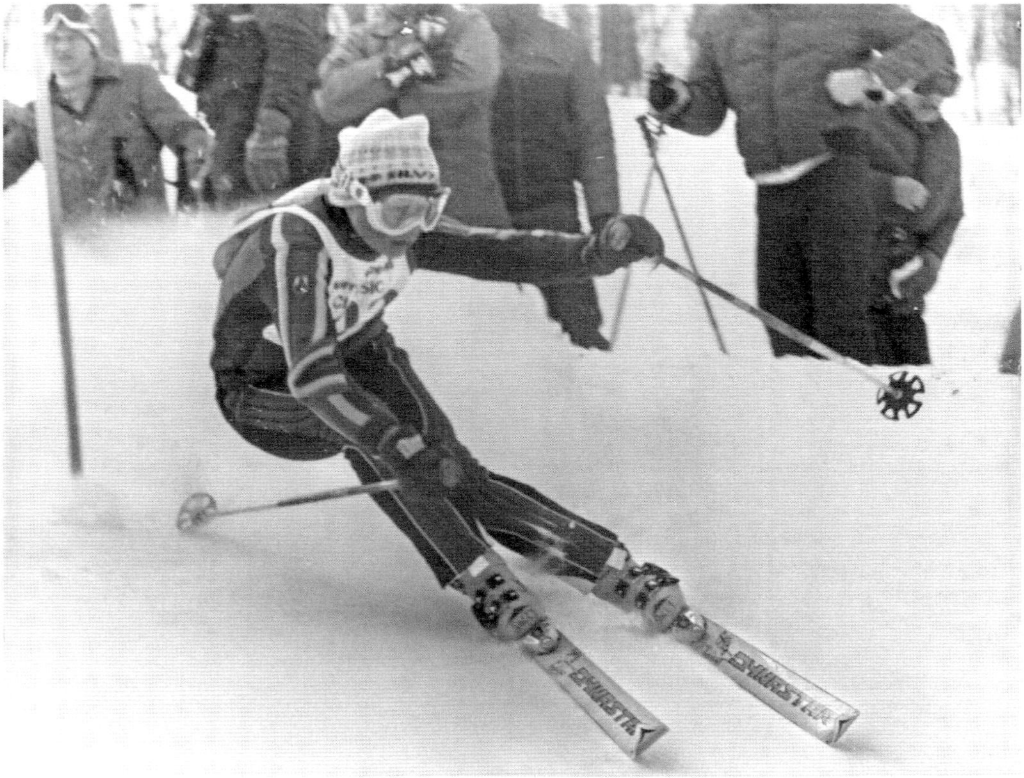

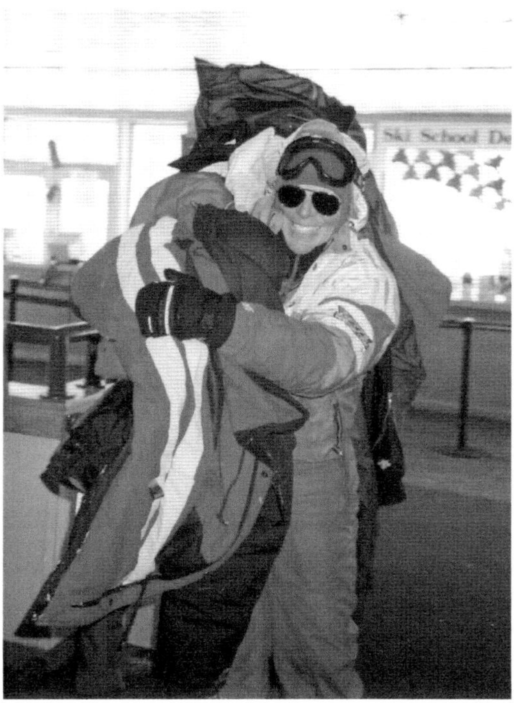

Green Mountain Valley School graduate Sally Knight of Waitsfield, shown here as a young student at GMVS, raced on the U.S. Women's Pro Ski Tour in the 1990s and excelled on the NCAA circuit as a student at the University of Vermont. But she counts among her proudest achievements the founding of Camp ForMe, a summer day camp dedicated to assisting adopted children in developing trust and self-esteem. (Photograph by Malcolm Reiss; courtesy of GMVS.)

At Jay Peak, Green Mountain Valley School instructor Al Hobart struggles beneath a pile of heavy outerwear that the school's racers discarded on a 25-below-zero race day. Faculty members at GMVS know well the motto that they never will ask a student to do something that they themselves cannot do, like heavy lifting. (Courtesy of Al Hobart.)

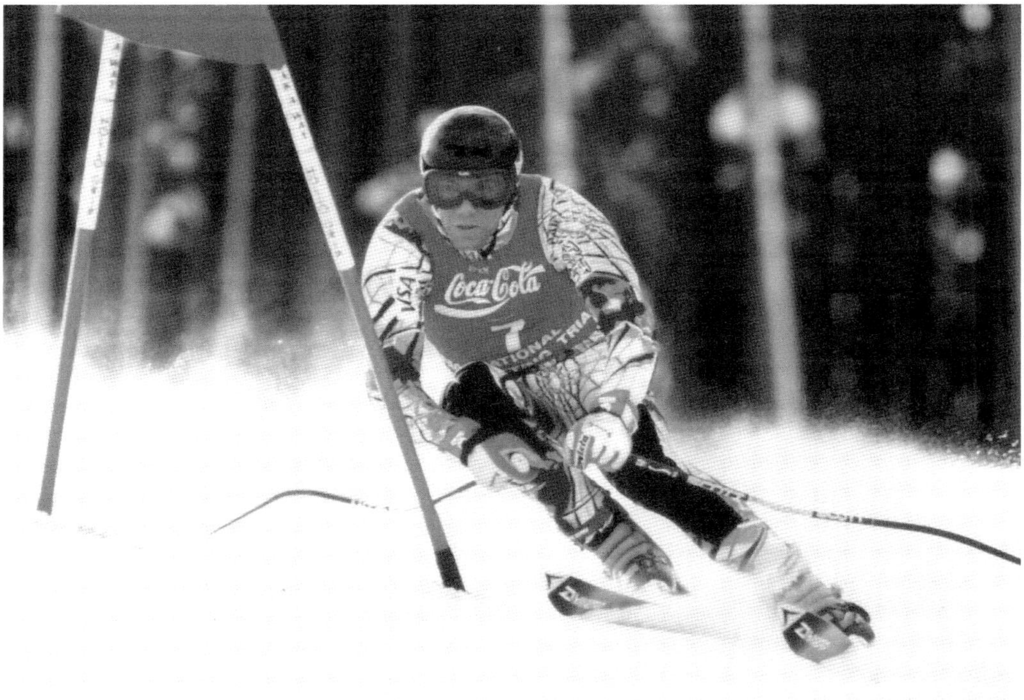

Green Mountain Valley School graduate A. J. Kitt skied the World Cup circuit for 11 years, from 1987 to 1998. A power skier, he won one World Cup race, a downhill in Val d'Isère in December 1991, had six World Cup podiums (five in downhill and one in super G), and had 21 World Cup top 10 finishes. At the 1993 World Championships, Kitt placed third in the downhill. (Courtesy of Al Hobart.)

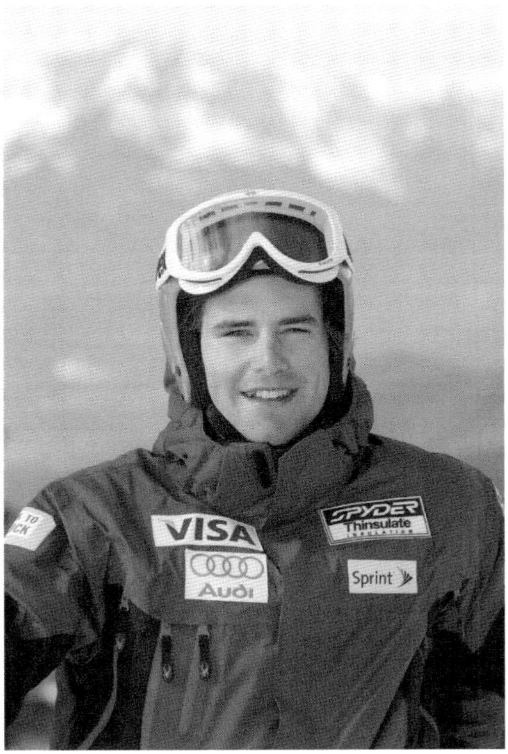

Nolan Kasper of Warren is one of the most recent valley skiers who made the U.S. Ski Team as an emerging racer. A quad silver medalist (giant slalom, slalom, super G, and overall) at the 2006 Chevrolet U.S. Junior Olympics, Nolan was elected to the U.S. development team soon after. He is a graduate of the Burke Mountain Ski Academy in Vermont. (Photograph by J. Selkowitz; courtesy of the U.S. Ski Team.)

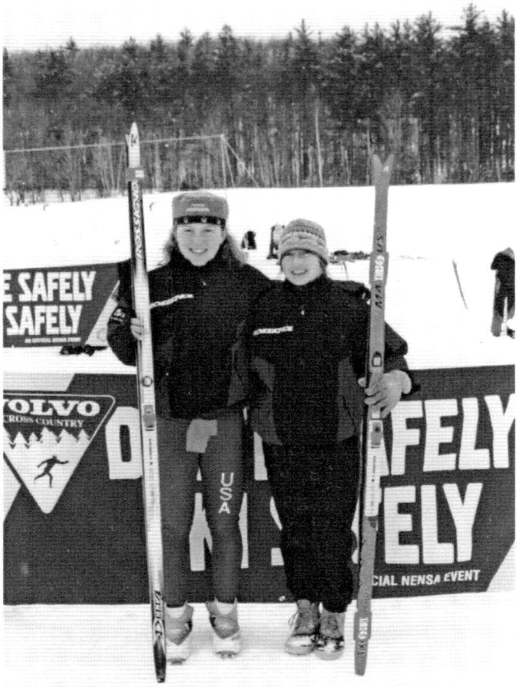

Caitlin Compton (left) and Creepy Phillips skied cross-country in the valley as kids. Compton, who was a member of the U.S. Olympic Team in 2010, forsook the ski academy route to achieve other goals. As a Harwood Union High School skier, she won a state title. At Northern Michigan University, she was a three-time NCAA National Champion. Phillips is an elementary school teacher in the valley. (Courtesy of *Valley Reporter*.)

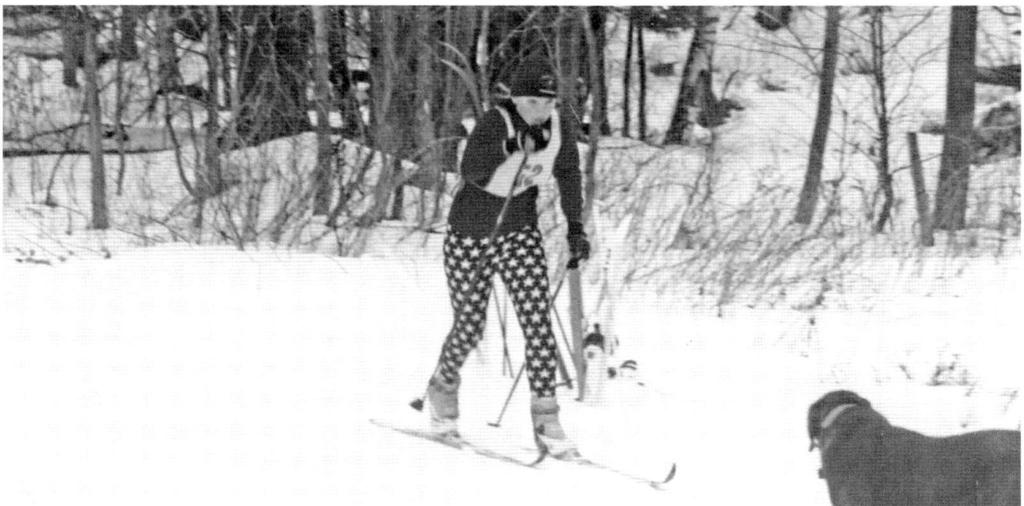

Sarah Simpson, shown here in a 1998 race, was an outstanding valley cross-country skier at Harwood Union High School, whose team was coached by John Kerrigan. Sarah, who went on to study veterinary medicine in New Zealand, regularly finished in the top five in statewide high school competitions. Her sister Katya was number two in Vermont in the mid-1980s. (Courtesy of *Valley Reporter*.)

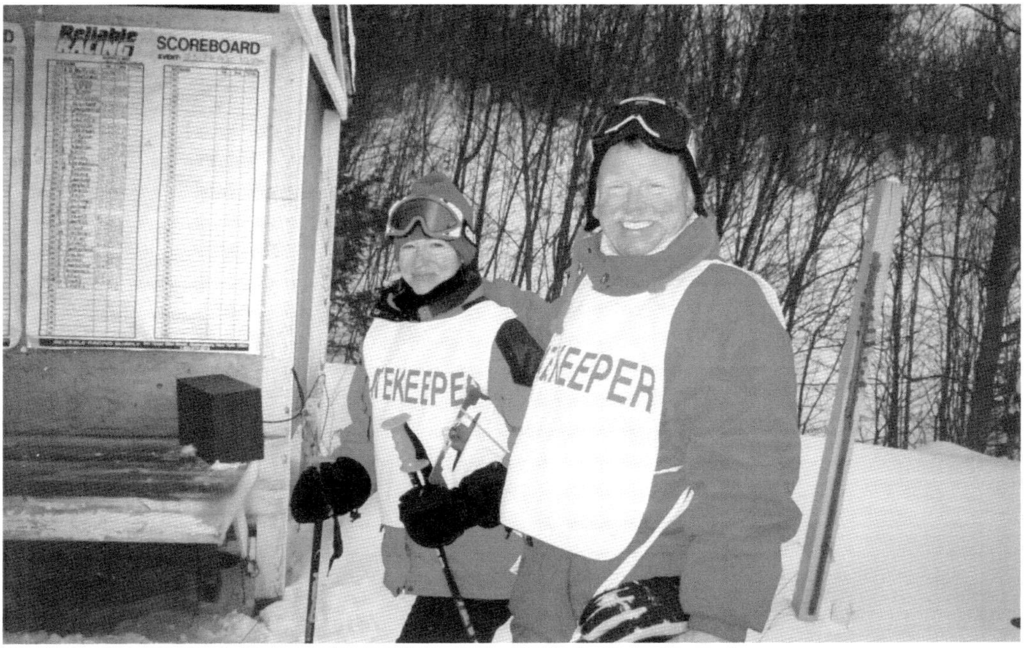

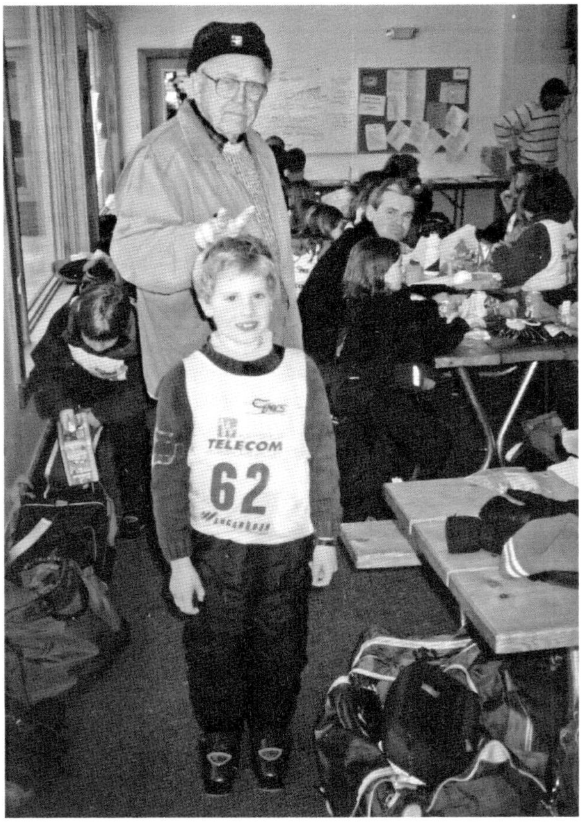

No racing program is a success without a squadron of parent volunteers to handle the job of gatekeeping. In the above photograph, Holly and Rob Buck did the duty during a weekend race involving their son Christian on Inverness in 2000. Holly is a local dental hygienist, and her husband Rob is a retired airline pilot. In the photograph at right, Christian, who was eight years old on this race day in 1998, had support from his granddad Bob Buck. The elder Buck was a pioneering pilot who wrote several books on how pilots should handle severe weather conditions. His research in the 1940s flying through thunderstorms and severe icing conditions in B-17s and a P-61 Black Widow airplane earned him a Civilian Air Medal from Pres. Harry S. Truman. (Courtesy of Holly Buck.)

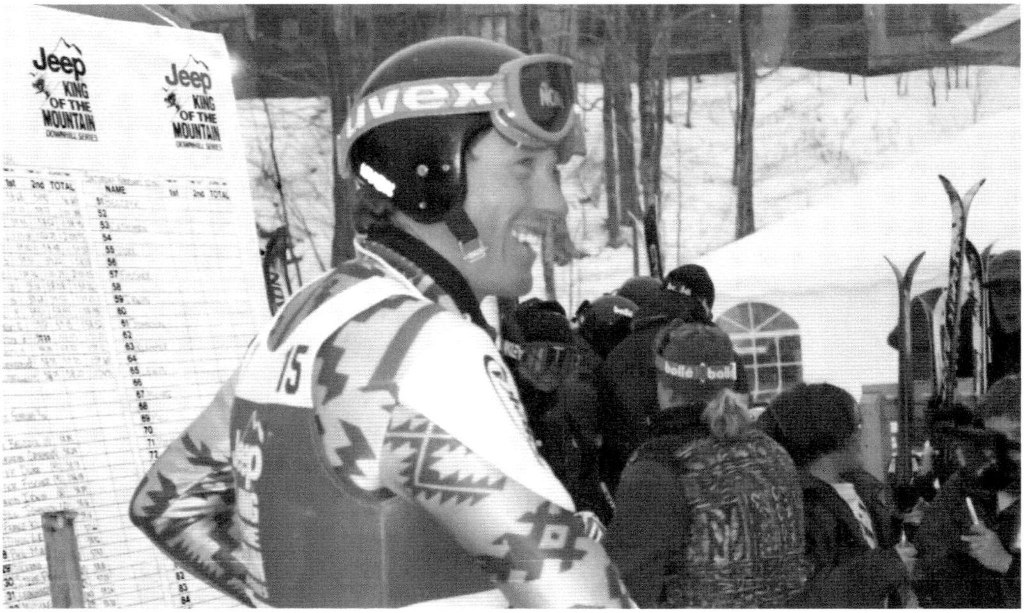

Pirmin Zurbriggen, shown here at Sugarbush in 1996, was 33 years old and one of many of the world's top racers who participated in the Jeep "King of the Mountain" downhill series after the prime of his career. The Swiss-born champion won the overall World Cup title four times, an Olympic gold medal in 1998 in downhill, and nine World Championship medals—four gold, four silver, and a bronze. (Photograph by Ellie Hilferty.)

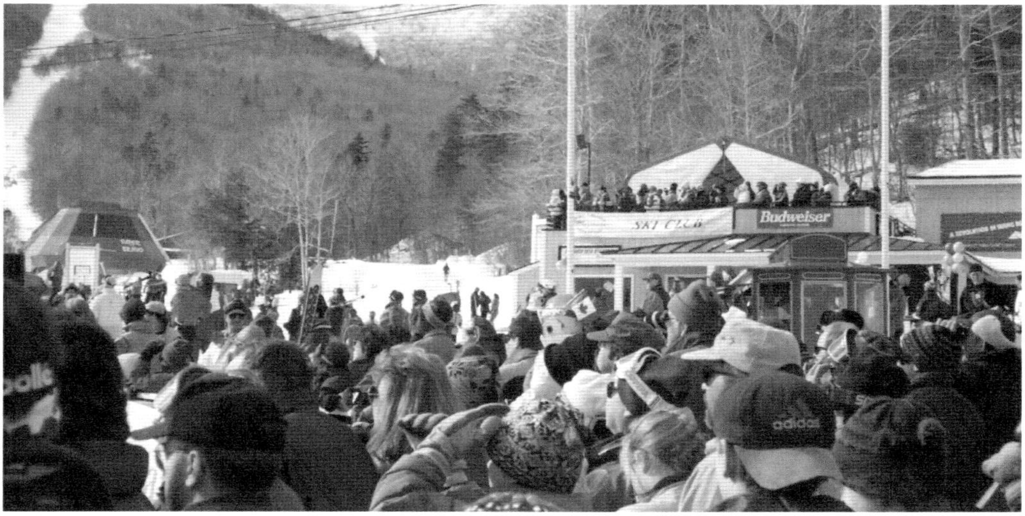

Huge crowds of ski racing fans were treated to some of the world's best during the Jeep "King of the Mountain" series held annually at Sugarbush in the 1990s. Among the racing champions were local Doug Lewis, Phil Mahre, and Bill Johnson of the United States; Franz Klammer, Leonard Stock, and Peter Wirnsberger of Austria; Pirmin Zurbriggen and Franz Heinzer of Switzerland; and Michael Veith of Germany. (Photograph by Ellie Hilferty.)

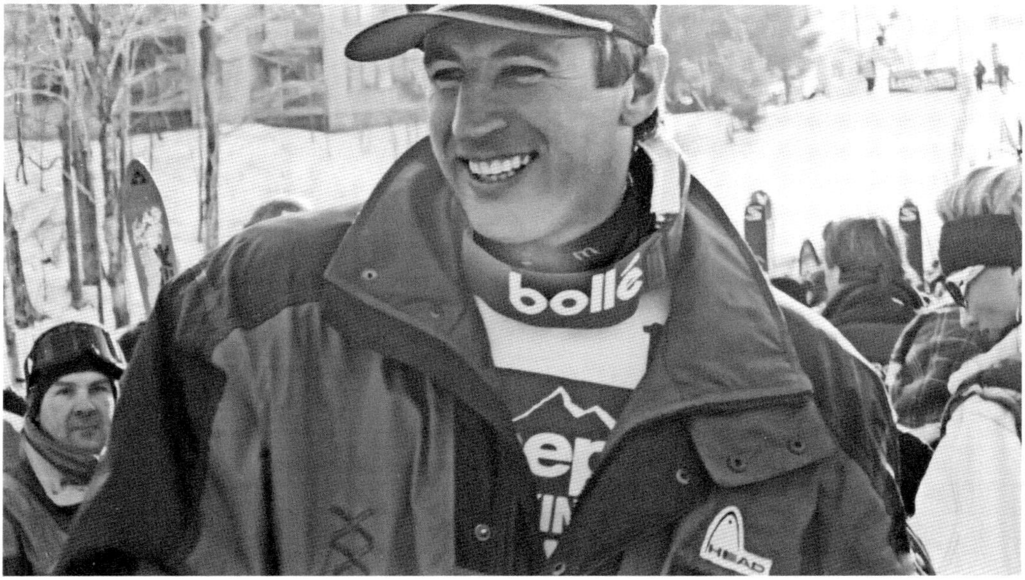

Leonard Stock is happy at the Jeep "King of the Mountain" series downhill race at Sugarbush in 1999. He was a great downhill skier for the Austrian team, succeeding Franz Klammer as the most successful downhiller of his time. He won Olympic gold in Lake Placid in 1980 and also in 1984 in Sarajevo. (Photograph by Ellie Hilferty.)

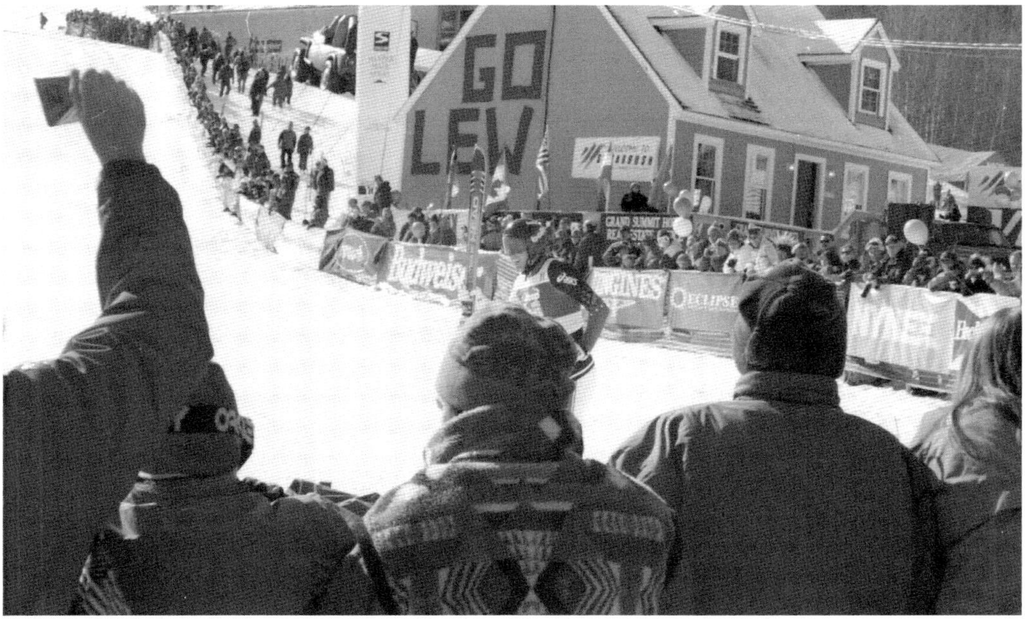

The large sign, "Go Lew," shows the locals' devotion for hometown hero Doug Lewis, who went from Green Mountain Valley School to World Cup racing and National Championships, to (in semi-retirement) the Jeep "King of the Mountain" series downhill race featured in this photograph. (Photograph by Ellie Hilferty.)

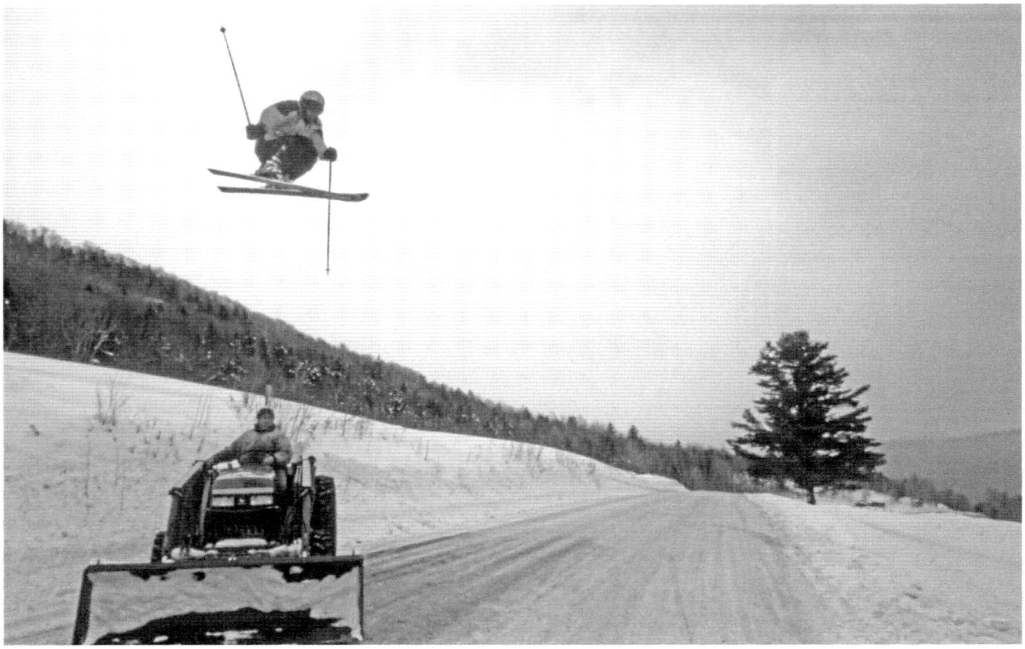

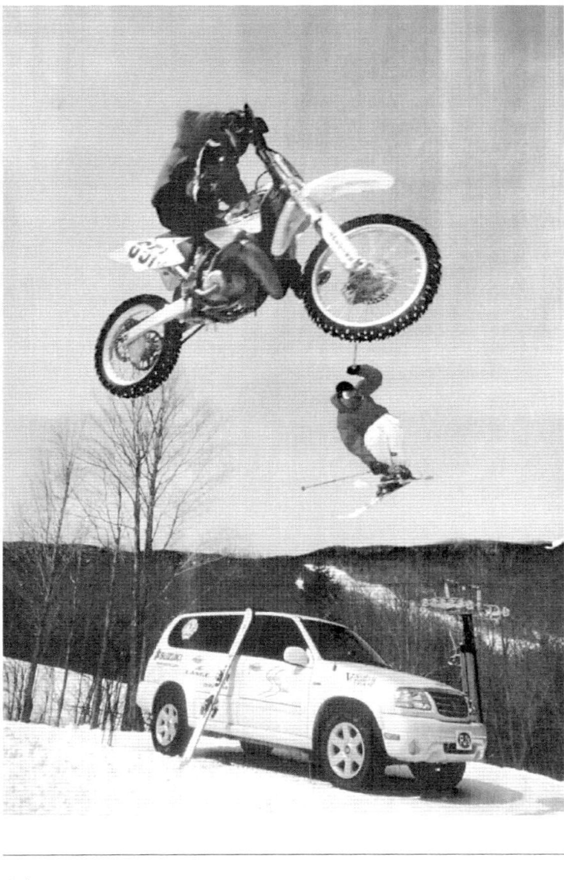

In the above photograph, Doug Lewis's 50-foot flyover of his neighbor Spike Vasseur on Bragg Hill Road defines both the culture and economy of the Mad River Valley. Farming was the occupation of choice for nearly three centuries, and still is for many, but as the driving economic force it has been replaced by the skiing and tourism industry. The acrobatics were nothing new for Lewis, a former member of the U.S. Ski Team, who once was recorded jumping 178 feet in the middle of a Legend's Downhill race. At left, Willy Bozack, a professional motocross rider on his dirt bike, and Roy "Bling" Tuscany, on skis, leap a Suzuki for a car commercial shot at Sugarbush's Mount Ellen Terrain Park. (Above, photograph by Michael Riddell; left, courtesy of John Egan.)

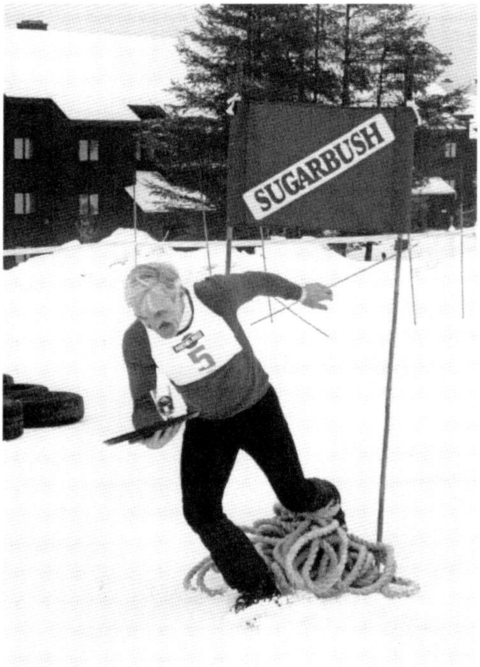

So, it is not World Cup nor the Olympics, but restaurateur Mike Ware participates in the annual Waiter's Slalom in the late 1970s at Sugarbush with the direst of handicaps, a bundle of rope around his foot. In another junk race at Sugarbush, it is learned that canoes work well on water but go a lot faster on snow, sometimes dangerously rivaling an unsteerable bobsled. Guisti Iter (left), Ned Marion, and Mike Ware bailed out after this run when their "sled" made a straight path for the woods at Mount Ellen. (Courtesy of Mike Ware.)

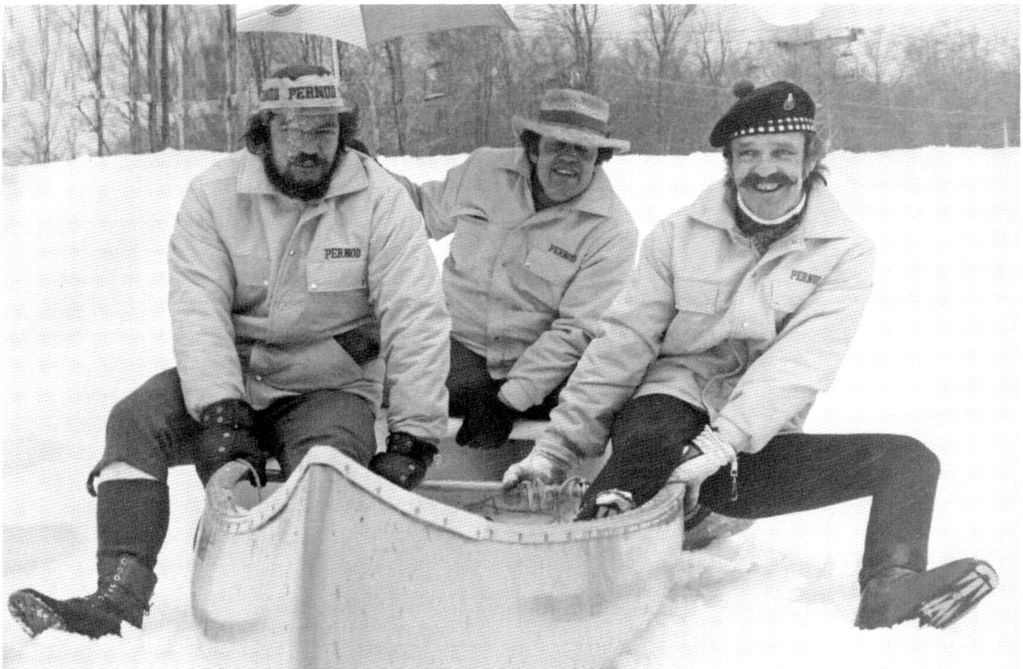

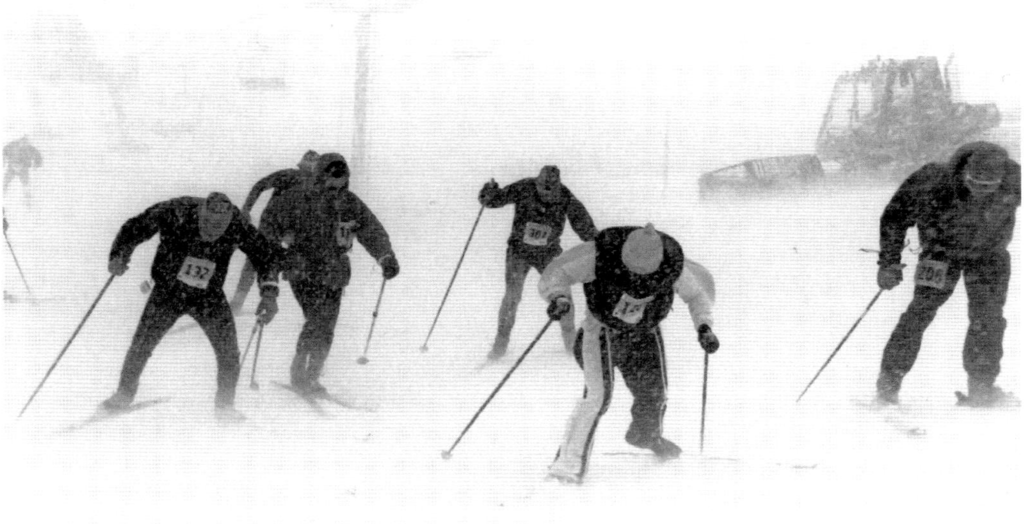

Through the rain and through the snow, over the route the skiers go. The Sugarbush four-legged triathlon is held in April, combining a 5-mile run through Warren and Waitsfield, 6 miles of canoeing on the Mad River, 8 miles of road biking along Route 100 up to Mount Ellen, and picking up cross-country skis for the final 5-kilometer leg. The weather can be anything from a roaring blizzard, as evidenced above, to a balmy spring afternoon (below). Why four legs in a "triathlon?" It happened in the 1980s when the run was substituted for the ski race during lean snow years, then kept. (Courtesy of the *Valley Reporter*.)

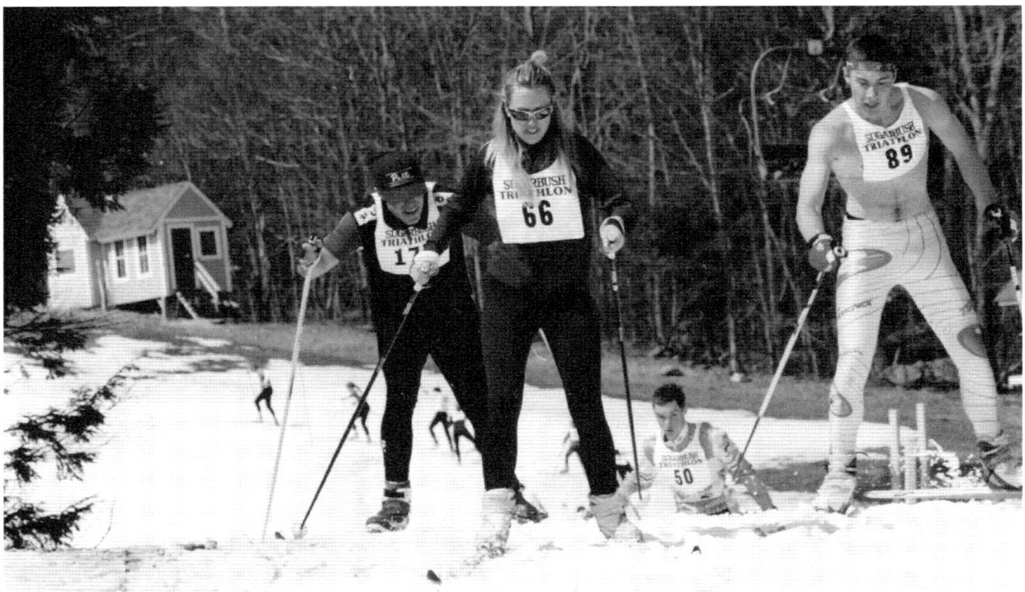

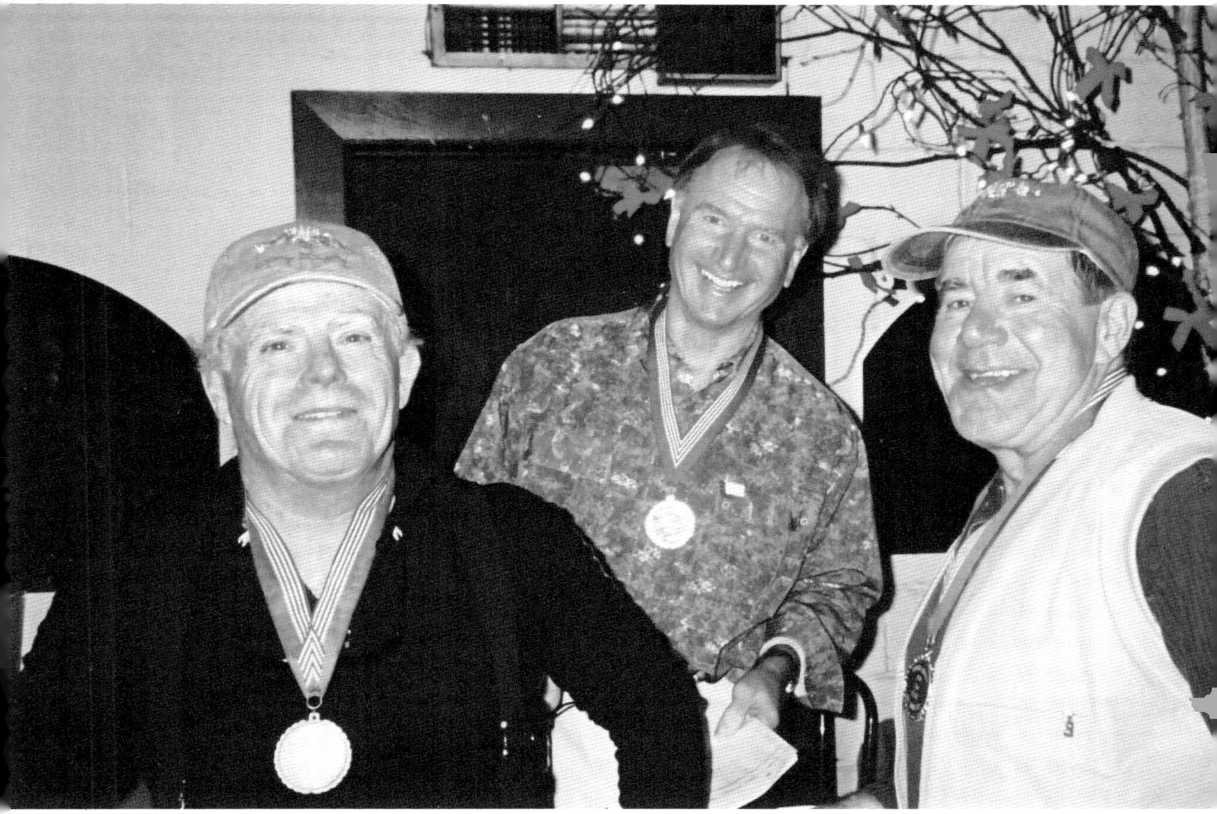

Medalists in the annual Chez Henri race enjoy their moments of stardom in Henri Borel's restaurant sometime in the 1990s. From left to right, they are Rich Jones; Sigi Grottendorffer, former director of the Sugarbush Ski School; and Paul Ruetzler. The amateur race is one of several held on Spring Fling at Sugarbush. Jones is one of many retirees who went the opposite direction after retirement. Instead of seeking sunshine in the south, the schoolteacher from New Jersey joined dozens of other retirees from lower states who found the cold weather of Vermont agreeable. Ruetzler, a native of Austria, first came to Sugarbush in 1961 as an employee of Dopplemayer, the ski lift company. He became acquainted with Jack Murphy and joined the ski school team of Stein Eriksen. He also had a ski lodge in the Mad River Valley for many years. (Courtesy of Henri Borel.)

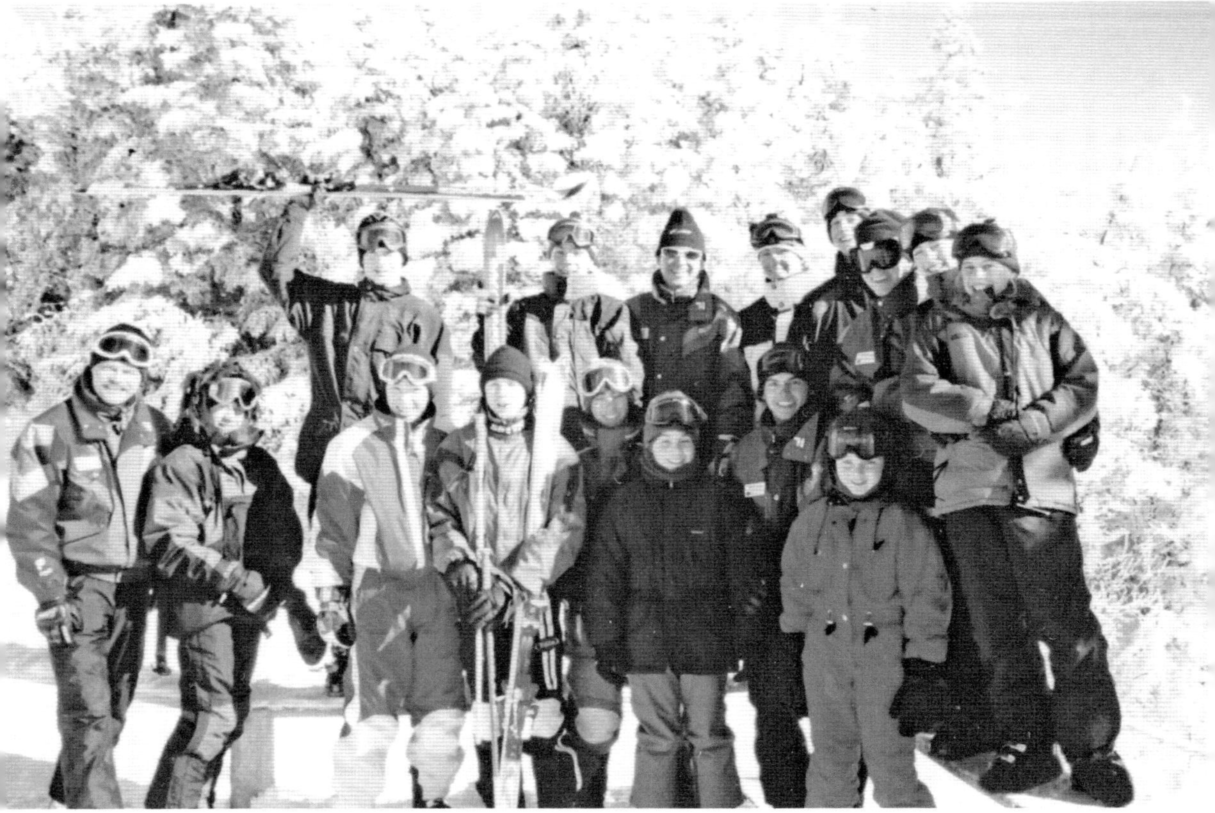

The Diamond Dog Freestyle Team of 1996 takes time out for a class photograph at Sugarbush. From left to right are (first row) coach Kevin Wry, unidentified, Sean Breen, Bruce Hyde, Jamie Schibuk, Jack Fleisher, coach Justin Ayers, and Allison Keenan; (second row) Andrew Woods, Roy Tuscany, coach Chris Parkinson, Rachel Kort, Kasey Wry, coach Darrell Mays, Lindsey Wry, and Matilda "Scooter" Urie. Among their noteworthy distinctions: Sean Breen was a Junior Nationals winner; Andrew Woods won the U.S. Open in halfpipe; Kasey Wry is a free ride coach at Squaw Valley, California; Kevin Wry is still coaching the Diamond Dogs; and Chris Parkinson is a coach for the Sugarbush Bush Pilots. Roy Tuscany suffered a debilitating injury and founded High Fives, a nonprofit organization devoted to raising funds and awareness for athletes who have suffered a life-altering injury while pursuing their dream in winter sports. (Courtesy of Sugarbush.)

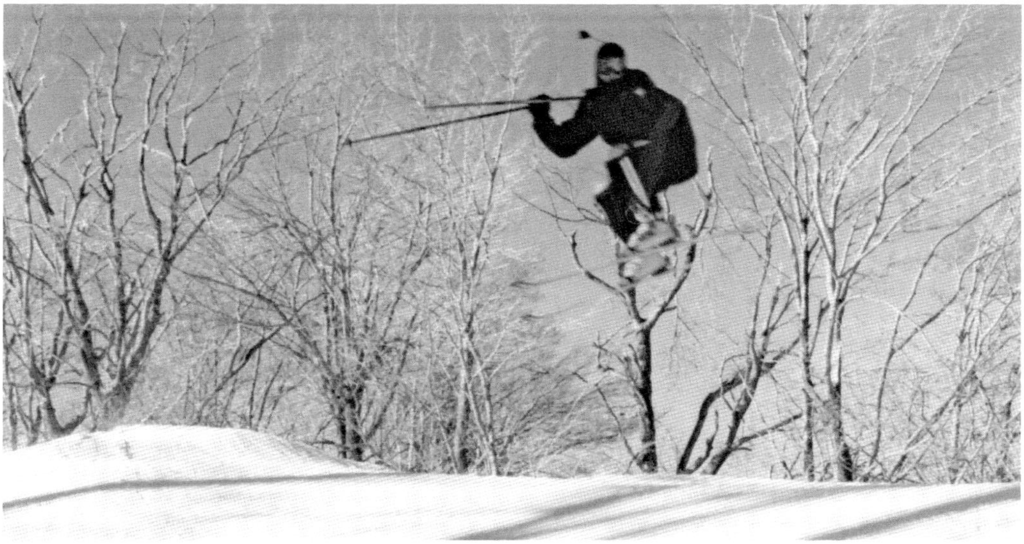

As a teenager, Kasey Wry, shown here doing a UFO at Sugarbush in 1998, was a member of Sugarbush's Diamond Dog freestyle team coached by his father, Kevin Wry. Kasey, who won many championships, became an architect in California, and coached the Squaw Valley freestyle team. (Photograph by Kevin Wry; courtesy of *Valley Reporter*.)

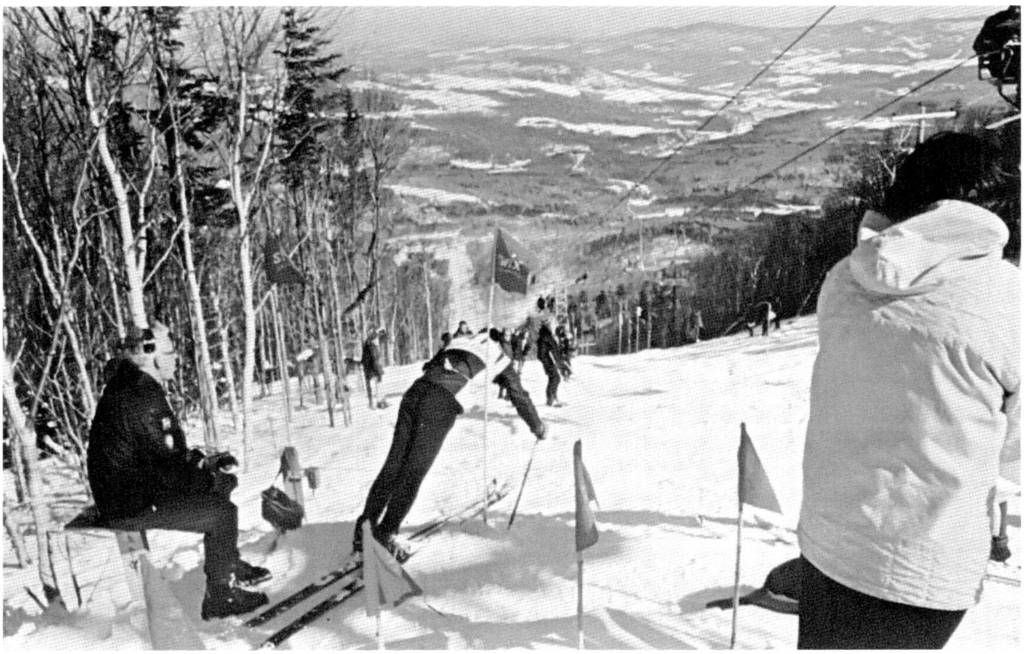

A racer launches from the top of The Cliffs at Mount Ellen when the mountain was part of the Glen Ellen resort, which was the third alpine location in the valley until it was absorbed as Sugarbush North in 1978. The new owner, Roy Cohen, installed snowmaking the next year and kept the summit chairlift open into May. (Photograph by Peter Miller; courtesy of Bill Bozack.)

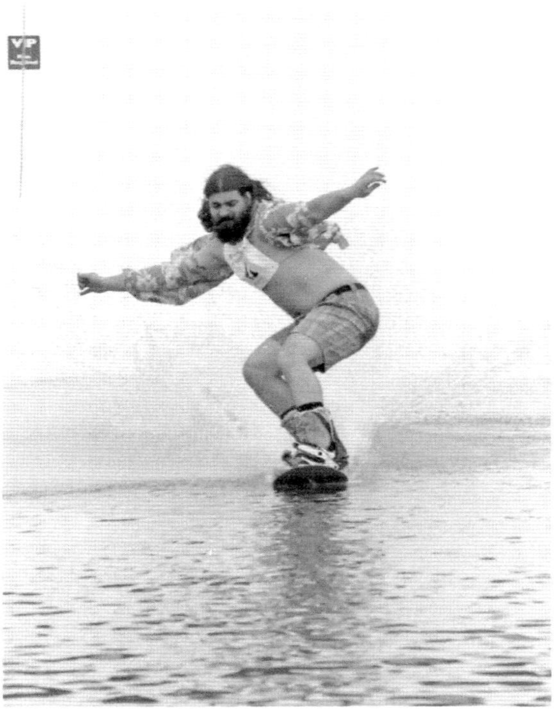

This is one rite of passage where the participant most often fails, literally, to pass to the other side. Held annually in the spring, young and old skiers and riders, most of them dressed in glaringly ridiculous costumes, sign up for the Sugarbush Pond Skim for meager prizes and lasting glory—sometimes 5 or 10 minutes worth. (Courtesy of the *Valley Reporter*.)

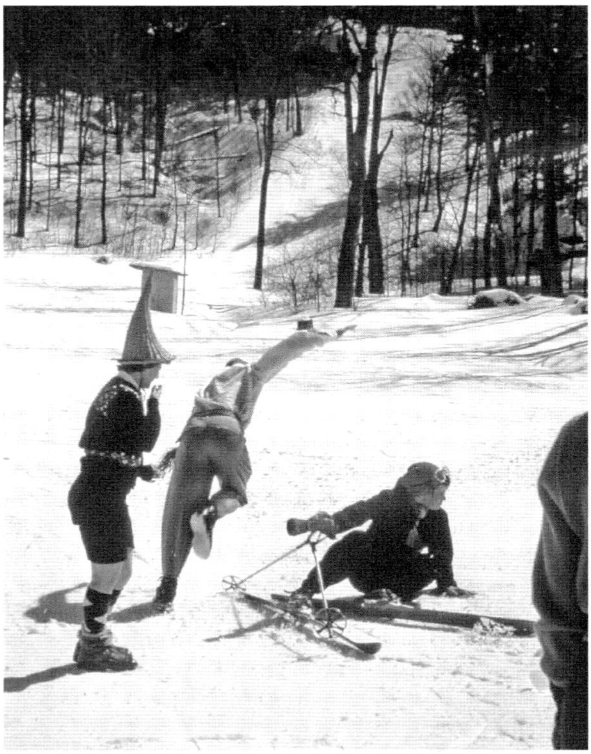

Long before Comedy Central, entertainments in the valley were manufactured on the spot, as this photograph from the Easter parade at Mad River Glen in 1956 illustrates. The spontaneity of the action came about by accident, and the skier on the ground could honestly say, "If I knew how it happened, it wouldn't have happened." (Courtesy of Ann Day.)

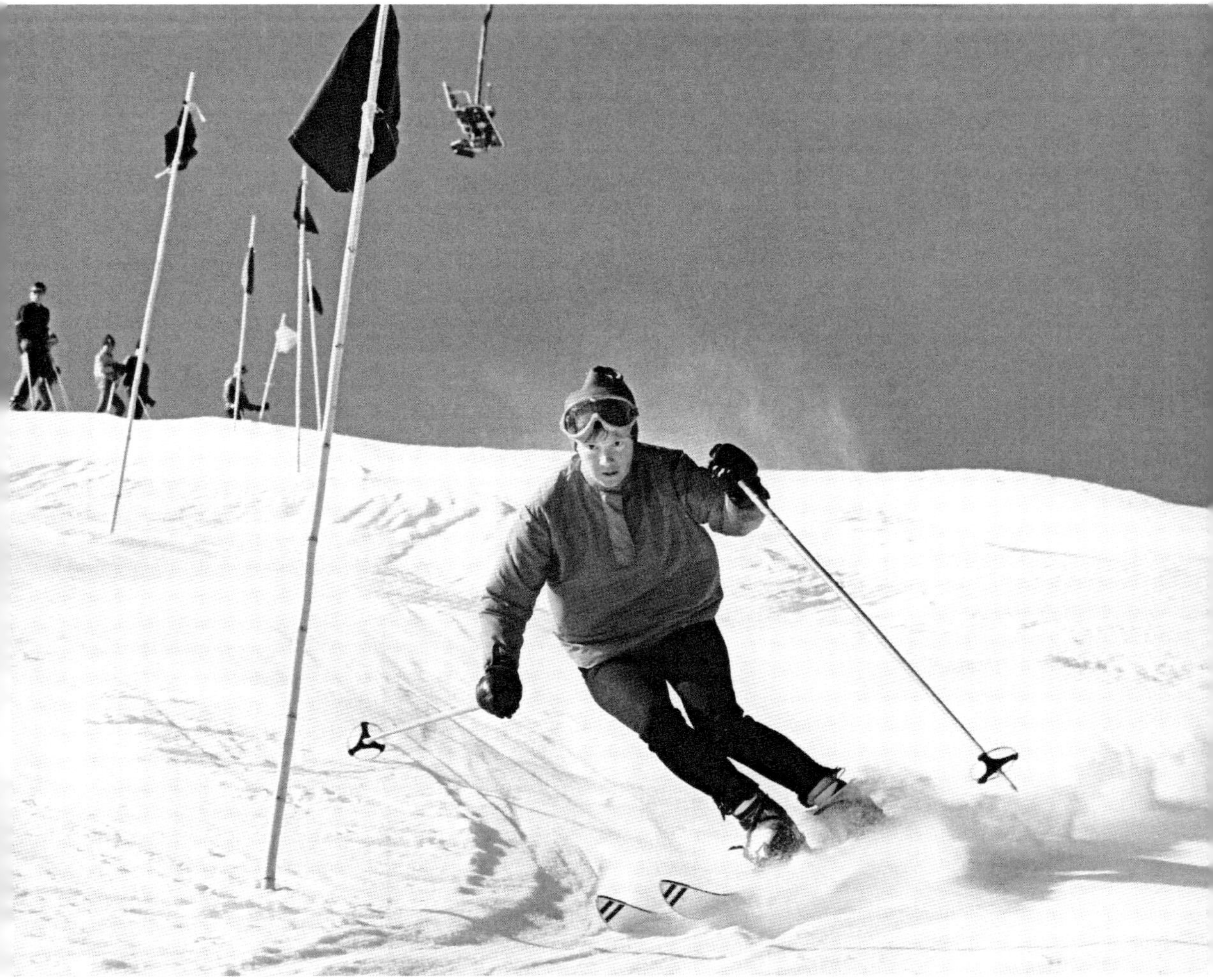

Olivia "Lee" Hall Delfausse made the leap from being a childhood skier at Mad River Glen and Sugarbush to prominence on the U.S. Ski Team and then to the World Cup circuit, where she enjoyed a reputation as a fearless downhill skier, participating in races along with another valley racer on the U.S. team, Rosie Fortna. A slalom racer, Fortna competed in many FIS World Cup races from 1967 to 1971, joining a large list of Vermonters who made skiing history. A phenomenal 10 athletes who call Vermont home participated in the 2010 Winter Olympics held in Vancouver. Included in that group was Caitlin Compton, who lived in the valley and skied at Harwood Area High School. (Courtesy of Lee Hall Delfausse.)

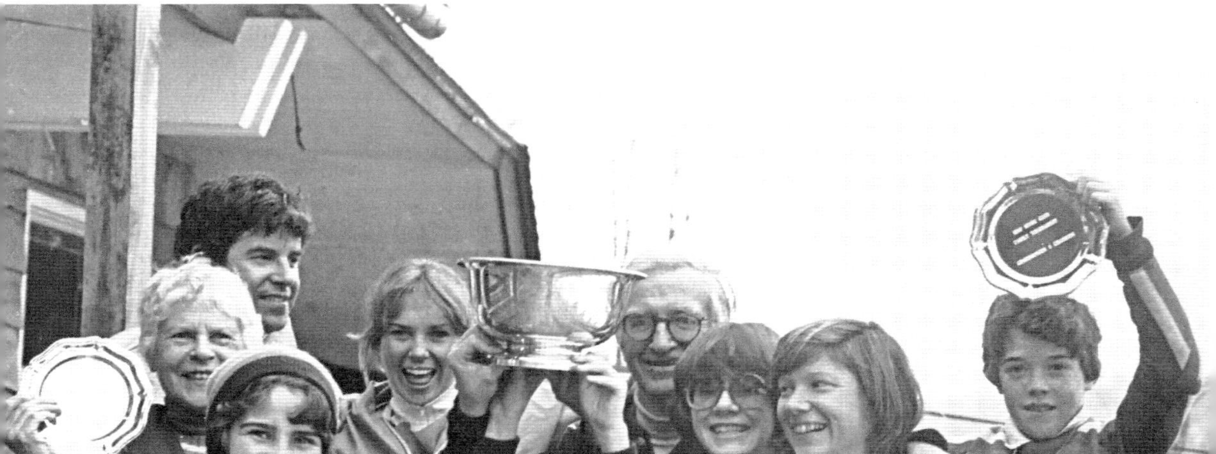

In 1982, it was all in the family at Mad River Glen. Posing with their winning trophies in the Family Race were members of the Hall family. They are, from left to right, Sally, with Geordie behind her and Tamsin in front, Ellen, Sarah Delfausse Olsen, George Hall, Elisha Hall, Lee Hall Delfausse, and Pierre Delfausse. Lee, who went on to national fame as a member of the U.S. Ski Team, excelled in tennis also, as did her daughter, Sarah Delfausse Olsen, who coaches and recently published a children's book, *Tennis for Me*. Lee and Sarah have won three mother–daughter national championships. Lee was inducted into the New England Tennis Hall of Fame in 2009. She is a graduate of Concord Academy in New Hampshire and, in an interview with the school's magazine said, "I've won national titles in skiing, but it doesn't compare to a team effort with my daughter." (Courtesy of Lee Hall Delfausse.)

4

Eat, Sleep, Shop, and Carouse

The storm would rage, pelting snow BBs horizontally across the roads and fields. It would be a Friday night, anywhere between 9:00 p.m. and midnight, or even 2 a.m., and there would be a knock on the farmhouse door—a tired city man with a woeful look, pleading, "My car is stuck in a ditch about a half-mile down the road."

And, thus, over many weekend nights, what had been pegged by *Holiday Magazine* as "a little, sleepy corner of Vermont" was magically transformed as a destination for tourism. Its target: the newly opened Mad River Glen. Then, when Sugarbush happened in 1958, condos and large second homes appeared on the yonder hills. People came in the winter, then the summer, and especially the fall, when the trees burned with brilliance, presaging the cold and snow that was to be welcomed, hopefully as early as November.

But the valley never burst with the usual commercial clutter that swept over other ski towns, where main roads leading to the lifts were clogged with traffic edging past bars, restaurants, and shopping malls.

Considering the popularity of Sugarbush and Mad River Glen, development has been relatively sparse. Zoning and the environment put the brakes on expansion. Getting a permit is a slow, often painful process. Lawyers prosper. But again, it is the trade-off that counts, leading to a couple of massive playgrounds that are still surrounded by small towns with small enterprises.

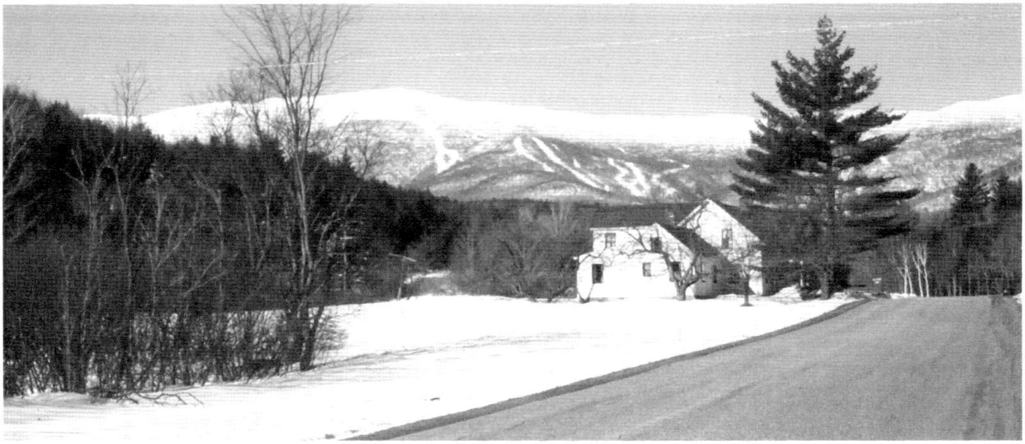

Millbrook Lodge, a Cape-style farmhouse built at the end of the Civil War, was one of the first inns met by visitors as they left Route 100 in Irasville and drove up the alternately snow-filled, muddy, or frozen McCullough Turnpike going to Mad River Glen. It was owned by Ginny and Henry Perkins, later by Thom and Joan Gorman, who opted for the innkeeping life after leaving their jobs in New York City. As a way of pushing the state to pave the road, Perkins put up his own money for the first few miles from Route 100. (Photography by Sewall Williams.)

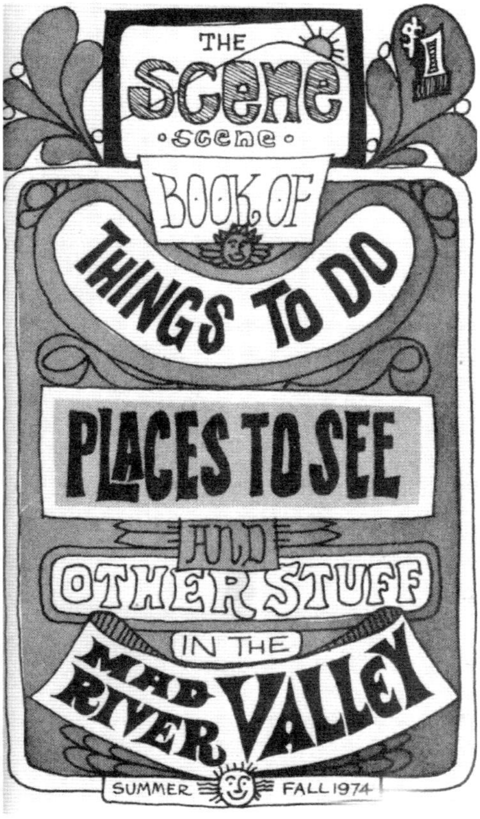

As the crowds of skiers came to enjoy what Roland Palmedo had correctly called "the extra-good, real old-fashioned Vermont winter in the snow corner of New England," marketing began in earnest. The "Scene Scene" was a folksy invitation not to just entertain visitors but to attract permanent residents to the valley. Its author, Felix von Moschzisker, was one of many ex flatlanders who visited the valley and found it so difficult to leave that he finally settled here, shucking off the urban excesses of Philadelphia, where he had been a newspaperman.(Courtesy of Tony Egan.)

When skiing began to attract fun seekers from urban New York and New England in the late 1940s and 1950s, Hap Gaylord, back from service during World War II, was often awakened in the middle of the night by someone asking if his tractor could pull their car out of a snowy ditch on Route 100 or some of the other dirt roads leading up to Mad River Glen or Sugarbush. Many of the chilled-to-the bone tourists stayed the night at the Gaylord farmhouse and enjoyed a hearty breakfast before finishing the day on the mountain. (Courtesy of the *Valley Reporter.*)

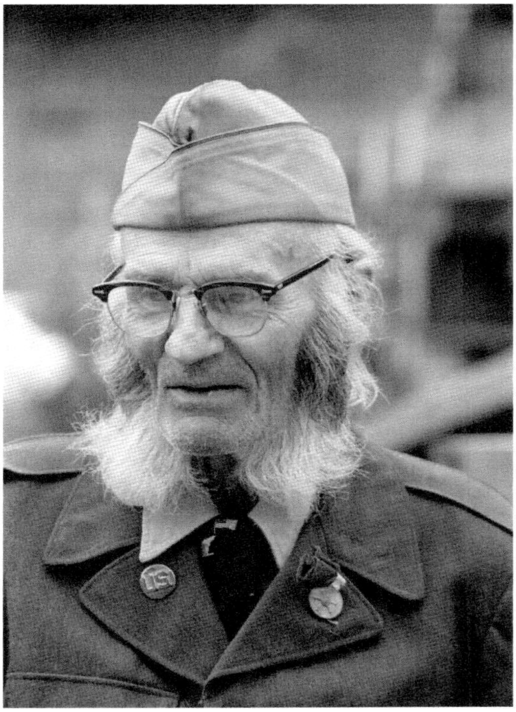

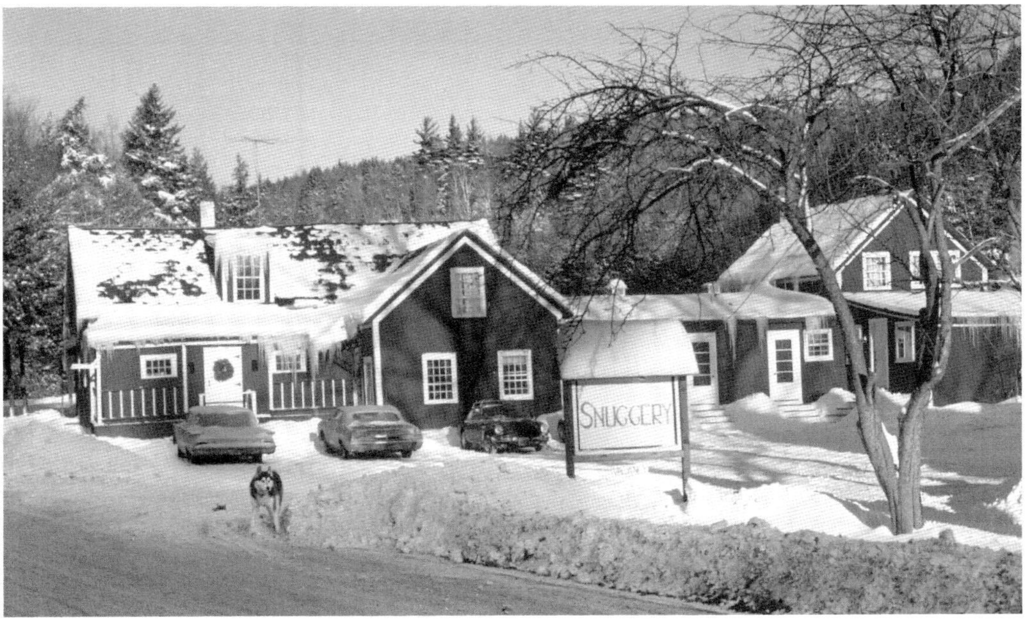

The Snuggery on Route 17, just east of German Flats Road, hosted overnight skiers for many years. Known today as The Hyde Away, the inn was first known as the Ulla Lodge, owned by brothers Sewall and Arthur Williams. Damon Gadd, one of the founders of Sugarbush, also owned the inn in the early 1950s. (Courtesy of Sewall Williams.)

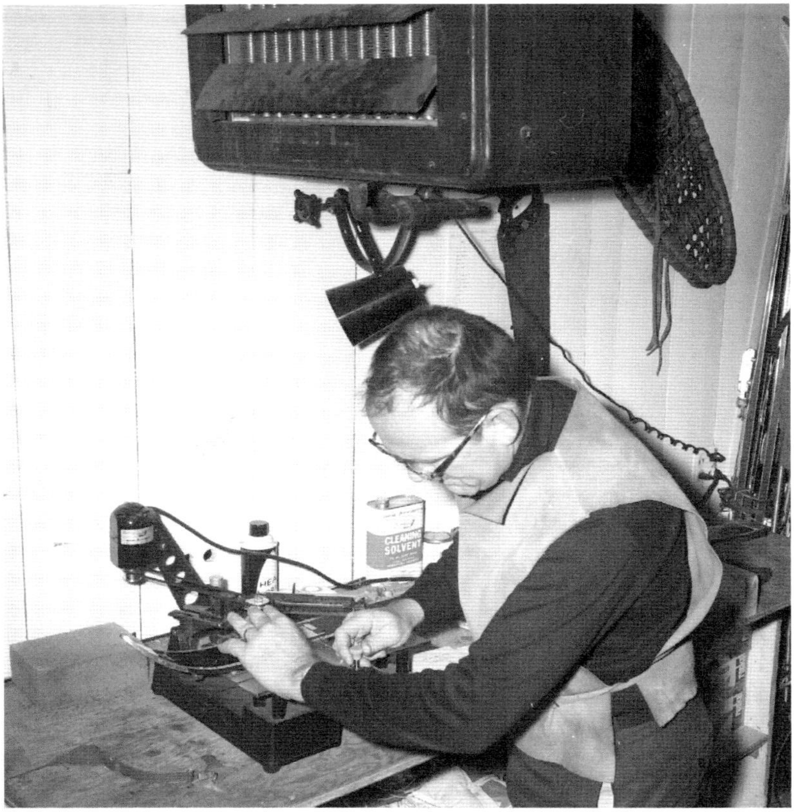

Sewall Williams, working here at ski engraving in his ski shop in 1965, was one of the most widely known figures in the Mad River Valley. An innkeeper, photographer, and veteran of the 10th Mountain Division in World War II, he is also a member of the Ski Hall of Fame. (Courtesy of Sewall Williams.)

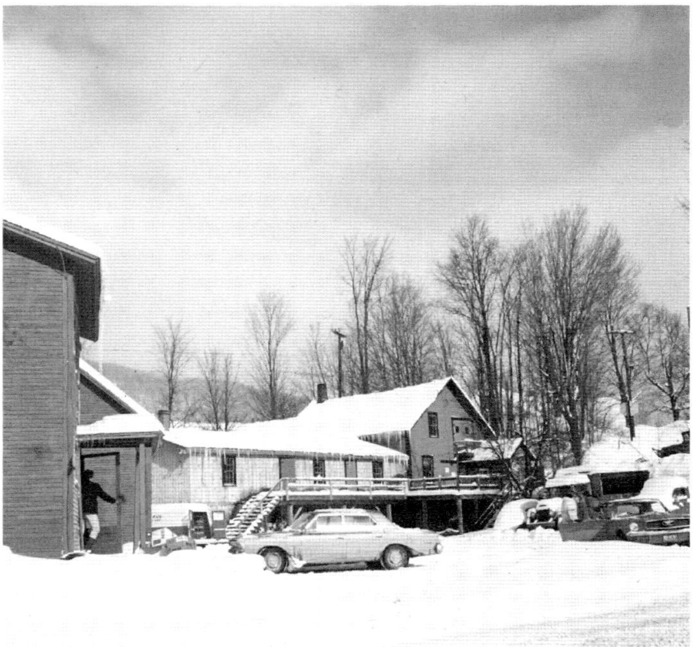

At the crossroads of Route 17 (the McCullough Turnpike leading up to Mad River Glen and Mount Ellen) and Route 100 were and are several watering holes and restaurants, one of the early ones being Gallagher's, which is now occupied by John Egan's Big World Restaurant. Back in the 1970s, Gallagher's boasted a $2 Sunday night special and featured a menu that "starts at hamburger and goes right up to filet mignon." (Photograph by Sewall Williams.)

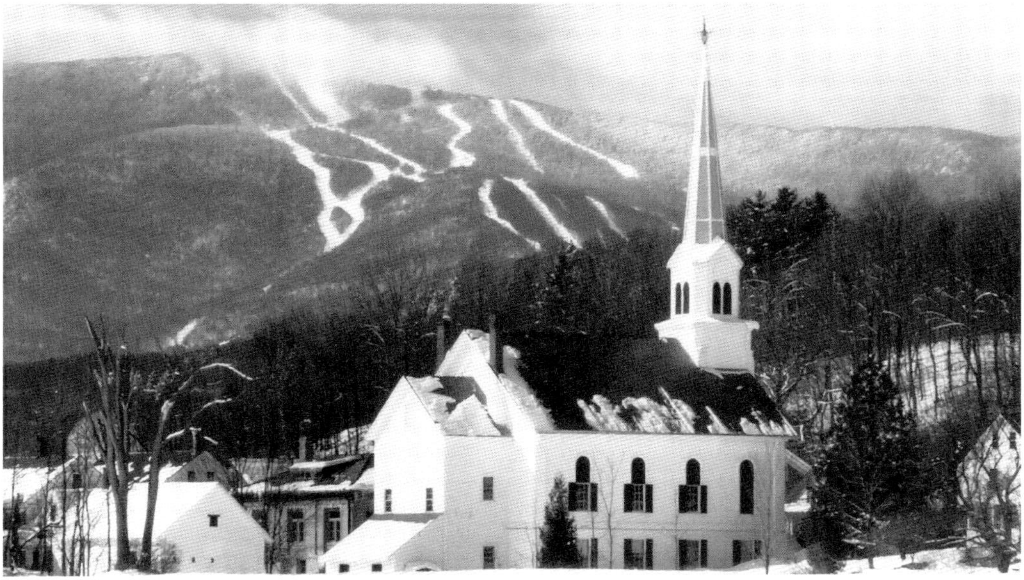

The United Church of Christ in Waitsfield, with the backdrop of ski trails behind it, was and is the centerpiece of historic Waitsfield, a pure New England village with a covered bridge, craft shops, restaurants, town clerk's office, Masonic hall, library, and grocery. The nearby Mad River flows through the village beneath the Great Eddy Covered Bridge built in 1833. (Courtesy of Sugarbush.)

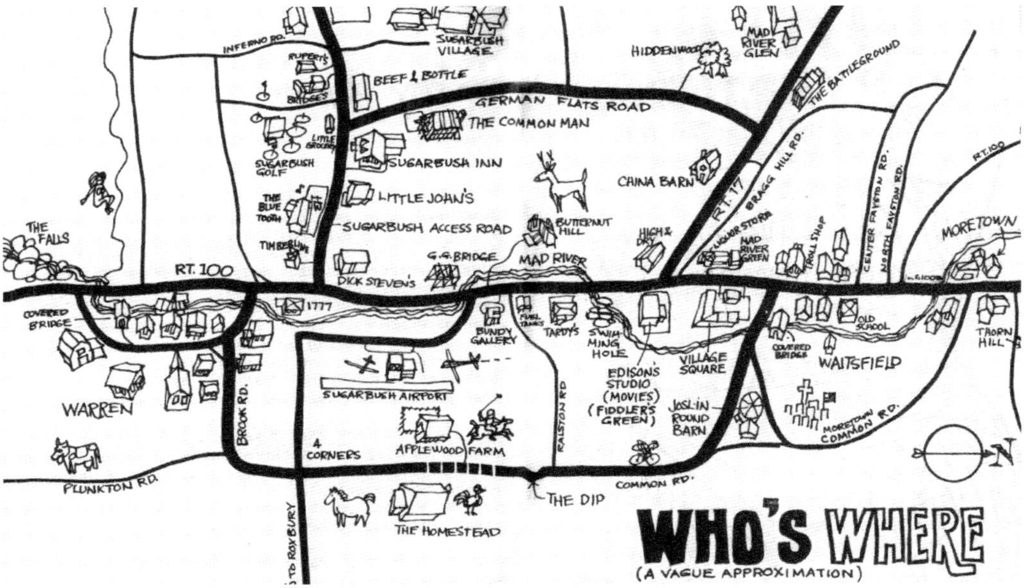

This early map will still get a person anywhere in the Mad River Valley, and much of the scenery remains, except for inns and restaurants that changed ownership through the years. Though it may seem hard to believe to urbanites from Boston, New York, and other metropolises, Route 100 was one of less than a half-dozen north-south thoroughfares running through all of Vermont. (Courtesy of Tony Egan.)

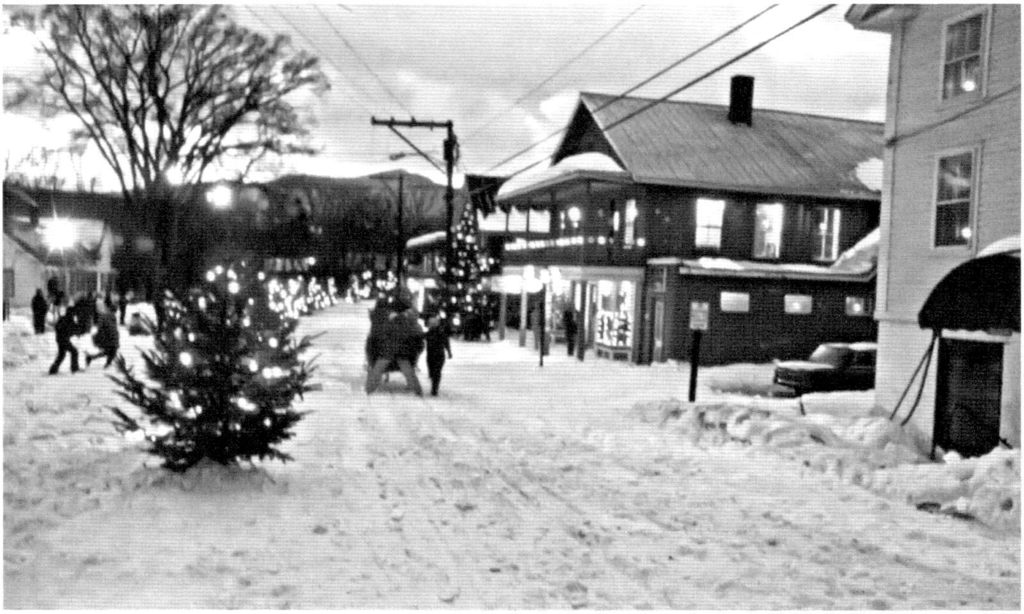

For several years, television viewers nationwide were treated to this scene of Bridge Street in Waitsfield when it became part of a Miller Beer Christmas commercial in 1977. Oddly, some of the snow pictured was manufactured by Sugarbush's snowmaking guns. Camera crews also photographed the jingling sleigh riding on North Road past the Carpenter Farm. (Courtesy of the *Valley Reporter*.)

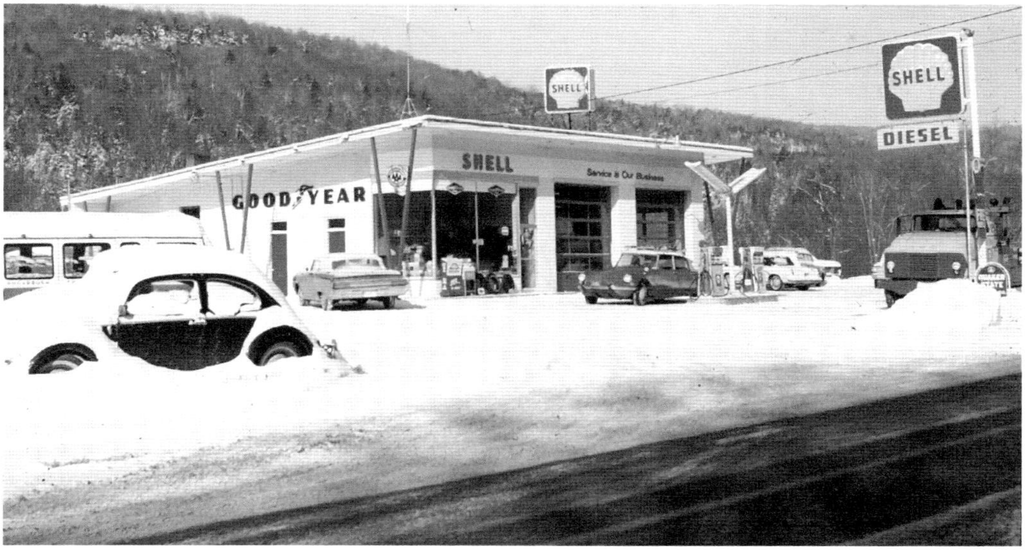

Kingsbury Service Station on Route 100, Waitsfield, was a welcoming gas stop for arriving skiers in the 1960s. Travelers getting to the valley from New York and Boston late on Friday night had to gas up for the return trip. As many as 2,500 visitors came to Sugarbush each weekend in the beginning. (Photograph by Sewall Williams.)

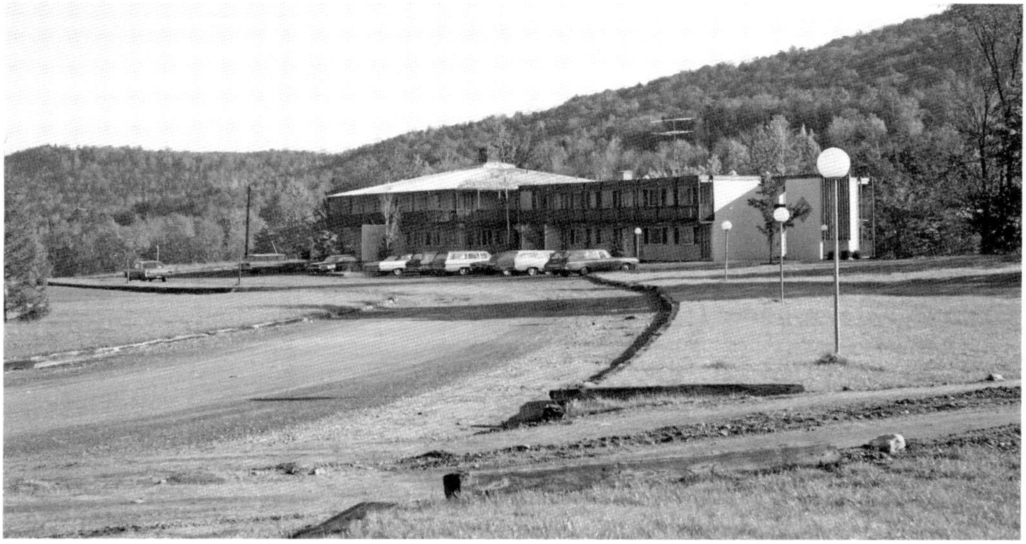

Driving from the south up Route 100 from Granville, Berghof Lodge would be one of the first inns encountered in the mid-1960s for travelers intent on finding lodging near Sugarbush and Mad River Glen. The lodge is now the Seasons Resort. By 1967, there were 40 lodging establishments serving tourists. (Photograph by Sewall Williams.)

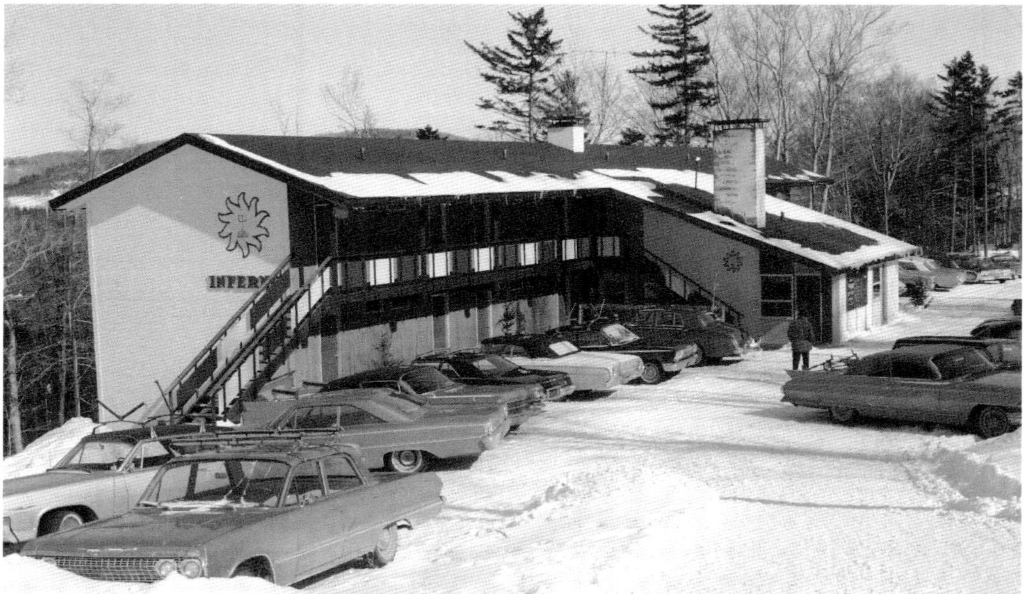

The Inferno Lodge and Club 10 were near the Valley House. Membership read like a Cholly Knickerbocker column in the old *New York Journal American*. Cholly himself (Igor Cassini) was a member, as were Oleg Cassini, Igor's brother; Armando Orsini; shipping tycoon Stavros Niarchos; catsup maker H. J. Heinz II; filmmaker Spyros Skouras Jr.; publisher Whitelaw Reid; and bandleader Skitch Henderson. (Photograph by Sewall Williams.)

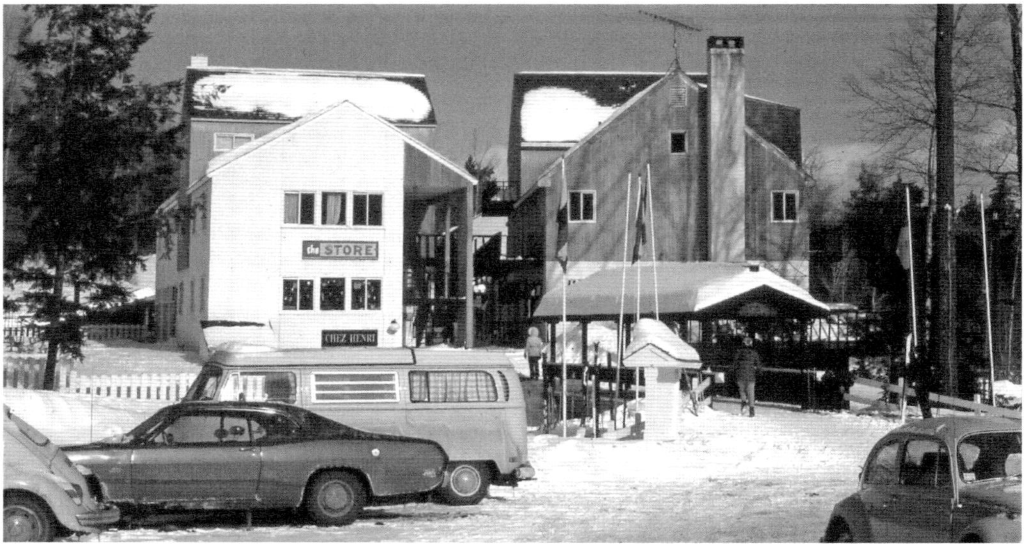

Ski in/ski out for lunch. Restaurateur Henri Borel added an exquisite international ambience to rural Vermont when he opened Chez Henri Bistro at the base of Sugarbush's Lincoln Peak in 1964 with its romantic fireplace, Italian marble bar, 1850s mirrors, "speakeasy" booths, and Vermont scenes and murals. (Courtesy of Sugarbush.) Below, innkeeper Sewall Williams (left), co-owner of the Ulla Lodge, and Hap Gaylord, who welcomed overnight guests to his farmhouse in the 1940s and 1950s, are en route to the Fourth of July parade in Warren. Williams wears "winter whites," as he did as a member of the U.S. Army's 10th Mountain Division. Gaylord operated a gas station and a badly needed towing service in the valley, inspired by tourists dropping their cars in ditches on snowy roads. (Courtesy of *Valley Reporter.*)

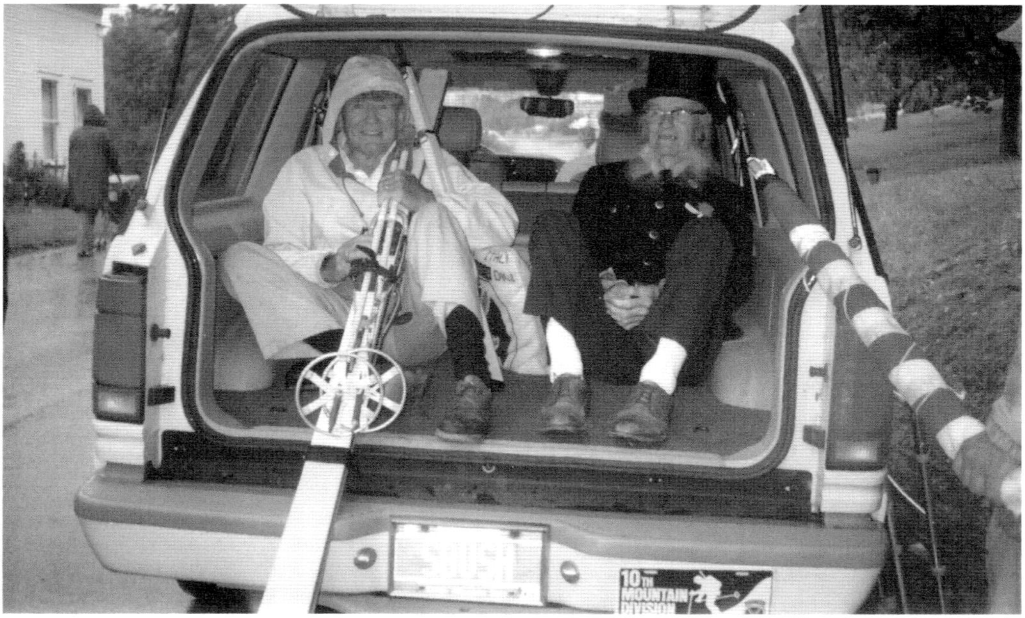

This menu from Armando Orsini's La Pasta restaurant on German Flats Road during the 1962–1963 season reveals one of the first examples of fine dining in the Mad River Valley. Orsini, known as the "Playboy Prince of Pasta," was one of Lili St. Cyr's six husbands and owned another Orsini's restaurant on 56th Street in New York. (Courtesy of Mike Ware.)

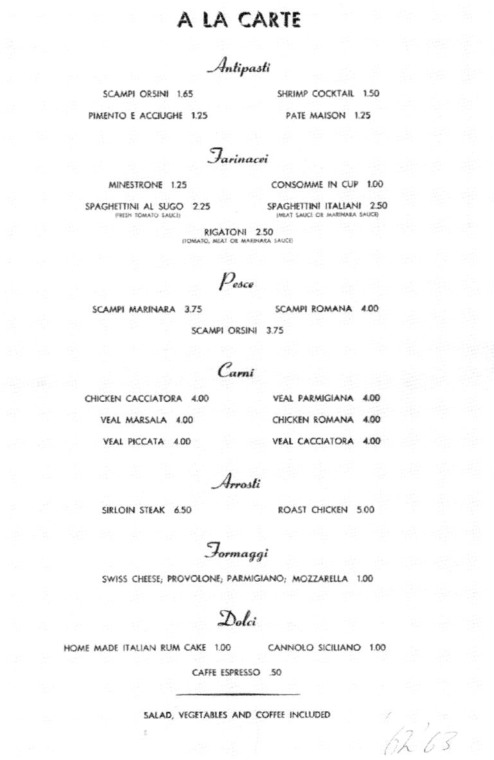

A LA CARTE

Antipasti

SCAMPI ORSINI 1.65 SHRIMP COCKTAIL 1.50
PIMENTO E ACCIUGHE 1.25 PATE MAISON 1.25

Farinacei

MINESTRONE 1.25 CONSOMME IN CUP 1.00
SPAGHETTINI AL SUGO 2.25 (FRESH TOMATO SAUCE) SPAGHETTINI ITALIANI 2.50 (MEAT SAUCE OR MARINARA SAUCE)
RIGATONI 2.50 (TOMATO, MEAT OR MARINARA SAUCE)

Pesce

SCAMPI MARINARA 3.75 SCAMPI ROMANA 4.00
SCAMPI ORSINI 3.75

Carni

CHICKEN CACCIATORA 4.00 VEAL PARMIGIANA 4.00
VEAL MARSALA 4.00 CHICKEN ROMANA 4.00
VEAL PICCATA 4.00 VEAL CACCIATORA 4.00

Arrosti

SIRLOIN STEAK 6.50 ROAST CHICKEN 5.00

Formaggi

SWISS CHEESE; PROVOLONE; PARMIGIANO; MOZZARELLA 1.00

Dolci

HOME MADE ITALIAN RUM CAKE 1.00 CANNOLO SICILIANO 1.00
CAFFE ESPRESSO .50

SALAD, VEGETABLES AND COFFEE INCLUDED

62 63

The Common Man fine-dining restaurant has been at its location on German Flats Road since the early 1960s, beginning as La Pasta and owned by widely known New York restaurateur Armand Orsini, who sold it to Scotsman Mike Ware and Englishman John Meyer. (Courtesy of Sugarbush.)

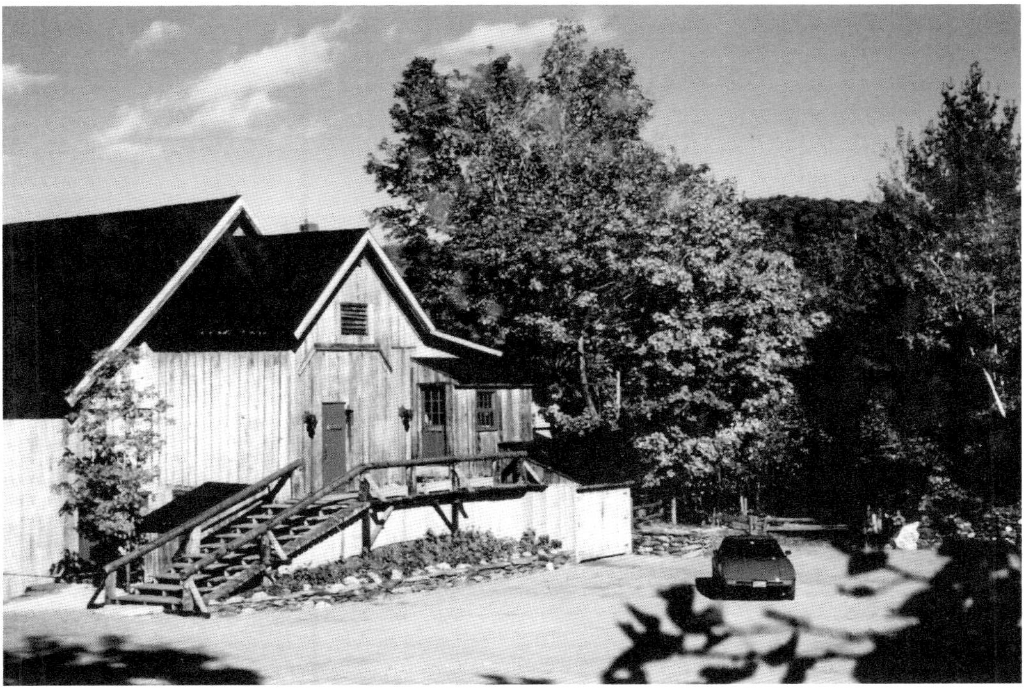

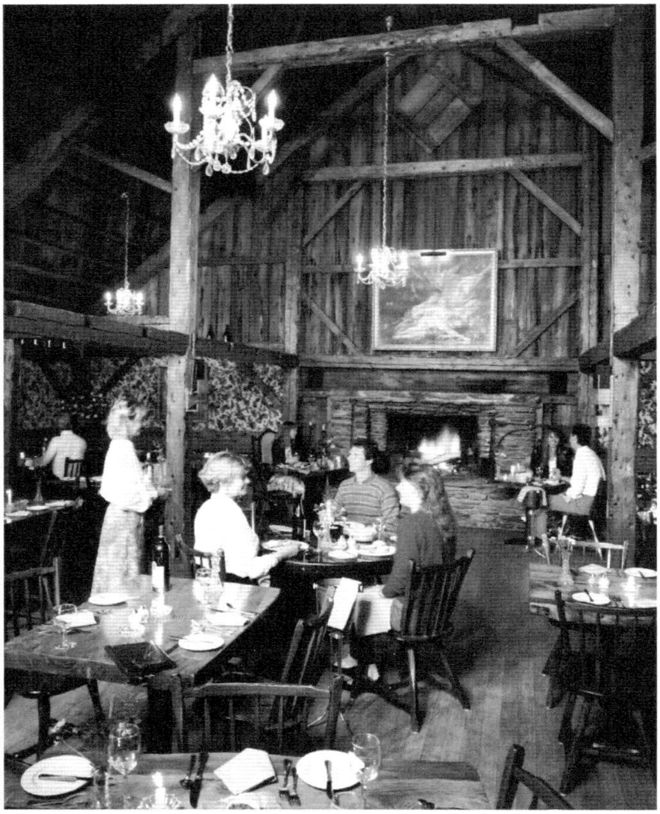

The interior of the Common Man restaurant, with its massive, hand-hewn beams and rafters, reflects the sturdy architecture of the valley. Even the tables were made of thick wood, and a large stone fireplace stands at one end. Barn-like building notwithstanding, the ambience was fine dining. The photograph below was taken after fire destroyed the Common Man on February 5, 1987. It was reconstructed from a queen post barn, shown here, that had been built in 1854 in Moretown and was relocated to German Flats Road. The fire was spectacular enough to make page one of *USA Today*. (Courtesy of Mike Ware.)

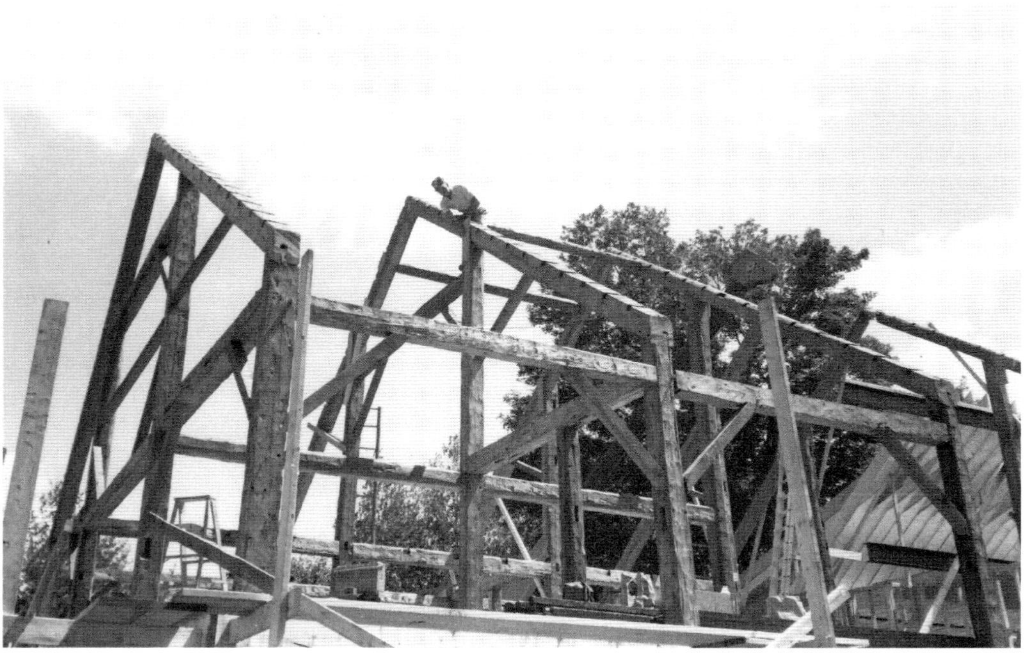

Ruth Henderson, wife of famous 1950s *Tonight Show* bandleader Skitch Henderson, was one of the entourage of musicians, artists, actors, and other celebrities to grace Sugarbush in its "Mascara Mountain" days. Others were restaurateur Vincent Sardi, conductor Leonard Bernstein, authors John Updike and Erica Jong, actress Kim Novak, New York mayor John Lindsay, Boston's Cabots, and the Kennedy clan. (Courtesy of Sugarbush.)

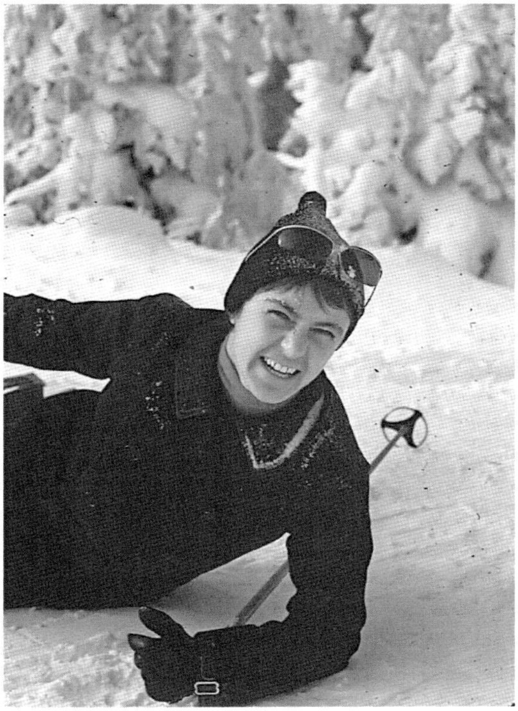

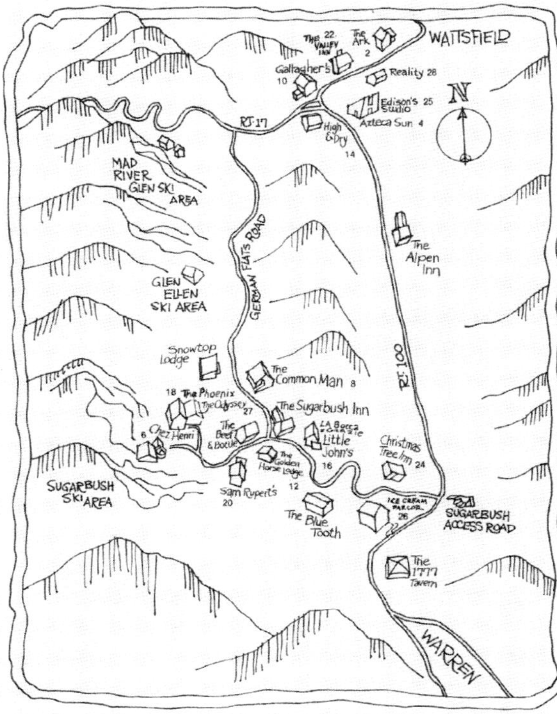

Gone but not forgotten are several valley restaurants and amusements whose ownership changed or vanished with the whims of economics: Eg., The Moveable Feast, The Ark, The Valley Inn, Edison's Studio, Bagatelle, Beggar's Banquet, China Barn, Alpen Inn, The Blue Tooth, Fox Hill, Golden Horse, Rogos, The Phoenix, and The Odyssey. (Courtesy of Vermont Ski Museum.)

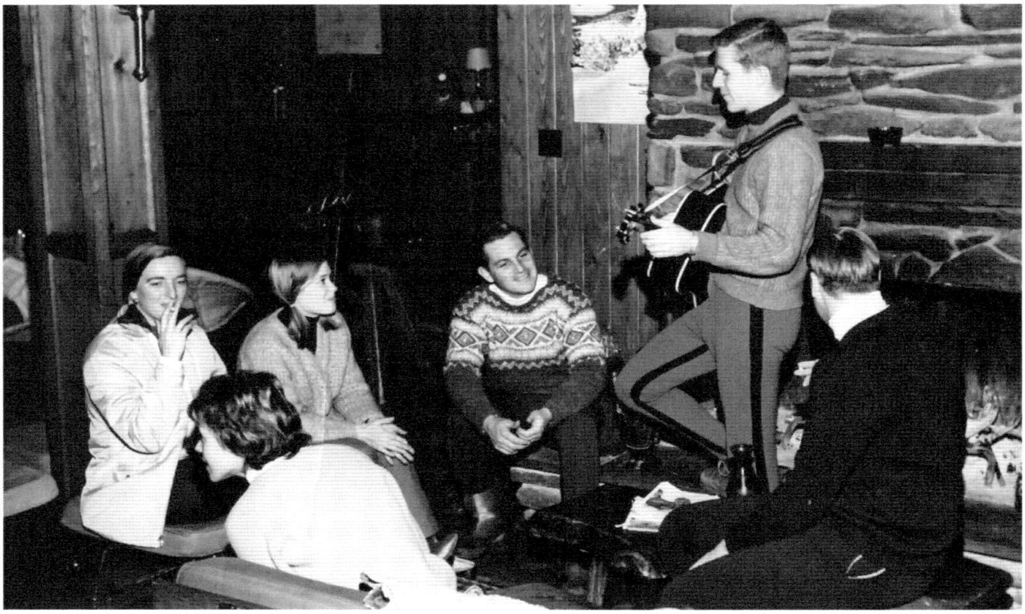

The Red Rose Room at the Christmas Tree Inn on the Sugarbush Access Road typified the end of a Vermont winter day, with a roaring fire, cocktail, and conviviality close at hand. Before Vermont became popular with tourists in the late 1940s, the state's reputation was cold and forbidding, leading the nation in the century before in per capita out-of-state migration. What Bertrand Russell, the British philosopher, was doing visiting Vermont is anybody's guess, but he noted that "Vermont is a great place to be born in, provided one emigrates when one is very, very young." (Courtesy of Charlie Brown Productions.)

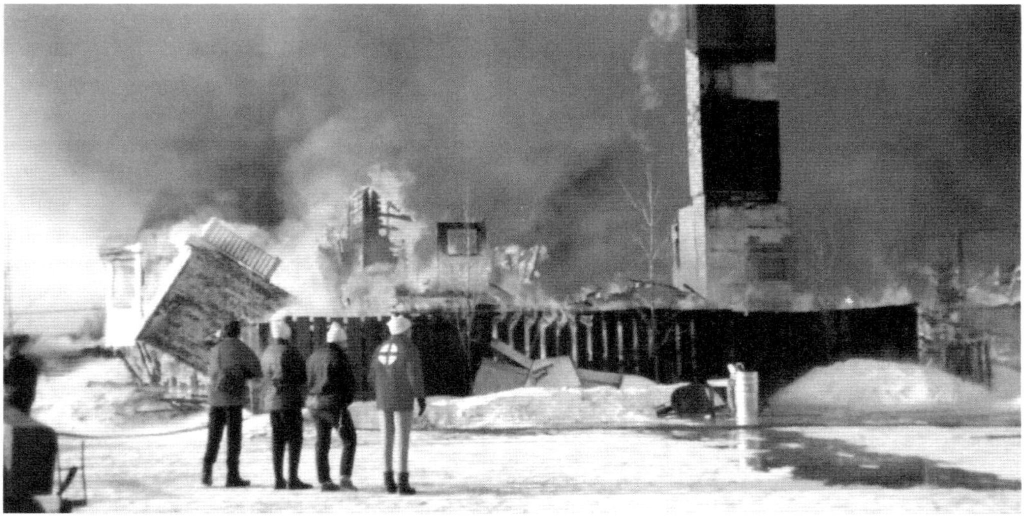

The spectacular burning of the Sugarbush Inn, a treasured landmark, was a fleeting memory after it was rebuilt at the same location at the Access and German Flats Roads soon after the fire in 1965. (Photograph by Sewall Williams.)

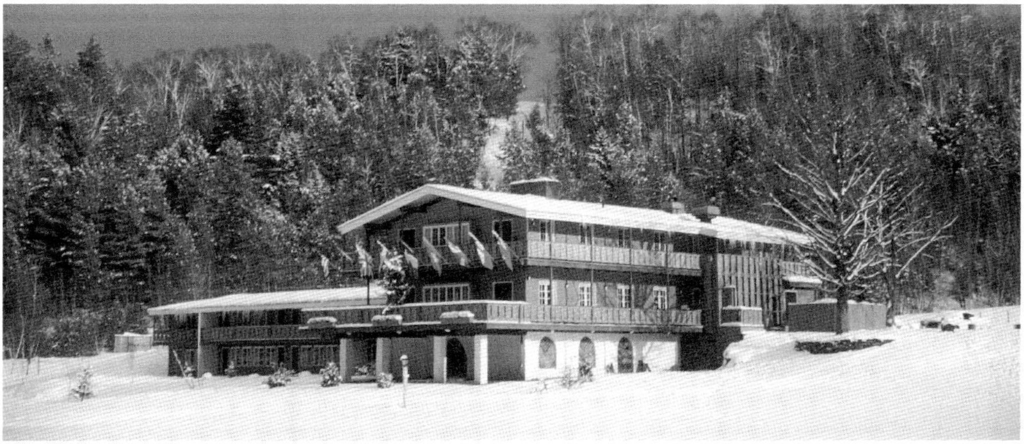

The Alpen Inn, Route 100, was a popular hotel owned and operated by John and Margo Macone. Located south of Bundy Road near the Waitsfield/Warren town line, it was abandoned for many years until reclaimed and refurbished by Yestermorrow, a design and building school. In the photograph below, it is New Year's Eve, and some people like to ring in the event on horseback, like Mike Ware at the Alpen Inn. Ware, who also owned and operated The Common Man restaurant, was Scotland-born and is a founder of the St. Andrews Society of Vermont. He often wore his kilt of Clan Gordon while skiing. (Above, courtesy of Charlie Brown Productions; below, courtesy of Mike Ware.)

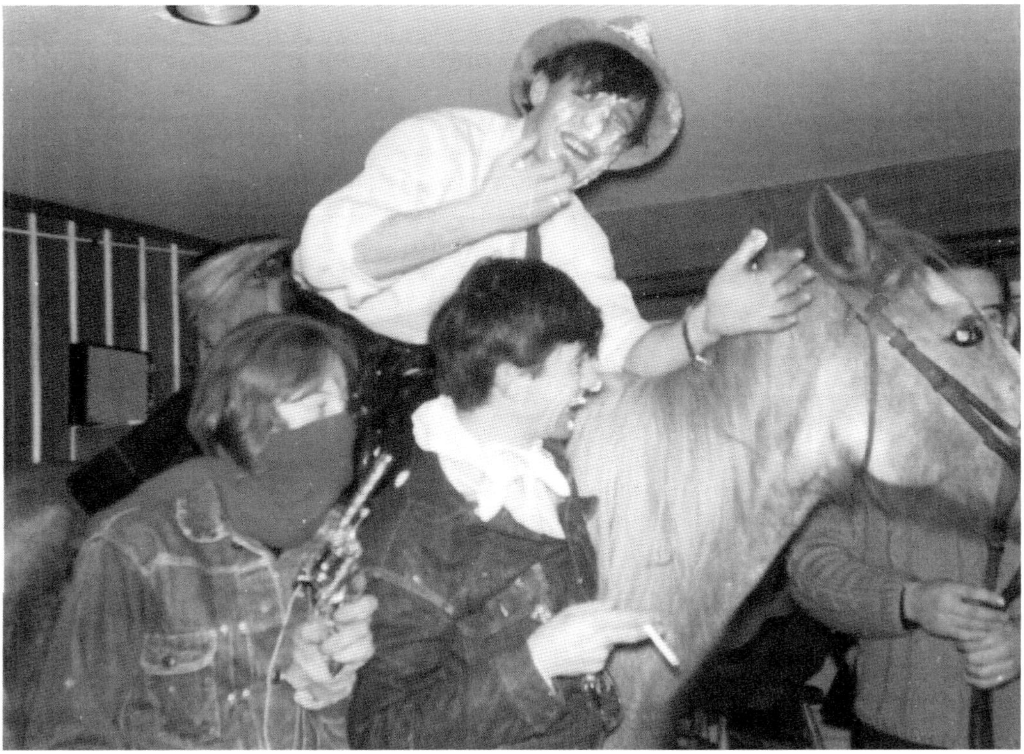

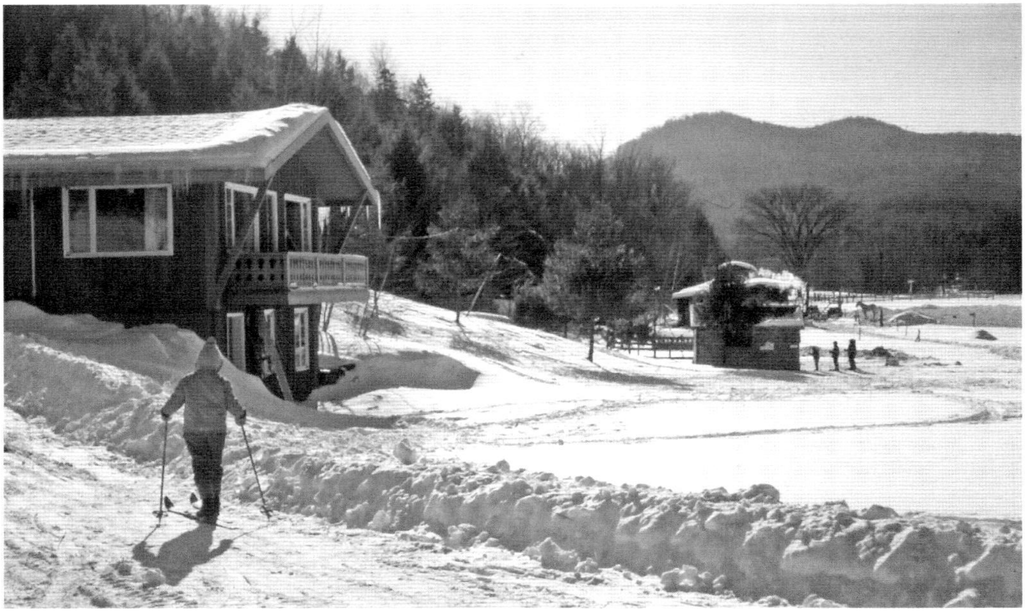

Just to the south of the Alpen Inn, Frank and Ann Day constructed a rope tow in 1963, five years after Sugarbush opened. The enterprise on Route 100 lasted two seasons, but later the Days built another rope tow, powered by an old Buick engine, which lasted a year on the site near where Shaw's supermarket exists today at Mad River Green in Irasville. In the photograph below, young skiers get ready to go uphill at the Alpen Inn lift. The warming hut came from the Ward Lumber Company in Moretown, and when the Alpen Inn lift was abandoned, the hut was moved to the new lift at Irasville. That lift was 1,500 feet long and approached the Knoll Farm on Bragg Hill Road. (Courtesy of Ann Day.)

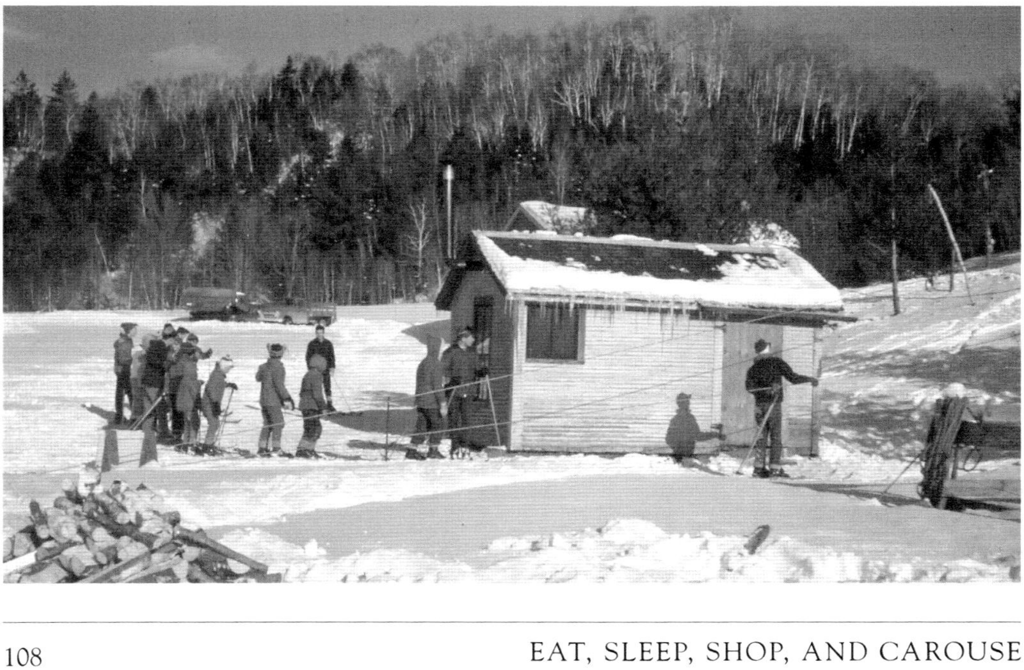

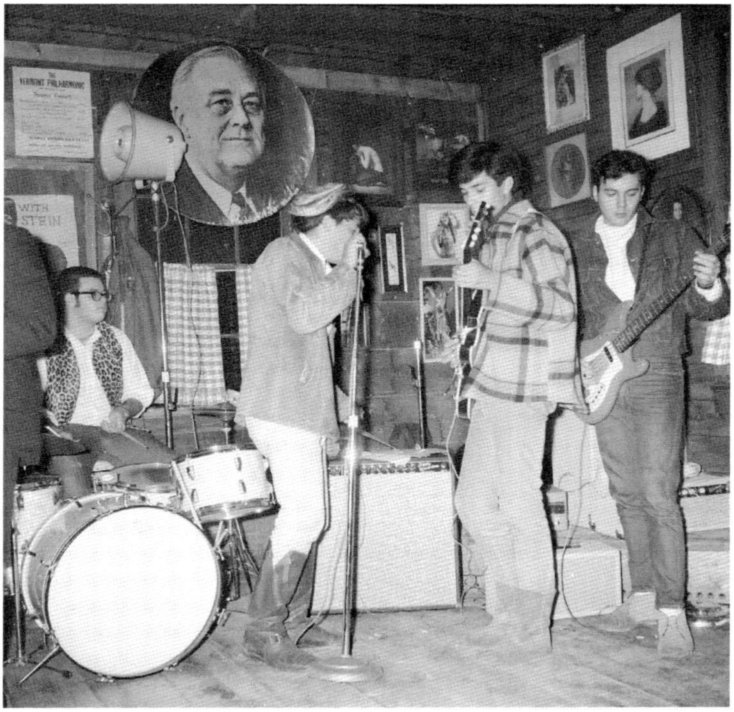

Small combos, the predecessors to rock 'n roll bands, were continuing highlights at the inns in Irasville, in this case, Gallagher's Steak House at Routes 100 and Bragg Hill Road. Note the photograph of FDR in the background. (Photograph by Sewall Williams.)

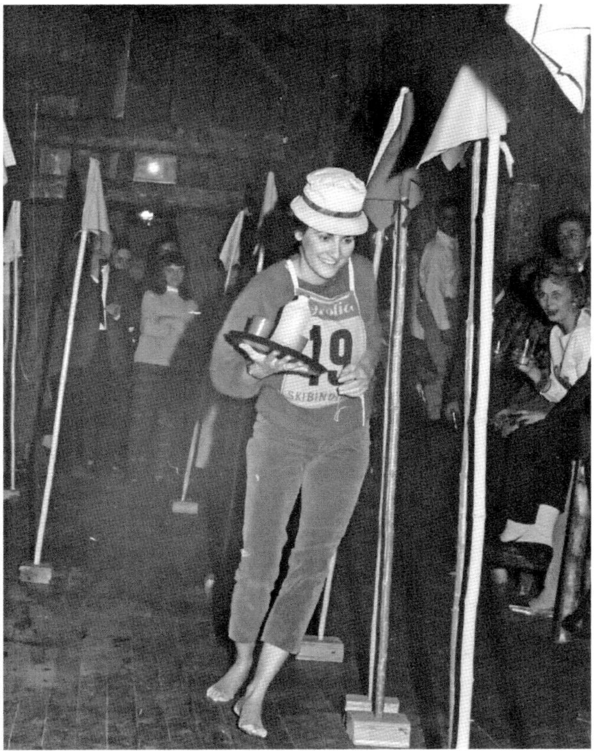

With skiing around the clock being out of the question, one of the next best things to do was participate in or be a spectator at an indoor slalom race—not too easy to handle when the racers are carrying trays of drinks, as this waitress is doing in the Waiters and Waitresses Slalom held annually for years. (Courtesy of Charlie Brown Productions.)

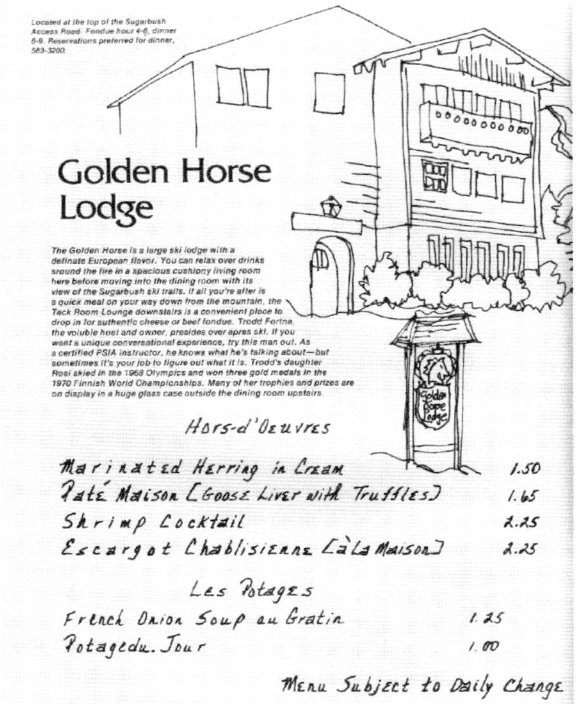
Located at the top of the Sugarbush Access Road. Fondue hour 4-6, dinner 6-9. Reservations preferred for dinner, 583-3200.

Golden Horse Lodge

The Golden Horse is a large ski lodge with a definate European flavor. You can relax over drinks around the fire in a spacious cushiony living room here before moving into the dining room with its view of the Sugarbush ski trails. If all you're after is a quick meal on your way down from the mountain, the Tack Room Lounge downstairs is a convenient place to drop in for authentic cheese or beef fondue. Trodd Fortna, the voluble host and owner, presides over apres ski. If you want a unique conversational experience, try this man out. As a certified PSIA instructor, he knows what he's talking about—but sometimes it's your job to figure out what it is. Trodd's daughter Rosi skied in the 1968 Olympics and won three gold medals in the 1970 Finnish World Championships. Many of her trophies and prizes are on display in a huge glass case outside the dining room upstairs.

Hors-d'Oeuvres

Marinated Herring in Cream	1.50
Paté Maison [Goose Liver with Truffles]	1.65
Shrimp Cocktail	2.25
Escargot Chablisienne [à la Maison]	2.25

Les Potages

French Onion Soup au Gratin	1.25
Potage du Jour	1.00

Menu Subject to Daily Change

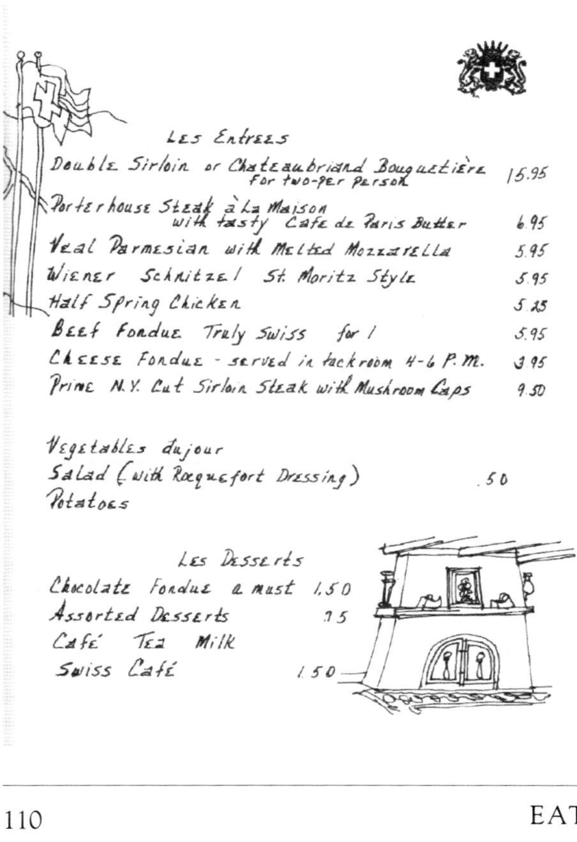
Les Entrees

Double Sirloin or Chateaubriand Bouguetière for two-per person	15.95
Porterhouse Steak à la Maison with tasty Cafe de Paris Butter	6.95
Veal Parmesian with Melted Mozzarella	5.95
Wiener Schnitzel St. Moritz Style	5.95
Half Spring Chicken	5.25
Beef Fondue Truly Swiss for 1	5.95
Cheese Fondue - served in tackroom 4-6 P.M.	3.95
Prime N.Y. Cut Sirloin Steak with Mushroom Caps	9.50

Vegetables du jour
Salad (with Roquefort Dressing) .50
Potatoes

Les Desserts

Chocolate Fondue a must	1.50
Assorted Desserts	.75
Café Tea Milk	
Swiss Café	1.50

In the dining out section of the "Valley Guide," published by Felix von Moschzisker in 1975, the Golden Horse Lodge, owned by Trodd and Lixi Fortna and located on the Sugarbush Access Road at Lincoln Peak, advertised fondue hour from 4:00 p.m. to 6:00 p.m. The most expensive meal on the menu—double sirloin or chateaubriand bouguetiere for two persons—topped out at $15.95. The lodge building continued to be a valley landmark after the restaurant closed and was sold to Sugarbush for use as its administrative offices. Lixi Fortna, who served as a state representative in the Vermont Legislature, was an original employee when Sugarbush opened in 1958. She, along with the Sugarbush founders Damon Gadd and Jack Murphy, took turns doing chores, from selling tickets to tending bar. The Fortnas' daughter, Rosi, competed in the 1968 Winter Olympics and won three gold medals in the 1970 World Championships. (Courtesy of Tony Egan.)

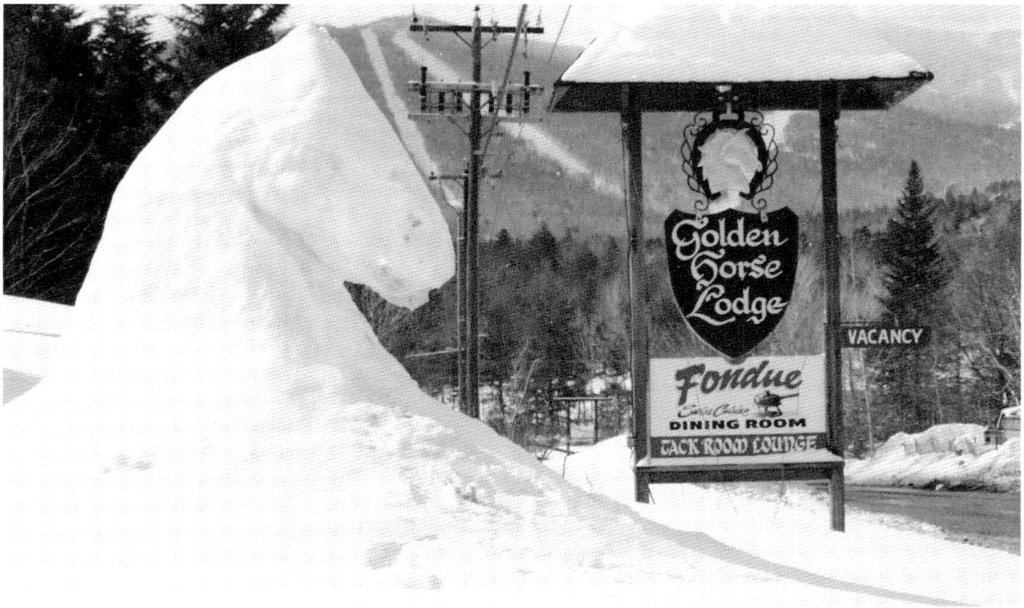

The Golden Horse Lodge, owned in the 1960s by Todd and Lixi Fortna, was a Tyrolean-style building with 40 rooms for sleeping, Tack Room bar, dining room, and living room with a fireplace. Overnight rates ranged from $10.50 to $16.50. (Photograph by Sewall Williams.)

Family connections run deep in the Mad River Valley, with sons and daughters becoming quickly absorbed in all kinds of activities with their parents, mostly outdoors. Seen here are, from left to right, Laurie Roth, daughter of realtors John and Ginny Roth; Chris Murphy, son of Jack and Audrey Murphy; and Megan Gadd, whose parents, Damon and Sara, founded Sugarbush with the Murphys. (Courtesy of Kelly Murphy Wood.)

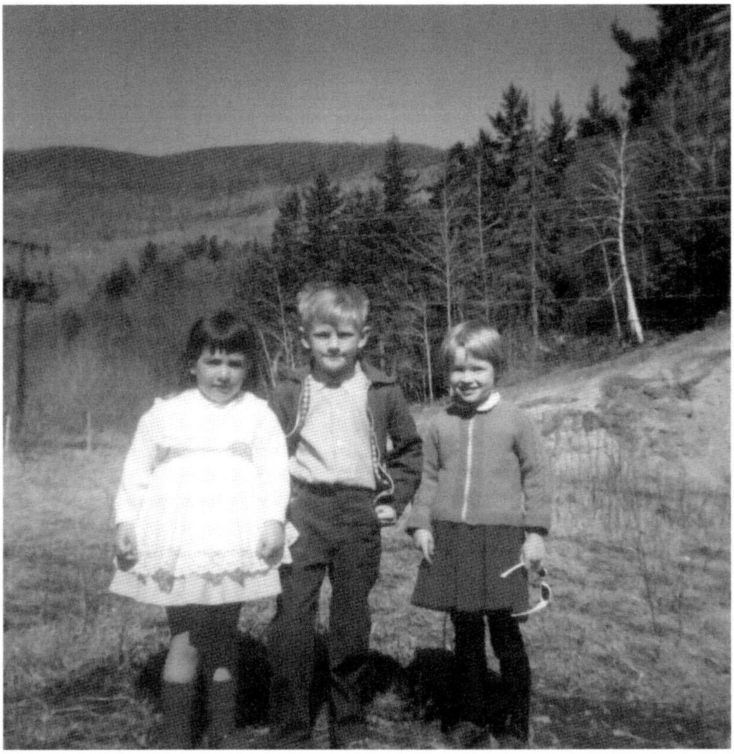

The High & Dry

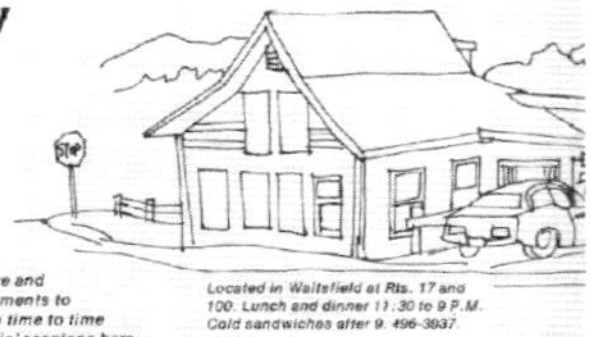

The High and Dry is a small ski lodge with restaurant and lounge attached. Its dining room has several large picture windows and holds about a dozen tables. The walls are decorated with color photographs of 12-meter sailboats in competition. The waitresses are friendly, and the meals—both lunch and dinner—are inexpensive: for example, you can get Eggs Benedict here on Sundays for $1.95. One thing that distinguishes the High and Dry is the fact that its cocktail lounge somehow draws a high number of native Yankee Vermonters. When these people get together here and the mood is right, it is not uncommon for musical instruments to appear. It's all very informal and unpredictable. But from time to time you will hear some fantastic old-fashioned country fiddlin' sessions here.

Located in Waitsfield at Rts. 17 and 100. Lunch and dinner 11:30 to 9 P.M. Cold sandwiches after 9. 496-3937.

"Crunch 'n Munch" Luncheon

French Fries .50

Browned Onion Rings .65

Salad
Tossed, Mixed and Thrown .65

Home-Made Soup de Jour
Bowl 75
Cup 45

Daily Special ex. Sat. *$1.95*

Open Rib Steak Sandwich w/French Fries	*$3.95*
Turkey Club Sandwich	*1.95*
with Bacon .50 additional	
Turkey "Monte Carlo" — Broiled Turkey w/swiss cheese & tomato on toast	*2.00*
Hot Roast Beef Sandwich	*2.00*
Grilled Roast Beef w/Swiss Cheese	*1.95*
Cold Roast Beef Sandwich	*1.75*
Hamburger Deluxe	*1.60*
with Bacon .15 additional	
Cheeseburger Divine	*1.75*
Cheddarburger w/French Fries	*2.25*
Reuben Sandwich w/Ham or Corned Beef	*2.10*
Broiled Ham Stack w/Swiss Cheese & Tomato	*1.75*
Grilled Ham & Cheese	*1.35*
Chef Supreme Salad Bowl	*2.50*
Tuna Salad Sandwich	*1.45*
Bacon, Lettuce & Tomato	*1.75*
Hot Dog — [9"] grilled or steamed	*.95*

Sandwiches are served with your choice of: sesame bun, rye or white bread, with cottage cheese, kosher dill pickle and potato chips.

14

The High and Dry, a favorite of both locals and apres ski crowds, was one of many restaurants to come and go at the busy intersection of Routes 17 and 100. The walls were decorated with photographs of sailboats. The menu promoted the restaurant's desserts as "Zurtz Happy Endings." (Courtesy of Tony Egan.)

Christmas Tree Inn

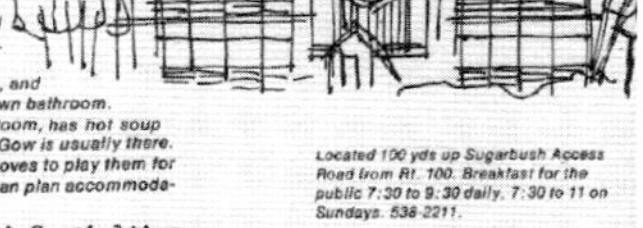

It's no secret you will be able to ski longer, harder and better if you approach the hill every day with a warm breakfast in your stomach. Conveniently located at the base of the Sugarbush Access Road, the Christmas Tree Inn is a natural place to stop and get that breakfast in calm wholesome surroundings. Should you choose to stay at this modern country lodge, there's always an open fire in the living room, and the bedrooms are bright and cheery, each with its own bathroom. In the evenings the cocktail lounge, the Red Nose Room, has hot soup and sandwiches available [4 to 11 p.m.]. Owner Bob Gow is usually there. He has a large collection of old 78 rpm records and loves to play them for his customers. Modified American plan and European plan accommodations.

Located 100 yds up Sugarbush Access Road from Rt. 100. Breakfast for the public 7:30 to 9:30 daily, 7:30 to 11 on Sundays. 538-2211.

Breakfast Specialties

No. 1 Choice of juice or fruit, muffins, two eggs with bacon, sausage or ham, toast, coffee, tea or milk. 2.50

No. 2 Home made pancakes with our own maple syrup. Juice or fruit, muffins, bacon, sausage or ham. Coffee, tea or milk. 2.50
Onion or Apple pancakes 2.75

No. 3 French toast made with home made bread and served with maple syrup. Choice of juice or fruit, muffins, bacon, sausage or ham, coffee, tea or milk. 2.50
Rum French Toast 3.00
Additional egg on French Toast or Pancakes .50

No. 4 Choice of juice or fruit, muffins, two eggs, toast, coffee, tea or milk. 2.00

No. 5 Choice of juice or fruit, muffins, one egg, bacon, Sausage or ham, toast, coffee, tea or milk. 2.00

We make our own bread, muffins and maple syrup. Our eggs are fresh from a local farm.

Juices .40 and .60
Fruit .45

Muffins .40
Buttered Toast .35
Cinnamon Toast .45

Single egg with toast .75
Two eggs with toast 1.25

Home Fried Potatoes .60

Bacon .60
Sausage .75
Ham .80

Assorted cold cereals or hot cereal served with toast .85

Pancakes and maple syrup 1.35
French Toast and Maple syrup 1.35
with rum 1.85

Coffee, tea or milk .25
Hot Chocolate .35

syrup.

DROP IN AT THE RED NOSE ROOM
FOR AN EVENING OR AFTERNOON SNACK
Soup, Sandwiches and Drinks
from 4 p.m. to midnight.

24

One of the early inns that is still at the same location serving overnight and drop-in breakfast guests, but no longer operating as a restaurant, is the Christmas Tree Inn at the base of the Sugarbush Access Road just west of Route 100. Bob Gow, the owner, had a large collection of 78-RPM records, which he played for his customers. (Courtesy of Tony Egan.)

No resort area was considered complete without an ice cream parlor. This one was part of the Kehoe Inn at Route 100 and the Sugarbush Access Road. It advertised a "gooey mess" as one of its favorite desserts. Most ice cream parlors of the age had serpentine marble bars, with the marble mined locally at a quarry in Moretown and other locations in Vermont. (Courtesy of Tony Egan.)

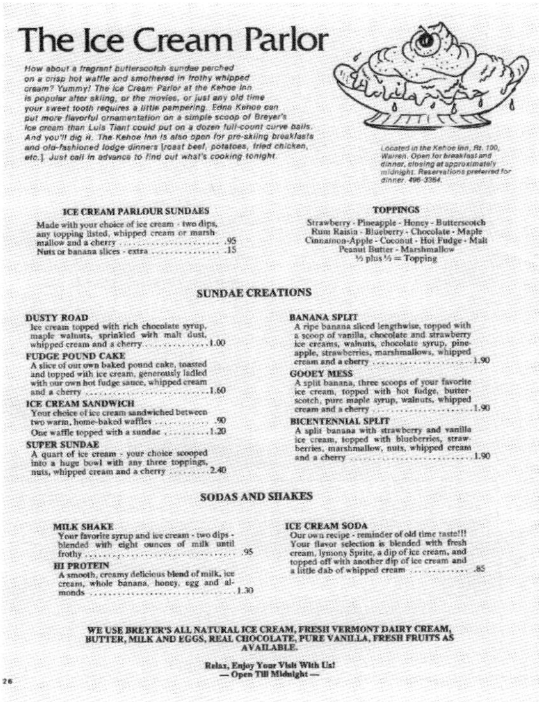

The Ice Cream Parlor

How about a fragrant butterscotch sundae perched on a crisp hot waffle and smothered in frothy whipped cream? Yummy! The Ice Cream Parlor at the Kehoe Inn is popular after skiing, or the movies, or just any old time your sweet tooth requires a little pampering. Edna Kehoe can put more flavorful ornamentation on a simple scoop of Breyer's ice cream than Luis Tiant could put on a dozen full-count curve balls. And you'll dig it. The Kehoe Inn is also open for pre-skiing breakfasts and old-fashioned lodge dinners [roast beef, potatoes, fried chicken, etc.]. Just call in advance to find out what's cooking tonight.

Located in the Kehoe Inn, Rt. 100, Warren. Open for breakfast and dinner, closing at approximately midnight. Reservations preferred for dinner. 496-3364.

ICE CREAM PARLOUR SUNDAES

Made with your choice of ice cream - two dips, any topping listed, whipped cream or marshmallow and a cherry .... .95
Nuts or banana slices - extra .... .15

TOPPINGS

Strawberry - Pineapple - Honey - Butterscotch
Rum Raisin - Blueberry - Chocolate - Maple
Cinnamon-Apple - Coconut - Hot Fudge - Malt
Peanut Butter - Marshmallow
½ plus ½ = Topping

SUNDAE CREATIONS

DUSTY ROAD
Ice cream topped with rich chocolate syrup, maple walnuts, sprinkled with malt dust, whipped cream and a cherry 1.00

FUDGE POUND CAKE
A slice of our own baked pound cake, toasted and topped with ice cream, generously ladled with our own hot fudge sauce, whipped cream and a cherry 1.60

ICE CREAM SANDWICH
Your choice of ice cream sandwiched between two warm, home-baked waffles .... .90
One waffle topped with a sundae 1.20

SUPER SUNDAE
A quart of ice cream - your choice scooped into a huge bowl with any three toppings, nuts, whipped cream and a cherry 2.40

BANANA SPLIT
A ripe banana sliced lengthwise, topped with a scoop of vanilla, chocolate and strawberry ice creams, walnuts, chocolate syrup, pineapple, strawberries, marshmallows, whipped cream and a cherry 1.90

GOOEY MESS
A split banana, three scoops of your favorite ice cream, topped with hot fudge, butterscotch, pure maple syrup, walnuts, whipped cream and a cherry 1.90

BICENTENNIAL SPLIT
A split banana with strawberry and vanilla ice cream, topped with blueberries, strawberries, marshmallow, nuts, whipped cream and a cherry 1.90

SODAS AND SHAKES

MILK SHAKE
Your favorite syrup and ice cream - two dips - blended with eight ounces of milk until frothy .... .95

HI PROTEIN
A smooth, creamy delicious blend of milk, ice cream, whole banana, honey, egg and almonds 1.30

ICE CREAM SODA
Our own recipe - reminder of old time taste!!! Your flavor selection is blended with fresh cream, lymony Sprite, a dip of ice cream, and topped off with another dip of ice cream and a little dab of whipped cream .... .85

WE USE BREYER'S ALL NATURAL ICE CREAM, FRESH VERMONT DAIRY CREAM, BUTTER, MILK AND EGGS, REAL CHOCOLATE, PURE VANILLA, FRESH FRUITS AS AVAILABLE.

Relax, Enjoy Your Visit With Us!
— Open Till Midnight —

26

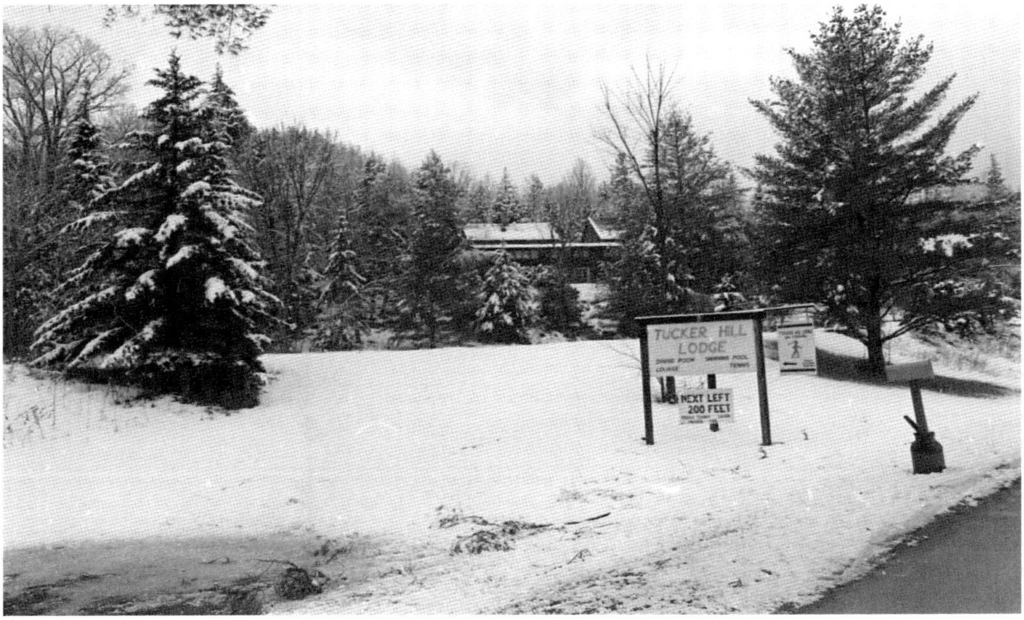

Tucker Hill Inn on Route 17 in Fayston remains a valley landmark, famous for its hospitality and its early tow lift. Rob Center, who owned the ski touring center, started the first-ever Tucker Hill triathlon in the valley. Thirty-two competitors took part in the cross-country ski racing, biking, and paddling event. It evolved into the Sugarbush triathlon. (Photograph by Sewall Williams.)

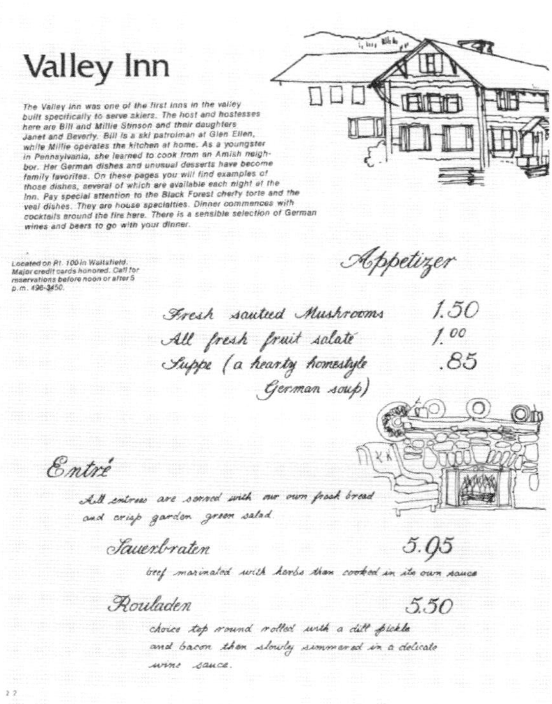

Valley Inn

The Valley Inn was one of the first inns in the valley built specifically to serve skiers. The host and hostesses here are Bill and Millie Stinson and their daughters Janet and Beverly. Bill is a ski patrolman at Glen Ellen, while Millie operates the kitchen at home. As a youngster in Pennsylvania, she learned to cook from an Amish neighbor. Her German dishes and unusual desserts have become family favorites. On these pages you will find examples of those dishes, several of which are available each night at the Inn. Pay special attention to the Black Forest cherry torte and the veal dishes. They are house specialties. Dinner commences with cocktails around the fire here. There is a sensible selection of German wines and beers to go with your dinner.

Located on Rt. 100 in Waitsfield. Major credit cards honored. Call for reservations before noon or after 5 p.m. 496-3450.

Appetizer

Fresh sauteed Mushrooms 1.50
All fresh fruit salate 1.00
Suppe (a hearty homestyle German soup) .85

Entré

All entrees are served with our own fresh bread and crisp garden green salad

Sauerbraten 5.95
beef marinated with herbs then cooked in its own sauce

Rouladen 5.50
choice top round rolled with a dill pickle and bacon then slowly simmered in a delicate wine sauce.

22

Bill and Milly Stinson, with their daughters Janet and Beverly, ran the Valley Inn on Route 100 in the heart of what was to become the Mad River Green shopping center. The inn was one of the first in the valley built purposely to attract skiers. (Bill was a ski patroller at Glen Ellen.) The menu featured dishes reminiscent of the Amish country in Pennsylvania, where Milly learned to cook such dishes as wiener schnitzel, sauerbraten, and Black Forest cherry torte. (Courtesy of Tony Egan.)

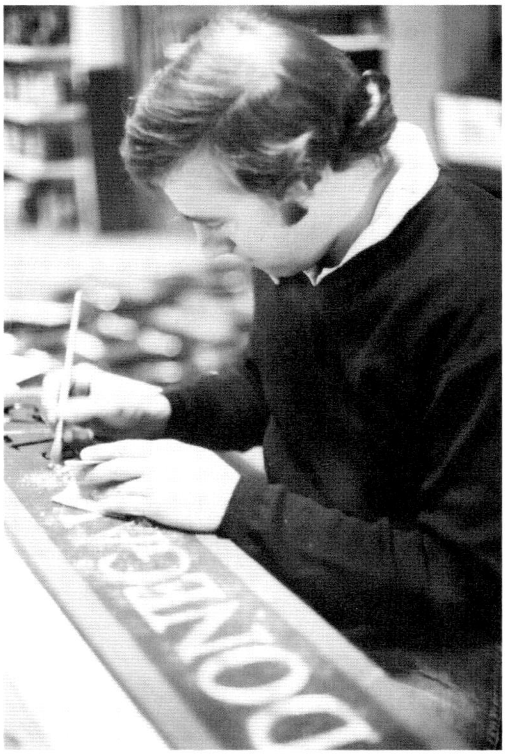

Shunning plastic and metal, Sparky Potter combined the rusticity of old Vermont with old-world wooden signs, a business that he and his wife, Peggy, started in 1972. Sparky was also a photographer and longtime ski patroller at Sugarbush. (Courtesy of Ski Vermont.)

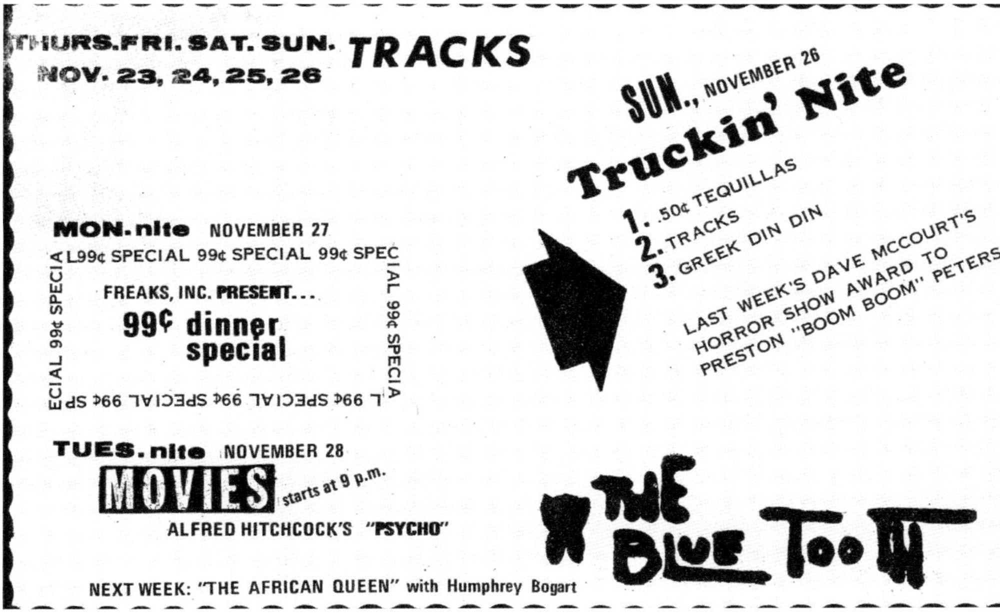

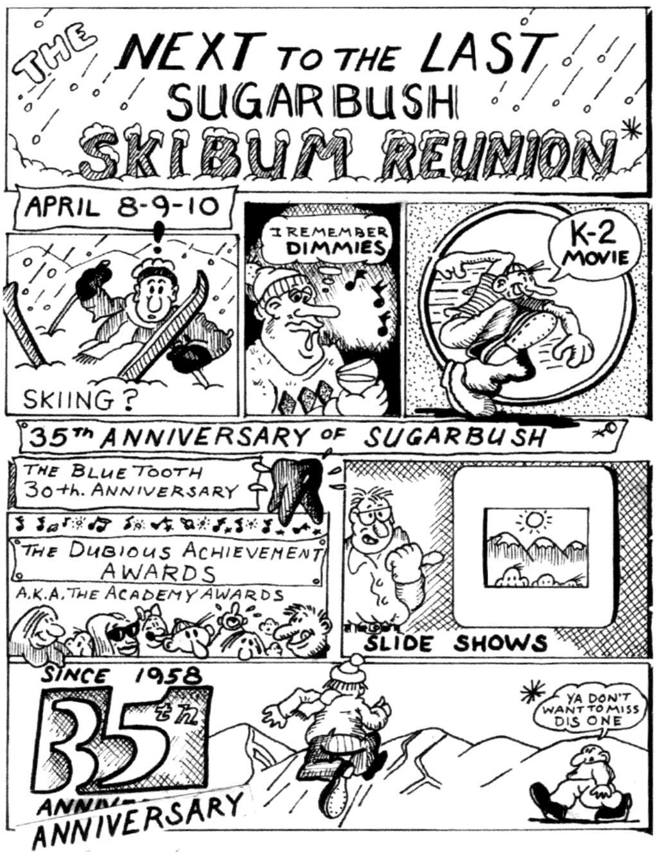

The Blue Tooth on the Sugarbush Access Road was demolished in 2009, leaving only some wild memories behind, as evidenced by the advertisement above. Keepers of the flame were a succession of owners: Tom Storrs and J. C. Conley, Charlie Brown, and Bill Rogowski. The cartoon at right was drawn by David McCourt in 1993, announcing the annual Ski Bums Reunion at the Blue Tooth. The owner then was Charlie Brown, who admitted ranking among the top valley ski bums. Typical of many, he caught valley fever and transplanted himself to Vermont after renting a house on German Flats Road in Warren with 15 friends in 1964. He began his restaurant career as a dishwasher but is more widely known today as a photographer. (Courtesy of Charlie Brown Productions.)

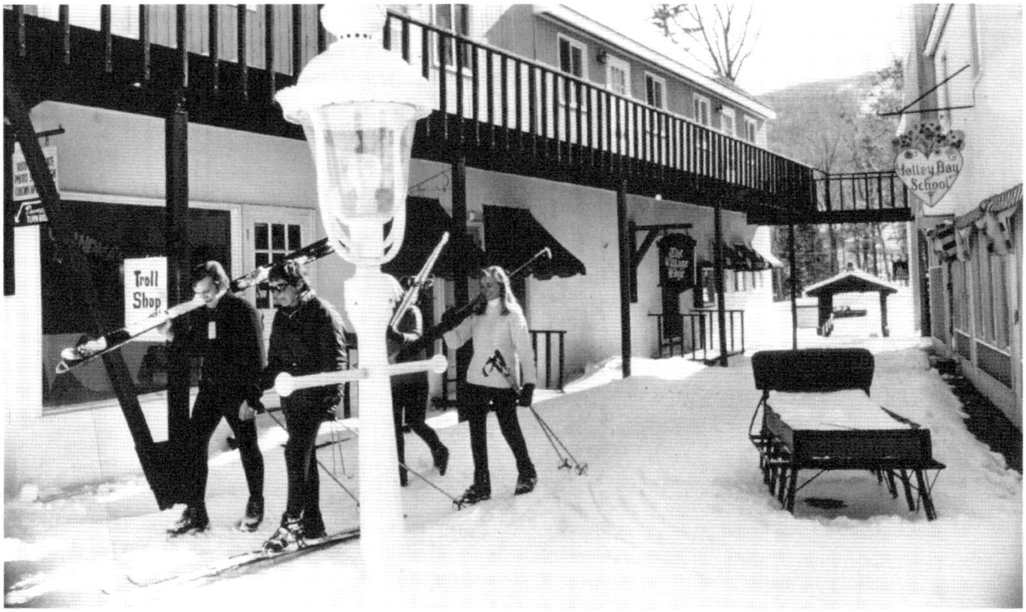

Sugarbush Village, which was developed at the base of Lincoln Peak, grew rapidly, beginning in 1970 with the construction of the Forum and Clariere, then Middle Earth, and Unihab. When completed, the village held the Valley Day School, Chez Henri, The Store, and the Village Edge Restaurant. Off slope, condos sprung up through the valley: the Battleground, the Bridges, Sugar Run, and Drumleys. (Courtesy of Vermont Ski Museum.)

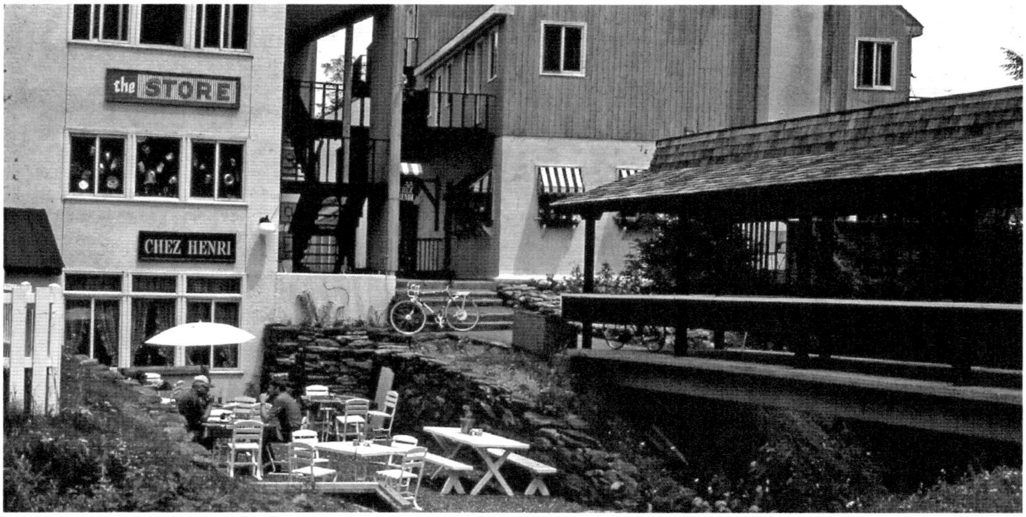

The core Sugarbush Village, entered via a Vermont covered bridge, has remained architecturally unchanged since the 1960s when it was developed. However, The Store, a gift shop that was located one floor above Chez Henri, was moved by its owner, Jackie Rose, to Route 100 in Irasville. The Store was later purchased and renamed Wares both for the housewares it sold and for its owner, Mike Ware. (Photograph by Sewall Williams.)

5

Through Fields and Trees on Skinny Skis

Nordic, or cross-country, skiing could be called a poor person's winter outlet because most everywhere the lift tickets are free and nonexistent. Besides the scant equipment, in many cases, all that is needed is a set of well-working lungs and a landowner's permission.

Even paying for the privilege is a relative bargain—especially if one is from out of town and does not know the lay of the land. There are many sets of trails to choose from that test various abilities, from beginner to expert.

But what is best about cross-country skiing in the Mad River Valley is the wide sweep of pastures, meadows, frozen ponds, and mountains—a landscape that breathes in rhythm along with its visitors. Occasionally one can spot a rabbit, moose, or beaver, and if skiers cannot see a cow, they are definitely in the woods, where, as Robert Frost said, in Vermont it is always "lovely, dark and deep."

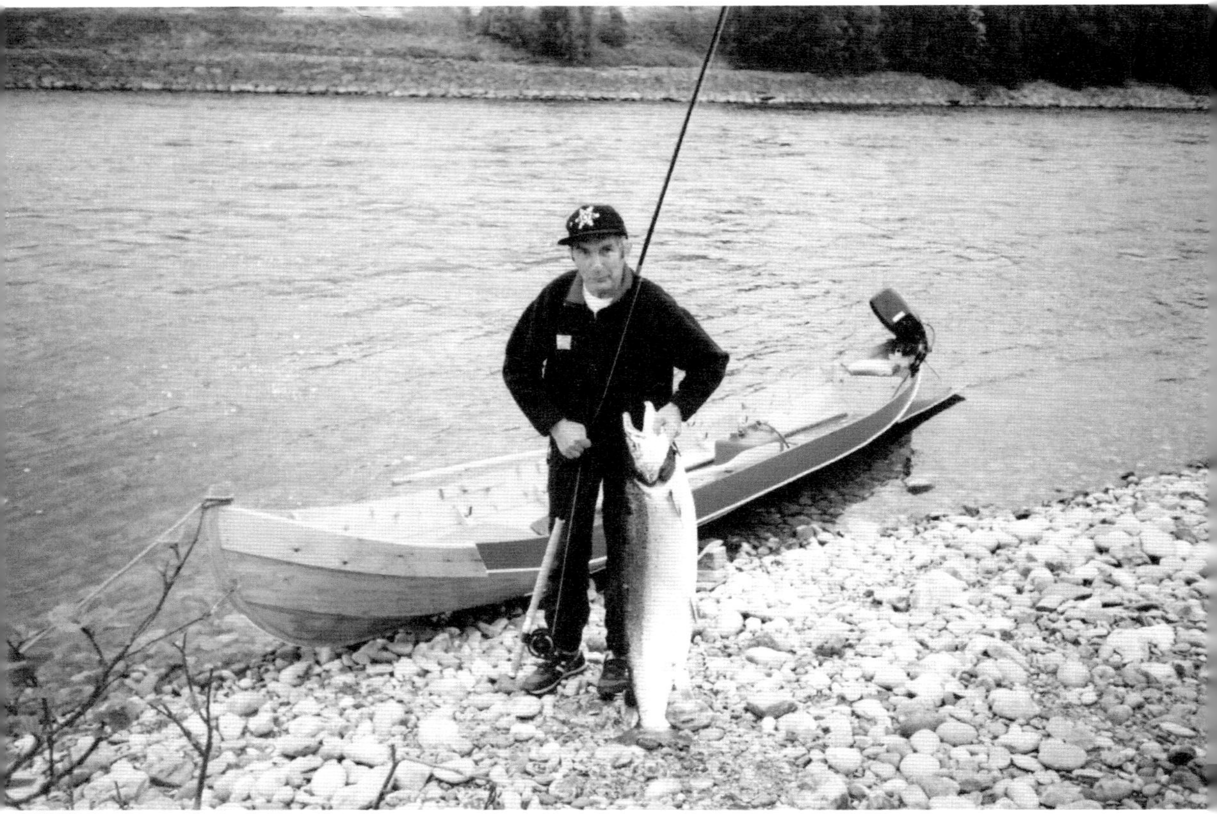

Ole Mosesen comes from a long line of Norwegian salmon fishermen. He increased his passion for nordic skiing in the 1960s, coming to Vermont to run the Sugarbush Inn Cross-Country Ski Center. Later he founded Ole's Cross Country Ski Center at the Warren Airport. (Courtesy of Ole's Cross Country Ski Center.)

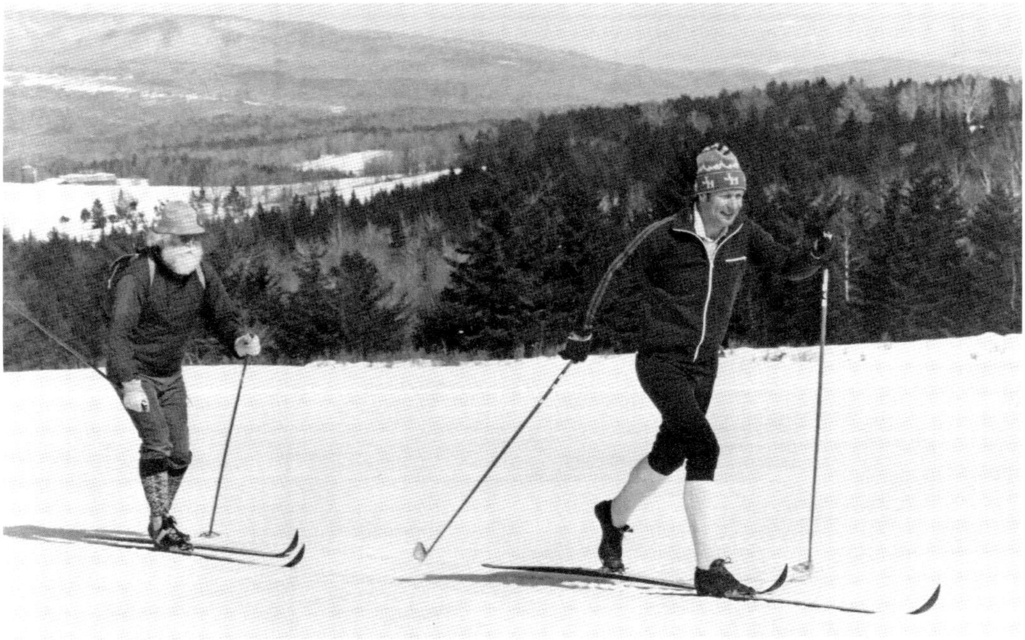

Warren, with its rolling hills, welcoming woods, and open pastures, has attracted cross-country skiers for decades, allowing them a plentitude of geographical freedom. Many crisscrossing, winding trails are maintained by mechanical groomers and shared with skimobiles. (Courtesy of Ski Vermont.)

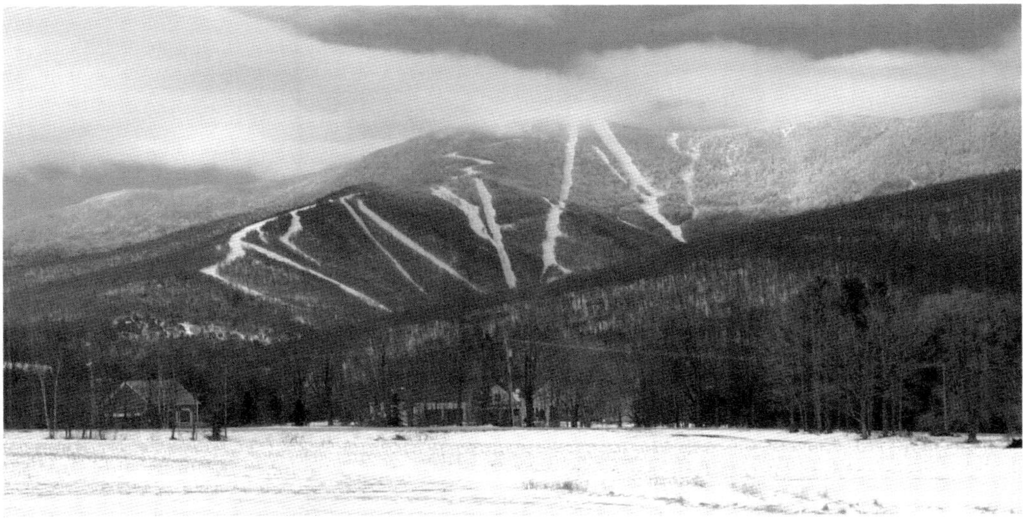

Running across the summit ridge of the three mountains is the Long Trail, which Roland Palmedo and friends first visited as a possible touring trail for cross-country skiing on April 6, 1951. "Scenically, this portion of the Long Trail is unsurpassed," wrote Palmedo in an article in *Appalachia*. "The ridge being as sharp as a church roof most of the way, one can frequently look down on the parallel valley on either side." (Photograph by Ellie Hilferty.)

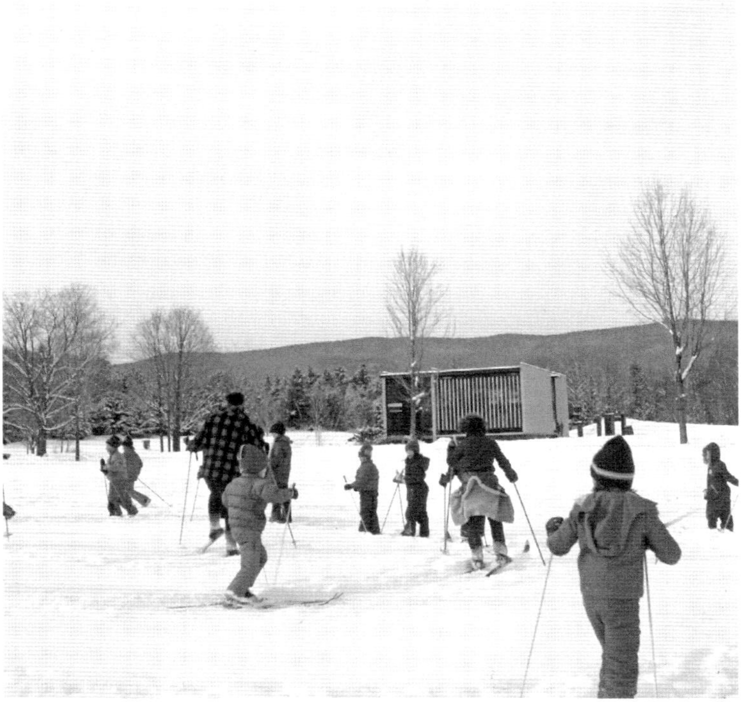

Nordic trails slice through the property of the Bundy Gallery in Waitsfield, which, considering the homespun architecture of the historic valley, was an anomaly built by Harlow Carpenter in the 1960s. It functioned as a contemporary country museum, a school, a location for weddings, and until recently, the home of the Mad River Chorale. (Photograph by Sewall Williams.)

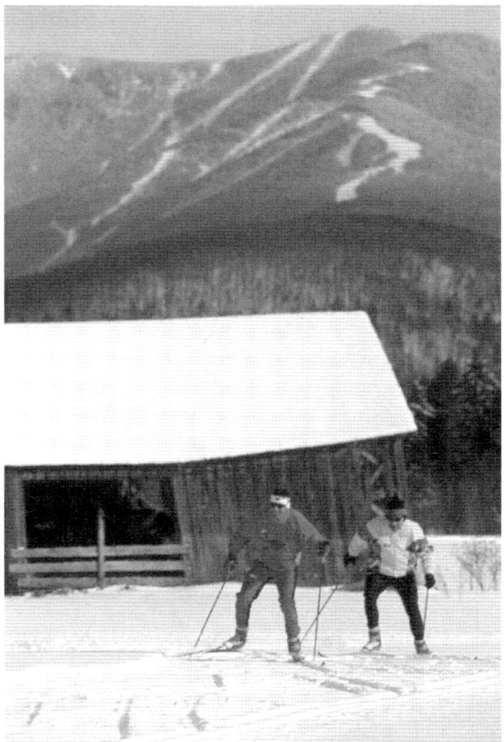

From the 6-kilometer Folsom Brook Trail near the Bundy Gallery down to the south of Airport Road, Ole's Cross Country Ski Center comprises a dozen trails of nearly 50 kilometers through woods, meadows, and even over a frozen beaver pond. And not many nordic ski areas have an airport as their headquarters. (Photograph by Dennis Curran; courtesy of Ole's Cross Country Ski Center.)

This 1993 poster advertising the Tucker Hill Telemark Ski Party in Fayston illustrates the long history of this difficult sport. Telemark has become a Mad River Valley staple through the Waitsfield-based North American Telemark Organization (NATO). (Courtesy of NATO.)

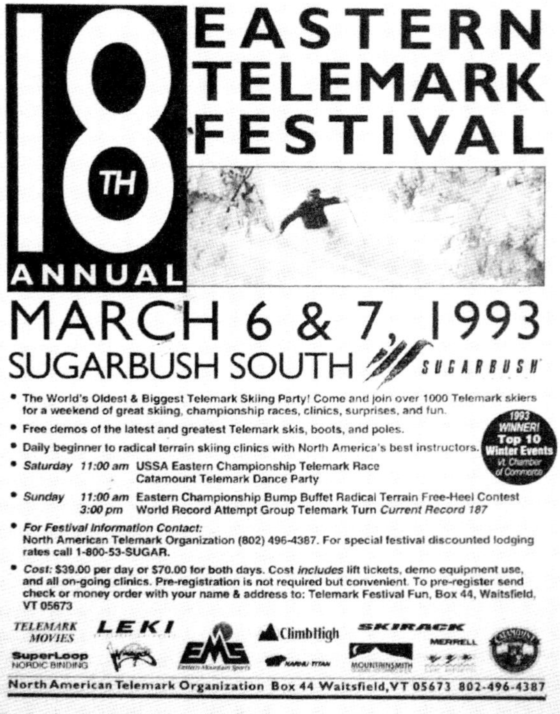

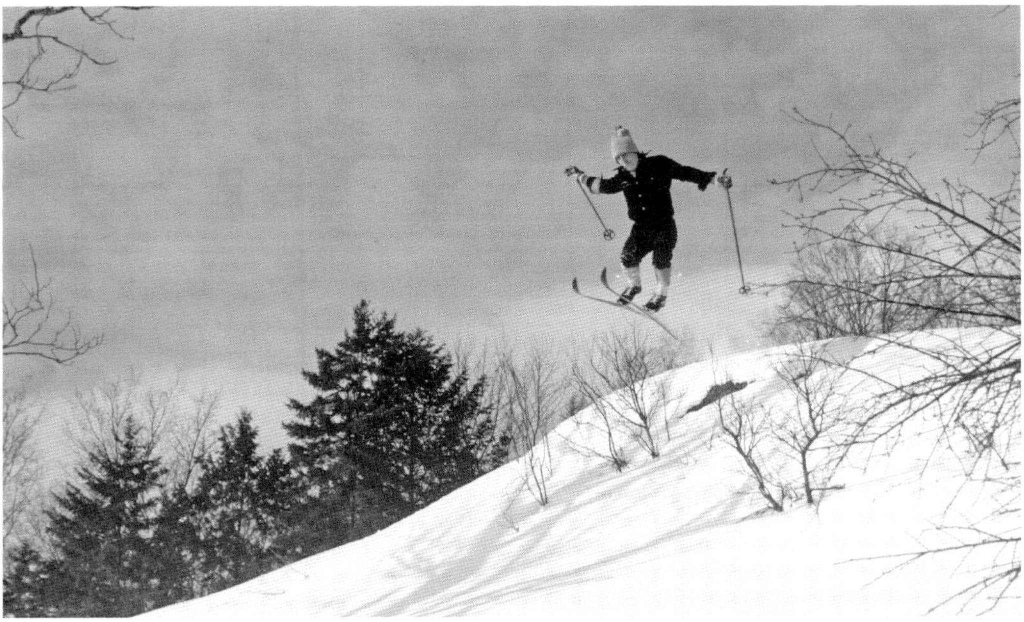

Dickie Hall of Waitsfield leaps a growth of weeds at the old Gaylord Farm in 1978. Hall, who is the founder of the North American Telemark Organization, is wearing a pair of Bonna 1600 Woodie telemark skis. (Courtesy of NATO.)

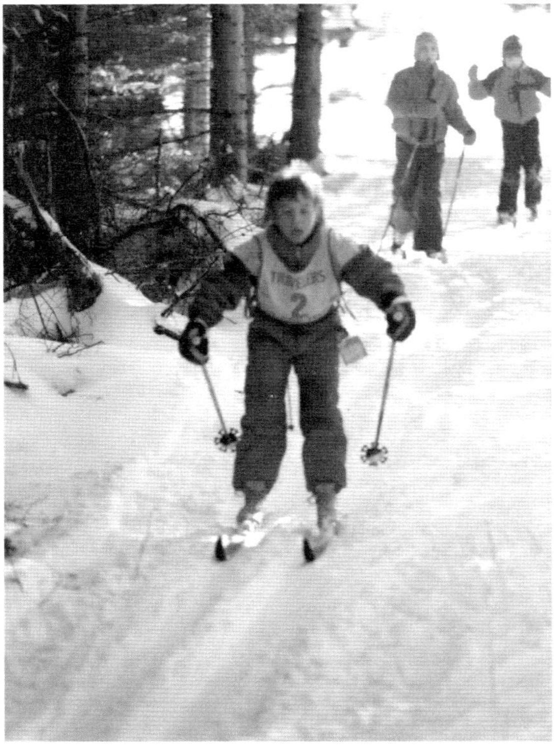

Jennifer Watkins, who has skied at the Blueberry Lake Cross Country Center owned by her grandfather, Lenord Robinson, since she was a toddler, is seen here in a Bill Koch race. Watkins later competed internationally as a biathlete. She was good enough to compete in the Biathlon World Junior Championships in 1996. In the photograph below, taken during the year she placed third in the World Cup Biathlon Finals in Nagano, Japan, she poses with Robinson—who played a major role in teaching her to ski. (Courtesy of Blueberry Lake.)

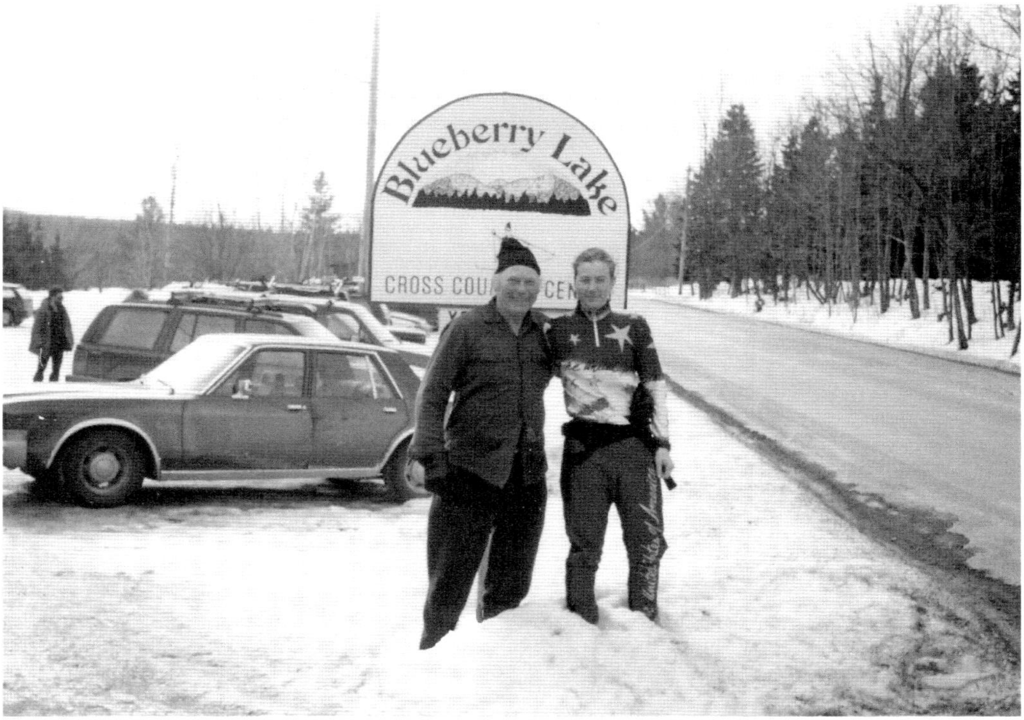

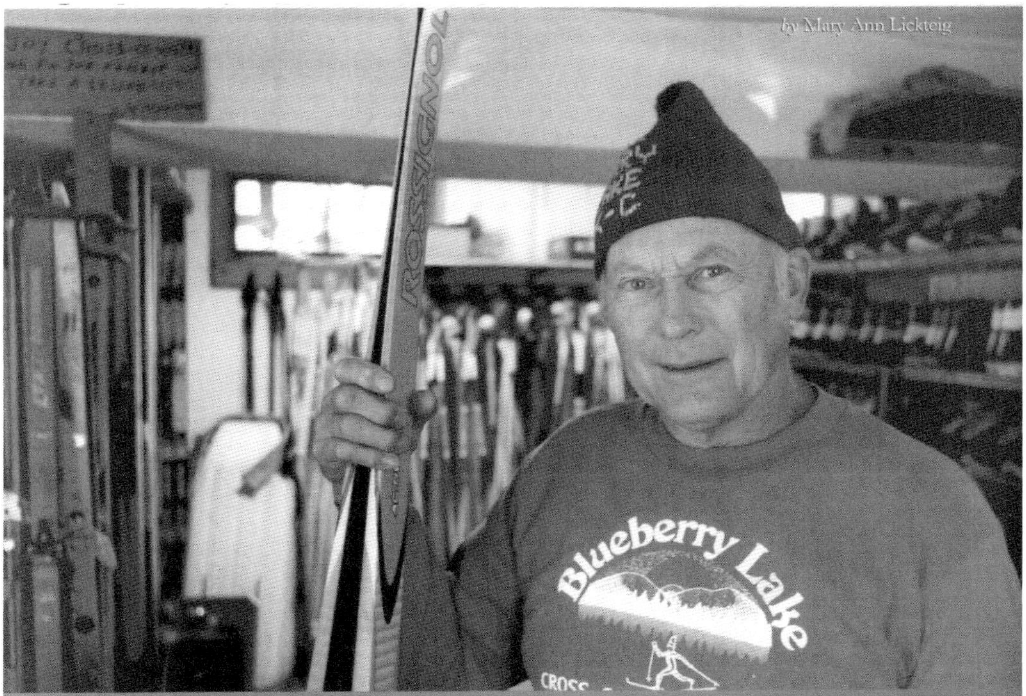

LIFE ACCORDING TO LENORD

No one can say with accuracy just when cross-country skiing came to the Mad River Valley (it dates back centuries with Nordics). It has certainly been here longer than alpine. Blueberry Lake Cross Country Center opened in 1984. Lenord Robinson, shown here, is the owner/operator, overseeing 11 trails that run for 30 kilometers through the woods and meadows of beautiful Blueberry Lake on a plateau on Plunkton Road in East Warren. (Courtesy of Ski Vermont.)

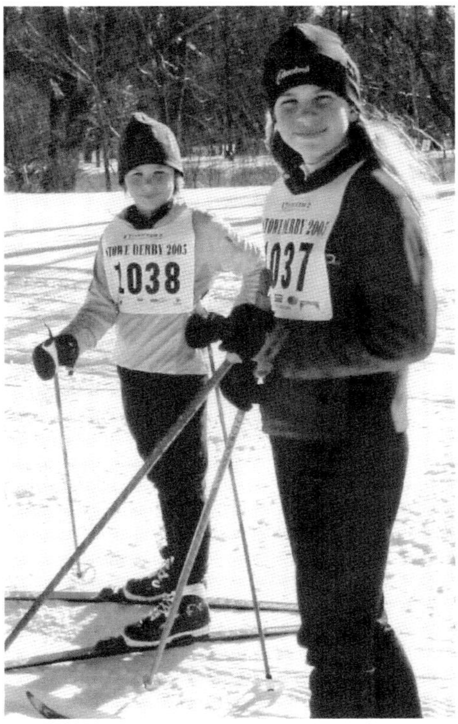

Sam and Chelsea Robinson represent the third generation of the Robinson family's cross-country experience in the Mad River Valley. Shown here as participants in a Valley Cup race, they are grandchildren of Lenord Robinson. (Courtesy of Blueberry Lake.)

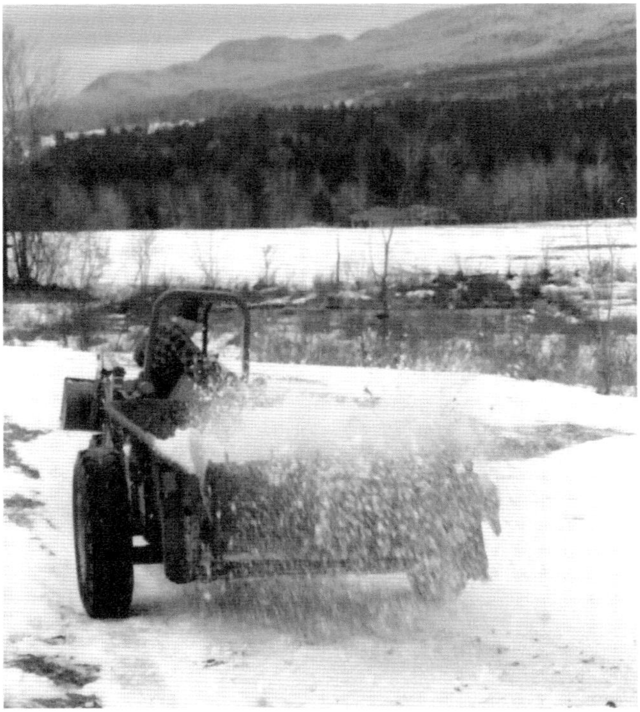

When Jack Frost declines to do his part by providing ample snow for nordic skiing in Vermont, Lenord Robinson's Yankee ingenuity takes over. Dairy farmer Robinson's manure spreader works just fine for laying down trails at the Blueberry Lake Cross Country Center in Warren. (Courtesy of Blueberry Lake.)

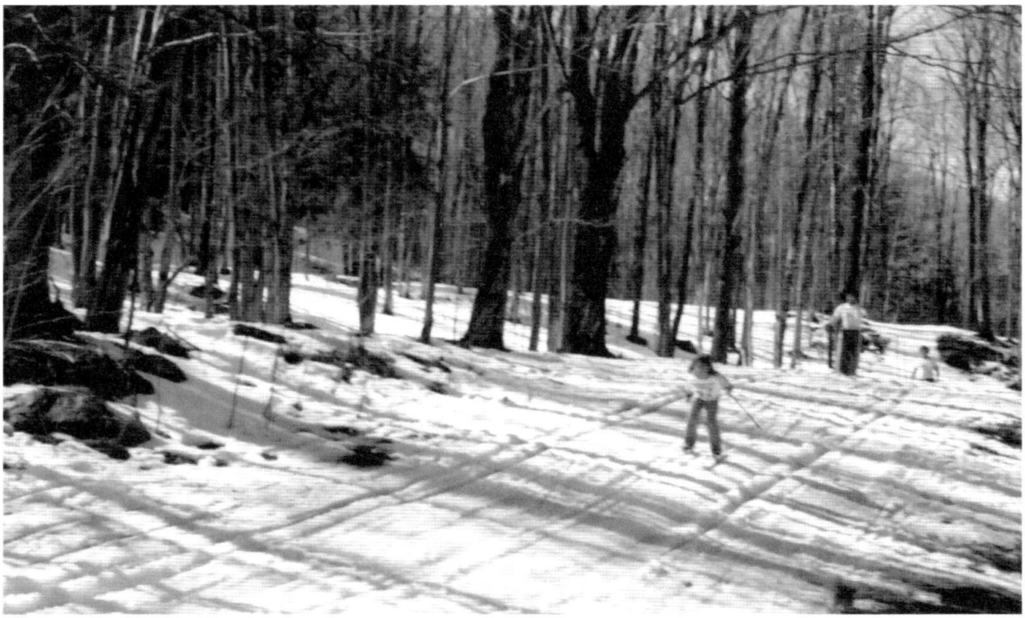

The Meadow, at 1,710 meters, is one of the easier of the 11 cross-country trails at Blueberry Lake that were laid out by Lenord Robinson, now an octogenarian who began adult life as a dairy farmer in Warren. Many of the nearby homes and outbuildings on his property were constructed by him using the spruce trees of his forest. (Courtesy of Blueberry Lake.)

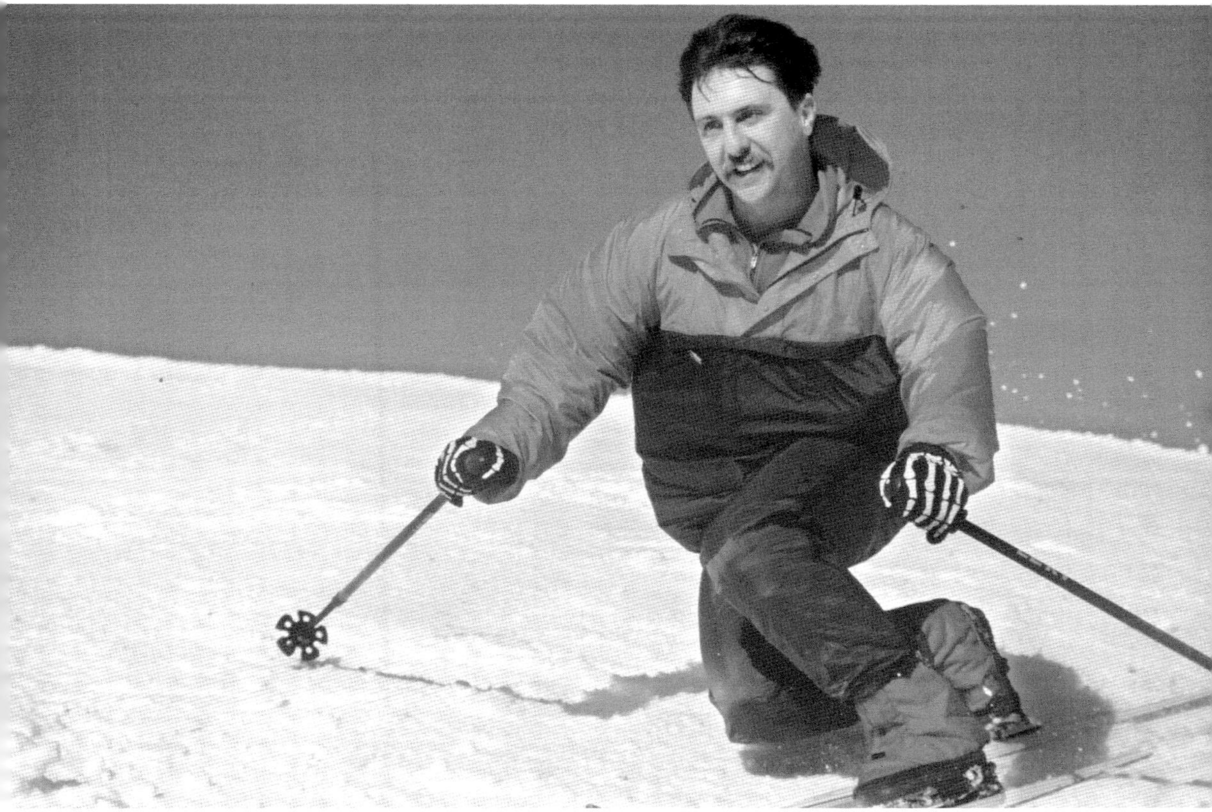

One way to compare telemark skiing with nordic and alpine might be to call it "a cross between them and a notch above" in difficulty and skill, combining alpine techniques with the free-heel ability to climb nearly anywhere. Dickie Hall, shown here, has taught thousands to master the technique since he learned to do it in the mid-1970s, soon after being fired as a ski patroller when he hijacked a lift at Killington to do a little midnight skiing. He founded a ski touring center in Stockbridge, Vermont, and then sought a mountain where he could operate a telemark school. Mad River Glen's General Manager Ken Quakenbush accommodated the idea, and, thus, the North American Telemark Organization was born at Mad River in 1980. It now counts thousands of skiers as members. NATO's headquarters are in Waitsfield, where Hall lives. (Courtesy of NATO.)

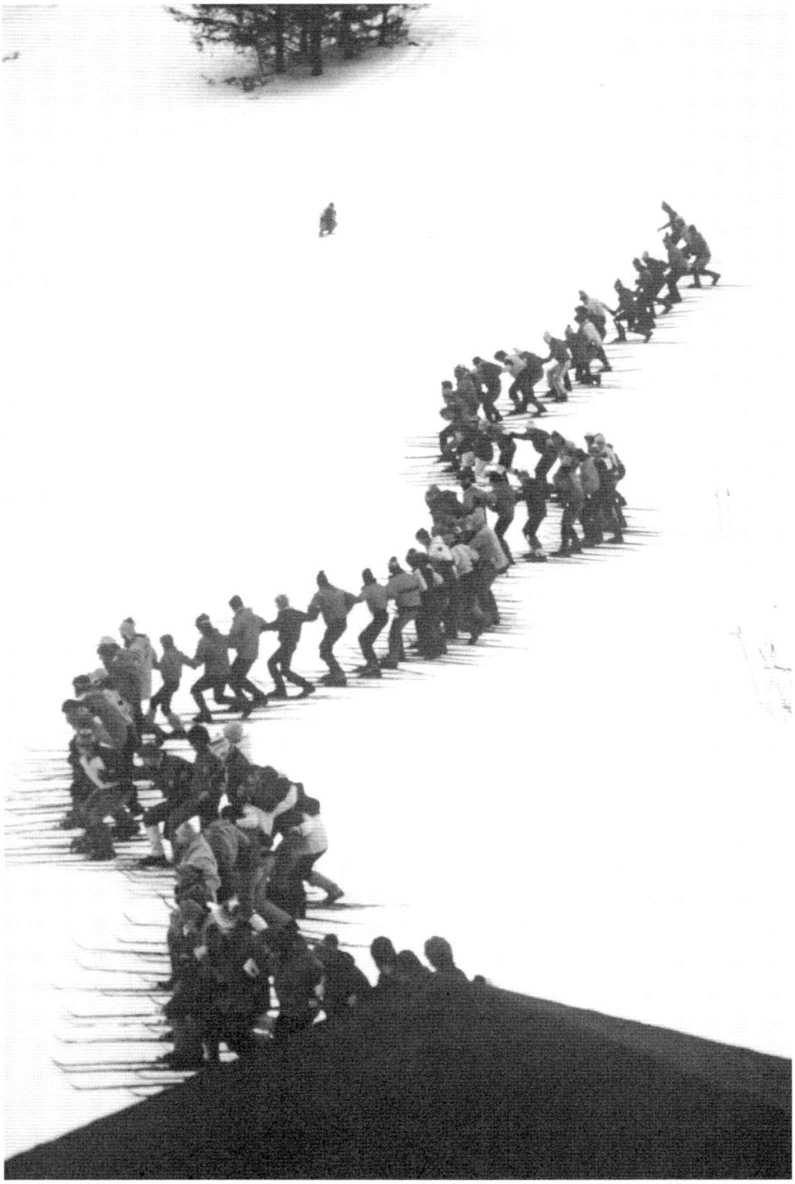

This is what a world record-setting telemark turn looks like: line up 187 skiers, who link arms, and turn. It is that simple. The feat was performed at Mad River Glen during the North American Telemark Organization's Telemark Festival in 1983. Sometimes referred to as a "Ski Party for Pinheads," the 35th annual festival was held in 2010, attracting more than 1,000 participants. (The nickname "pinhead" is suggested by the pin-type bindings of telemark skis.) *Cross Country Downhill*, a book written by Steve Barnett, who skied in Vermont while a student at Harvard, has become a bible for the sport. The first impression of people who have never tried the sport is that it takes knees of flexible steel. It also requires a great deal of patience to endure the many crashes while learning, according to those who have mastered it. (Courtesy of NATO.)

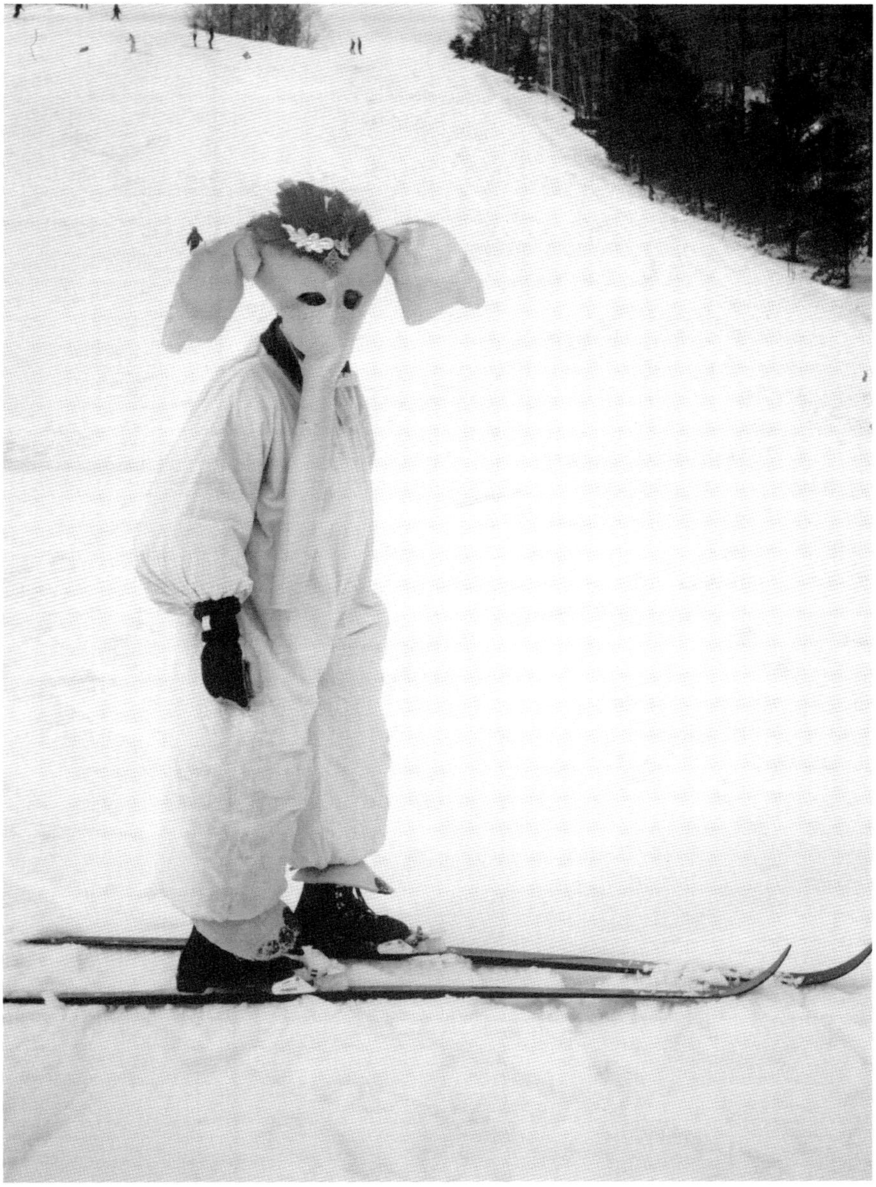

It is fitting to close out this book with an image from the end of a typical season at Mad River Glen. This is the Easter Bunny at the annual parade at the base lodge. Often there is enough snow for participants to take a few runs—just one last turn. If not, the camaraderie of the day provides enough happy memories to last through the summer and fall until the first flakes visit once more for a new season. *Holiday Magazine* wrote about the beginning of alpine skiing in the Mad River Valley as bringing life to "a little, lost corner of Vermont." Despite the thrills, the restless challenges, and the hard-fought competitiveness of skiing in general, in the valley there is one common denominator among all skiers, young or old, skilled or unskilled, and that is, above all else, having a good time. (Courtesy of NATO.)

Discover Thousands of Local History Books Featuring Millions of Vintage Images

Arcadia Publishing, the leading local history publisher in the United States, is committed to making history accessible and meaningful through publishing books that celebrate and preserve the heritage of America's people and places.

Find more books like this at
www.arcadiapublishing.com

Search for your hometown history, your old stomping grounds, and even your favorite sports team.

Consistent with our mission to preserve history on a local level, this book was printed in South Carolina on American-made paper and manufactured entirely in the United States. Products carrying the accredited Forest Stewardship Council (FSC) label are printed on 100 percent FSC-certified paper.

MADE IN THE USA